CONTENTS

PREFACE

My aim in preparing *Gospel, Church, and Kingdom* for publication has been to provide students and teachers of world missions—along with missionaries, pastors, mission executives, lay mission interpreters, and church leaders generally—with resource material for the study of recent developments in the theology of mission. A secondary aim has been to offer a synoptic view on recent mission theology from an ecumenical perspective, in the hope of promoting greater contact, understanding, and possible dialog between representatives of all groups engaged in common obedience to the Great Commission. A final aim has been to attempt to clarify issues of mission theology for my own church by way of challenging it both to deeper reflection on the issues and to more active involvement in forwarding the unfinished task.

The plan of the book is straightforward. After an introductory chapter which spells out the challenge of the new missionary era, and the reasons which now make the study of the theology of mission a critical necessity, I devote separate chapters to a Lutheran profile of mission, ecumenical or conciliar mission theology (two chapters), evangelical mission theology, and Roman Catholic mission theology. In the final chapter I comment briefly on questions and issues which are likely to loom large in the coming period, and which may require dialog among the three traditions, without attempting to provide definitive answers. The various chapters may be read independently with profit.

My special thanks are expressed to the Lutheran World Federation in Geneva, Switzerland, for permission to make generous use of materials which appeared earlier in an LWF study book (. . .*That the Gospel May Be Sincerely Preached throughout the World: A Lutheran Perspective on Mission and Evangelism in the 20th Century*, Geneva, 1982). Material from that book has been substantially revised and updated in the present volume. Acknowledgment is also made of the kind permission granted by the World Council of Churches, the Lausanne Committee on World Evangelization, and the United States Catholic Bishops Conference to quote pertinent extracts from ecumenical, evangelical, and Roman Catholic documents. For the interpretation of the materials quoted I alone am responsible.

My thanks are expressed to Lutheran Brotherhood of Minneapolis for a faculty sabbatical grant which has greatly eased the task, and to the Lutheran School of Theology at Chicago for making time available for this undertaking.

In the present volume I have employed the term *the two-thirds world* in preference to the more customary *the Third World* because I think it more accurately fits the reality of the situation in Asia, Africa, Latin America, Oceania, and the Caribbean, with their rapidly growing Christian communities.

ABBREVIATIONS

AACC	All Africa Conference of Churches, Lusaka, Zambia, 12-24 May 1974
AG	*Ad Gentes* (document from Vatican II)
CELAM	Conferences of Latin American bishops
COWE	Consultation on World Evangelization (sponsored by LCWE)
CWM	Commission on World Missions, LWF
CWME	Commission on World Mission and Evangelism, WCC
DFI	Dialogue with People of Living Faiths and Ideologies, WCC
DWM	Division of World Missions, LWF
DWME	Division of World Mission and Evangelism, WCC
E-O	Evangelizing of nominal Christians (see Chap. 5 and notes 39-41)
E-1	Evangelizing of non-Christians who are in proximity to a Christian community
E-2, E-3	Cross-cultural evangelistic efforts
EFMA	Evangelical Foreign Missions Association
EN	Pope Paul VI, *Evangelii Nuntiandi*

7

ERCDOM	"Evangelicals and Roman Catholics Dialogue on Mission, 1977–1984: A Report" (see Chap. 6, note 51)
GS	*Gaudium et Spes* (document from Vatican II)
IBMR	*International Bulletin of Missionary Research*
IFMA	Interdenominational Foreign Missions Association
IMC	International Missionary Council
IRM	*International Review of Mission*
LCWE or LC	Lausanne Committee for World Evangelization
LG	*Lumen Gentium* (document from Vatican II)
LWF	Lutheran World Federation
LOP	Lausanne Occasional Paper (see bibliography)
MARC	Mission Advanced Research and Communication Center (see bibliography)
NA	*Nostra Aetate* (document from Vatican II)
NCC	National Council of Churches of Christ in the United States of America
UR	*Unitatis Redintegratio* (document from Vatican II)
WA	Weimar edition of Luther's works; Weimar, 1883—
WCC	World Council of Churches
WEF	World Evangelical Fellowship
WSCF	World's Student Christian Federation

1

INTRODUCTION: FROM AN OLD TO A NEW MISSIONARY ERA

In the nearly 2000-year history of the Christian church there have been many fruitful missionary periods—the age of the first apostles, the journeys of medieval monks, the era of the padres who accompanied 16th-century explorers and conquistadors, the beginnings of Protestant evangelical missions in the 18th century—to mention only a few instances of committed individual Christians and groups who crossed frontiers in often dangerous and heroic efforts to reach previously unevangelized territories.

Following these isolated and disconnected efforts, there arose in the late 19th century a new missionary movement from the West which was to become global in scope and which would surpass all earlier movements in organization and resources. It literally set itself the task of completing the evangelization of the entire world within the lifetime of those then living. While this result was not attained, the 19th-century global missionary movement led to the gospel being more widely disseminated than ever before, and Christians were to be found living in more places than at any time since the birth of Christ.

Today, as the close of the 20th century approaches, the situation is very different. There are by far more Christians living in more places today than in the year 1900, even though the total number of Christians

9

as a percentage of the world's population has decreased slightly. In Africa south of the Sahara, for example, the number of Christians is expected to reach 50% of the total population of black Africa by the year 2000, compared to a mere 9% of the population in 1900. In China and Korea, the number of Christians continues to grow at a spectacular rate. Yet in the West, instead of being poised for a great new missionary advance, many Christians seem to assume that the "age of missions" is past, having been overtaken by the "ecumenical era," and that further work directed toward the evangelization of non-Christians is either unnecessary or inappropriate. Western Christianity, after four centuries of brilliant achievement, suffers from spiritual exhaustion and long-term decline, and seems unable or unwilling—apart from a few groups zealously committed to global evangelization—to gird itself for another great missionary effort.

Will there be another great missionary advance—a "new missionary era"—in our time? If so, what will it look like? We can be fairly certain that it will not be like the global missionary era which began in the mid-19th century, reached its zenith around the turn of the present century, and came to a decisive end before the middle of the 20th century! In the providence of God, and under the leading of God's spirit, the world mission of the church will continue and ever-new frontiers will be crossed. But the profile of the "new missionary era" will be very different from the Western-dominated movement that typified the 19th century.

In this chapter we examine that "old missionary era," look at the factors which produced its break-up, and consider the challenges and obstacles facing Christians and churches in all lands—above all, theological ones—as they seek to renew their missionary commitment. In the chapters that follow we shall examine in greater detail some of the theological issues that mark the transition from the old to a new missionary era.

THE GREAT CENTURY OF MISSIONS

Measured by any standard, "the great century of Christian missions" and its spill-over into the first half of the 20th century was a phenomenal achievement, whatever objections may be raised against it. Prior to the 19th century, Christianity had been primarily the hereditary faith of Europe and of some newly settled lands to which European emigrants or traders took their faith. Apart from Ethiopia and Egypt in Africa, the Philippines in Asia, and some parts of Latin America Christianized by Spain and Portugal, only scattered and miniscule Christian communities existed in the two-thirds world.*

Orthodox Russia was throughout the 19th century the leading Christian country of Europe. The United States was essentially a vast mission field, still in process of being evangelized. Europe, then the Christian heartland, was undergoing sweeping changes in the form of industrialization, urbanization, scientific and technical revolutions, and secularization. In western Europe the Enlightenment introduced a new period of free inquiry and rational speculation, and gave rise to a mood of skepticism toward established religious authority. A new anti-Christian ideology, Marxist atheism, made its appearance in the middle of the 19th century, and within another century it would dominate one-third of the globe. Signs of the steady collapse of Christendom were becoming more numerous.

Alongside these dechristianizing forces, however, movements for religious and spiritual renewal were also at work. Many of them poured their energies into the work of home, foreign, and diaspora mission societies. Through 19th-century movements of awakening, revivalism, and frontier missions, the United States of America would emerge as probably the most thoroughly Christianized nation by the year 1900, a fact which would have important implications for the evangelization of the rest of the world. Yet, as the end of the 19th century approached, the future status of Christianity in the world could not easily be predicted. Precisely at this time the world missionary movement burst unexpectedly and with surprising vigor on the scene, and dramatically altered the religious map of the world. No one could have foreseen such a development.

As the 20th century opened, with the rapid expansion of the Christian missionary movement from the West, the gospel was being preached and Christian churches planted in all continents and in virtually every open country of the globe. As never before, societies for the translation of the Scriptures into the known tongues of the earth were created, new missionary organizations by the thousands were organized by both Protestants and Catholics, and detailed surveys and analyses were made

*See the Preface for an explanation of the use in this book of the phrase *two-thirds world.*

of the forces available and the work to be done in each nation or region. Never before had the missionary forces of North America and Europe concentrated so single-mindedly on the global task.

Throughout the unevangelized world new Christian communities came into existence. These young churches were for the most part small, and still dependent on leadership and resources from Protestant and Roman Catholic mission agencies. But they were growing in both numbers and maturity of faith, and in many cases striving to attain the classical "three-self" marks of 19th-century Protestant mission theory: to be self-governing, self-supporting, and self-propagating. Here was the nucleus of a worldwide Christian community which would allow the worldwide ecumenical movement to emerge in the 20th century. In the 1940s this impressed Anglican Archbishop William Temple as "the great new fact of our time."

Never before could Christians be found living in so many different countries, amidst widely diverse customs, cultures, and religions, and employing so great a variety of languages. Suddenly the Christian community gained a breadth and universality which was its right by scriptural promise but which had eluded it through nearly two millenia.

What had produced this unique explosion of Christian faith and community into the entire world, nearly 19 centuries after the era of the primitive apostles? What was there about the late 19th century that generated such a surge of missionary commitment, and led some to entertain the literal hope of "evangelizing the world in this generation"? The factors have been comprehensively analyzed by historians, but several stand out.[1] Undoubtedly the *spiritual* factor was paramount. But the movement of the Spirit did not operate in isolation from powerful *political* forces at work, or from the *technical* developments of the late 19th century.

Stated somewhat too simply, student Christian activism and idealism, seeking to spread Christ's kingdom, allied with the rising forces of European colonialism and American imperialism, and supported by vast improvements in global commerce, transport, and communication, made the great century of Christian missions a possibility. This combination of factors was a unique product of late 19th-century history, and is not likely to occur again.

STUDENT MISSIONARY VOLUNTEERS

In 1886, 251 college students from 90 colleges gathered on the campus of the Mt. Hermon School in Northfield, Massachusetts, for a month-long Bible conference under the direction of the great evangelist Dwight L. Moody.[2] Under the urging of a missionary speaker, A. T. Pierson, who declared that "All should go, and go to all," 100 students committed themselves to undertaking foreign missionary service. The Student Volunteer Movement for Foreign Missions (SVM) came into being, with Robert Wilder as its central figure and John R. Mott, then still a student at Cornell, as the first chairman of its executive committee. Its watchword was: "The evangelization of the world in this generation."

By the time of the 1887 Northfield Student Conference, more than 2000 students had signed the pledge, "I am willing and desirous, God permitting, to become a foreign missionary." By 1890 more than 4000 volunteers, both young men and women, were offering their services to their own churches and preparing to go abroad. The SVM under Mott's dynamic leadership became the "missionary department" of the Intercollegiate YMCA and YWCA as well as the Inter-Seminary Missionary Alliance. Similar student movements for mission were organized in Great Britain, Scandinavia, on the European continent, and in several Asian countries.

In 1895 Mott was instrumental in organizing the World's Student Christian Federation (WSCF) in Sweden as an alliance of six regional student Christian movements. Its objectives were to lead students to become disciples of Jesus Christ, to deepen the spiritual life of students, and to enlist students in extending the kingdom of Christ throughout the world. Wherever Mott traveled and met with students, he secured from them a covenant to keep the "morning watch," to engage in Bible study and to pray regularly for guidance in doing God's will. Out of these and similar student-led organizations were to come the world missionary movement and the ecumenical movement of the 20th century.

What is most significant about these movements is that they were, at least at that time, *student* led, *voluntary,* and *spontaneous* in character. They were neither created nor controlled by the churches. The denominations were at a later stage to become major beneficiaries of student missionary idealism which enabled them to expand their overseas work rapidly. The denominations would also become regular participants in ecumenical organizations. In the initial phase, however, the *genesis* of these creative movements for Christian renewal, mission, and unity must be sought in the faith, dedication, and vision of a generation of students less interested in "church work" than in "exalting Jesus as king." Up until World War I this "student missionary uprising," as Mott called it, would provide a steady gusher of "volunteers" for overseas mission work and other forms of student endeavor.[3]

In America this flow of student missionary volunteers to foreign lands fitted hand in glove with the rising tide of American internationalism and humanitarian idealism which swept the country in the late decades of the 19th century. This movement to secure a larger place for America in world affairs climaxed with America's victory in the Spanish-American War of 1898, the acquisition of the Philippine Islands and Puerto Rico, and the emergence of the United States as a dominant power in the Caribbean and the Pacific. The 50-year-old slogan, "manifest destiny," confirming a historic Puritan conviction about America as a divinely *chosen* and covenanted nation, was now put to work as the rationale for America's entry into the big-power competition for colonial territories and prestige. Young missionary volunteers went out to China, Japan, Korea, the Philippines, and other lands with their own faith-convictions and missionary goals, but their actions were warmly applauded by a grateful American nation that was perhaps less interested in their theology than in their value as human expressions of America's civilizing obligation and humanitarian intention toward the rest of the world. To fulfill her role as a benevolent superpower on the world stage, America needed idealistic young men and women to represent her abroad. The "Christian" colonial powers of Europe were by this time fully supportive of Protestant and Catholic mission activities in colonial lands as instruments of their own national policies. Since the time of Constantine, seldom have imperial policy and the interests of God's kingdom—Caesar and Christ—been in such close and comfortable convergence.

EDINBURGH CONFERENCE, 1910

The World Missionary Conference at Edinburgh, Scotland, in 1910 was a watershed event which climaxed decades of regional missionary cooperation.[4] Edinburgh 1910 brought the movement to evangelize the world to a heightened state of global awareness and planning. It took place in the high tide of late 19th-century optimism, galvanized by the commitments of the volunteers—including the sacrifices of a number of early student martyrs—and in confident expectation that the entire world could be evangelized within the lifetime of those then living. This did not mean that the whole world would be *converted* to Christ; for Mott and others it meant that the *offer of salvation* in Jesus Christ would be "made known to all so that all might believe in him and be saved." The urgency of completing what came to be known as the *unfinished task* demanded that the Christian missionary forces of the world maximize their efforts and coordinate their planning, avoiding needless competition, so as to secure the best possible results. The statesmanlike leadership of the conference by John R. Mott as chairperson, and J. H. Oldham as secretary, combined evangelical fervor with businesslike efficiency in dealing with the conference agenda.

In overall character, Edinburgh 1910 was not a conference on the "theology of mission" as we now understand it. It was a conference to design the *strategy* for a final campaign by the concerted forces of the kingdom of God as they assayed what was needed to complete the "unfinished task." Given proper generalship and coordination of existing resources, the goal appeared to be achievable. The theological justification for mission work—the question, Why missions?—did not even occupy a place on the agenda at Edinburgh. An unspoken consensus existed that the Great Commission needed to be fulfilled. The actual agenda revolved more around the How? and What? of mission: the missionary message, the church in the mission field, education, missionary training, the home base, missions and governments, promoting unity, and the like.

Delegates to Edinburgh were impelled to missionary activity by such motives as God's love for the whole creation, compassion for the lost, Christ's command to preach the gospel, pity for the dying, expectation of the Lord's early return, and a grateful sense of stewardship. These and other motives blended together with the overriding reality of the Great Commission and a common perception that the world was eagerly waiting to hear the gospel message. The unity of the delegates was reflected as much in the daily periods of corporate intercession, when business was suspended to pray for Christian work in all parts of the world, and in the fellowship of working groups, as in their unspoken theological agreement. No signing of any theological statement was required at Edinburgh. In a word, Edinburgh demonstrated a unity of *spirit,* purpose, and common commitment to the task that did not need to be tested by explicit theological agreement.

ORIGINS OF THE FAITH AND ORDER MOVEMENT

Edinburgh 1910 thus launched a movement for missionary cooperation and consultation without prior doctrinal consensus. Persons with differing convictions were given the opportunity of working together and coming to know and trust one another; none was asked to compromise a denominational standpoint or theological conviction. Yet, theological issues were not overlooked. Stemming from the Edinburgh conference, and on the initiative of a missionary bishop from the Philippines, Charles H. Brent, there emerged a plan to convene "a world conference on faith and order" to deal expressly with theological problems excluded from the agenda of the Edinburgh meeting.[5] The Faith and Order movement, open to Christians of all communions that would accept "our Lord Jesus Christ as God and Savior," held its first world conference at Lausanne (1927) to deal with issues that divided Christian bodies, as well as with areas of agreement. Its mandate was "to proclaim the essential oneness of the Church of Christ" and to keep before the churches "the obligation to manifest that unity and its urgency for the work of evangelism."

The link between Christian unity and world evangelization was therefore prominent in the formation of the Faith and Order Conference, and it continued into the formation of the World Council of Churches, at Amsterdam in 1948. The Edinburgh conference had urged the planting of a *single united church* in each mission land as the best method of advancing the goal of world evangelization.

INTERNATIONAL MISSIONARY COUNCIL

The Edinburgh conference in its closing days decided to establish a "continuation committee" to conserve the gains that had been made, to give the mission agencies a continuing link, and to plan for further consultations.[6] The organizational expression of this was a modest "traveling secretariat" in the form of John R. Mott, who traveled indefatigably in the post-Edinburgh years, meeting with local church leaders—many of them veterans of earlier student movements—and helping to organize regional or national Christian councils. In 1921 the International Missionary Council (IMC) was formed as a "council of councils" in order to "manifest the essential spiritual unity already existing among Christians" through missionary cooperation. It had no doctrinal basis of its own, but its declared aim was "to further the proclamation to the whole world of the Gospel of Jesus Christ, to the end that all men may believe in him and be saved."

The IMC became a clearinghouse for the concerns of national missionary councils and Christian councils, and a coordinating and planning agency for mission organizations. Among its functions were to stimulate thinking and investigation on missionary questions, to make the results of studies available, to help coordinate activities of mission organizations in different countries, to bring about united missionary action where possible, and to help to unite Christian forces in seeking justice. The IMC was responsible for the publication of the *International Review of Missions,* and for calling a world missionary conference, if and when it were deemed desirable.[7] This last function would give the IMC worldwide visibility and insure its lasting influence on the world-missionary movement.

Over the years the IMC became what was probably the most respected ecumenical council for missionary cooperation and consultation. In addition to sponsoring a wide range of valuable studies, it helped to organize major world-missionary conferences like that of Edinburgh 1910: at Jerusalem (1928), on the Mount of Olives, and at Tambaram-Madras (1938), on the campus of Madras Christian College. Whereas Edinburgh had involved only a handful of representatives from the "younger churches" of the two-thirds world, younger-church leaders were to become increasingly prominent and vocal in later IMC meetings. IMC meetings also made solid and useful contributions to the emerging study of the "theology of mission," particularly in reference to the authority of the Christian message vis-à-vis other faiths, relations between "younger" and "older" churches, and the place of the local church in evangelism.[8] Matters related to the economic basis of the churches were extensively studied. As part of the preparation for the Tambaram-Madras conference (1938) Professor Hendrik Kraemer of the Netherlands was asked to write what was to become the most famous book about mission theology of all time, *The Christian*

Message in a Non-Christian World. In Chapter 3 of this volume we shall trace the theological contribution of the IMC.

EDINBURGH 1910 AND THE WORLD COUNCIL OF CHURCHES

In 1948, at Amsterdam, the World Council of Churches (WCC) was formally constituted by the merging of the Faith and Order movement and the Life and Work movement. The WCC held its own series of world assemblies: at Amsterdam (1948), Evanston (1954), New Delhi (1961), Uppsala (1968), Nairobi (1975), and Vancouver (1983). It was to become the most widely representative global council of churches in the world, with membership including most Protestant and Orthodox denominations. The Roman Catholic church is not a member, but collaborates with the WCC in many areas.

In 1961, at the Third Assembly of the World Council of Churches at New Delhi, the International Missionary Council was formally integrated into the structure of the WCC as a constituent movement. The former IMC now became the WCC's Commission and Division of World Mission and Evangelism (CWME/DWME). Its declared aim within the WCC was "to further the proclamation to the whole world of the Gospel of Jesus Christ to the end that all men may believe in him and be saved." Its functions included responsibility to "keep before the churches their calling and privilege to engage in constant prayer for the missionary and evangelistic work of the church" and "to remind the churches . . . of the unfinished task and to deepen their sense of missionary obligation."

With this act of integration the IMC, which, through the Edinburgh conference of 1910 had in some sense been the parent and progenitor of the modern ecumenical movement, was reunited with its conciliar child, the World Council of Churches, along with its other child, the World Conference on Faith and Order, and its closely related cousin, the Universal Christian Conference on Life and Work. The fact of integration would have important consequences (to be discussed later) not only for the ongoing work of the former IMC, but also for the post-Edinburgh conciliar missionary movement, of which it was the premier representative. Some evangelicals, for example, reacted to the integration of the International Missionary Council into the World Council of Churches by disaffiliating from the WCC's Commission on

World Mission and Evangelism, or holding it at a critical distance. The rise and rapid expansion of the Lausanne missionary movement and its predecessors in the 1960s and 1970s as an alternative to the ecumenical missionary movement (described in Chapter 5) follows the integration of the IMC into the WCC.

We have presented Edinburgh 1910 as the crowning achievement, midpoint, and symbol of the older missionary movement, and noted its legacy and achievements. Edinburgh crystallized a global movement of missionary cooperation, especially among Protestants in the West, gave increased direction and momentum to that movement, and stimulated the creation at the world, regional, and national levels of a network of cooperative missionary organizations. At a later point, this conciliar network would become an important part of the evolving ecumenical movement in all six continents.

Edinburgh 1910 and its successor, the International Missionary Council, pioneered in studies related to many aspects of missionary work. It held up the goal of the formation in each country or region of a single united church, deeply related to the culture of its own people, existing both as the people of God in that area and as the primary instrument for all further efforts for its evangelization. Edinburgh 1910 thus anticipated, though it did not fully realize, the concept of "partnership in obedience" of churches in all six continents in continuing and completing the unfinished task.

Closely related to these changes in church-to-church relationships between "older" and "younger" churches is the anatomy and development of *missionary vocation*. In the transition from the "old missionary era" to a newer era still in process of emerging, the earlier missionary role with its job description has become largely obsolete and subject to pressures for change and redefinition. These pressures vary according to location and the group concerned.

CHANGES IN THE MISSIONARY ROLE

The early missionaries had been pioneers: they mastered the languages, preached the gospel, baptized converts, organized fledgling churches, and generally laid foundations for the future. After them came a generation of missionaries who were managers and "directors": they headed institutions, trained the first generation of national Christian workers, oversaw organization and finances, shaped the strategy for the growing young church, and generally represented the interests of the sending body. These second-generation foreign missionaries, because of the authority they possessed and the respect they commanded, were often considered the religious version of Western colonial officials. Their avowed aim was to work themselves out of jobs so that their positions could be nationalized under a "three-self" type of church. In fact, however, they tended to hold on to power and to convey an image of missionary paternalism.

After 1945, with the movement of decolonization in the two-thirds world, the "missionary manager" position became no longer viable. The new crop of postwar missionaries had to learn new roles. They were no longer welcome as agents of a foreign sending body but were considered "invited guests" of a young Christian community in Asia, Africa, or Latin America, expected to work under the direction of the young church, to share its language, culture, and challenges, and to sacrifice personal power and ambition for the sake of the church.

Missionaries who began their service at the end of the "old missionary era" found the sudden change in roles threatening. The changes in missionary vocation were symptomatic of much greater changes that marked the transition from the old missionary era to the newer one. Missionaries, now valued for their "specialist" roles in teaching, medicine, agriculture, or development, and sometimes regarded as the ecclesiastical equivalent of the Peace Corps, found themselves wondering about the purpose of their missionary vocation. Was it to preach the gospel, or simply to be a temporary resource available to the local church, ready to step aside when no longer needed? In a period when nationals were taking over direct evangelism and local pastoral roles, many missionaries began to wonder whether they were *wanted*—or *needed*. This problem was likely to be less troubling where missionaries worked in pioneer situations, engaged in direct evangelism or service to the local population, and not under the direction of a local church. By the end of the "old missionary era," however, the role of the Western missionary had become increasingly *problematic*. In the decades after 1960, as young churches organized their own mission departments, developed their own mission fields, and sent out an estimated 16,000 missionaries representing the two-thirds world, the problem of competition and role confusion would only increase!

BREAKUP OF THE OLD MISSIONARY MOVEMENT

The late 19th-century missionary movement with its high profile of Western missionary presence in the lands of the two-thirds world was a singular phenomenon unlikely to be repeated in our day. The legacy of Edinburgh 1910, when a unique constellation of factors converged to set the stage for a great missionary movement from the "Christian" North into the "heathen" South, is simply not recoverable. Nor should it be, for the religious character of our world has decisively changed in the past century. Nostalgia for a past "golden age" of missions cannot be a motive for endlessly repeating the past or for avoiding today's issues. Seldom was it more true that:

> *New occasions teach new duties;*
> *Time makes ancient truth uncouth;*
> *They must upward still and onward*
> *Who would keep abreast of truth.*

(James Russell Lowell,
"Once to Every Man and Nation")

A new missionary commitment must be based on a realistic reading of the factors which make the older missionary era obsolete and call for change.

The Christian missionary movement today is in a state of *crisis* because the larger community of faith of which it is a part is also in a prolonged state of crisis. Gone for the most part are the simple faith, confidence, and activism of the student volunteers, and the conviction inspired by Mott in the Edinburgh 1910 delegates that they could literally accomplish the task of evangelizing the entire world within the generation of those then living.

Towards the end of the 20th century, despite an astonishing array of computers, electronic gadgets, and jet planes that give our own age technological superiority over our spiritual forebears of the 19th century, and which ought to make the evangelistic task infinitely easier today than it was in 1910, that evangelistic task may be even further from being finished. Moreover, the will to accomplish it simply does not exist in most of our Western churches, though there appears to be

a marked rise in missionary and evangelistic commitment in the churches of the two-thirds world. In the West, however, the optimism which
marked the late 19th-century scene, and the confident sense that God's
kingdom was dawning as the onward march of world evangelization
advanced from one nation to the next, are lacking today. Global mission
has now become a problematic task, fraught with fundamental theological problems about which Christians increasingly disagree—both
as to *what* it is and *whether* it should be done at all.

While not abandoning the task altogether, many churches formerly
in the vanguard of the world missionary movement appear to be merely
holding on. Some continue to do mission out of loyalty to past tradition
but without much present conviction. Confusion and perplexity reign
with regard to the continuing validity of missionary obligation, and the
appropriateness of witnessing to non-Christians about salvation in Jesus
Christ. Mainline denominations, while occasionally lamenting the loss
of missionary and evangelistic zeal, make relatively small plans and
set apart relatively meager resources. Pope Paul VI, in issuing the 1975
Apostolic Exhortation *Evangelii Nuntiandi,* asked a series of valid
questions:

> In our day, what has happened to that hidden energy of the Good News,
> which is able to have a powerful effect on man's conscience? To what
> extent and in what way is that evangelical force capable of really trans-
> forming the people of this century? What methods should be followed
> in order that the power of the Gospel may have its effect?[9]

Some 10 years after the Second Vatican Council, the Roman pontiff
wanted to know whether the Roman church found herself better
equipped than before to proclaim the gospel and to put it into people's
hearts with conviction. In one form or another serious Christians are
asking the same question today.

What accounts for the crisis in world missions? Why has the old
missionary order broken down? We shall attempt to show that factors
for *long-term change* are at work which make the end of the 20th
century and the period which follows qualitatively different from the
19th century.

COLLAPSE OF THE COLONIAL FRAMEWORK

The first blow to the old missionary order was the *dismantling of
the colonial framework* under which the gospel was first proclaimed

in the two-thirds world of Asia, Africa, Latin America, the Caribbean, and Oceania.[10] With minor exceptions these areas first saw the planting of the Christian church under the aegis of Western mission work aided and protected by colonialism. Since the middle of the 20th century the link between "Caesar and Christ" has been snapped. The dismantling of the centuries-old colonial setup began in Asia in the late 1940s and continued in Africa throughout the 1960s. Today the British, French, Dutch, Belgian, and Portuguese colonial empires have all virtually disappeared, though certainly not without trace. In Latin America, where colonial ties were broken in the 19th century, the struggle against neocolonial influence continues.

Today the friendly "protective umbrella" of colonialism has been abruptly withdrawn from Western missions and young churches, leaving them exposed as tiny minorities with dependent structures to sometimes hostile and unpredictable forces.

Needless to say, what was experienced in the West as "loss of empire" was welcomed by many in the two-thirds world, including the churches, as *liberation* from colonial tutelage and foreign oppression. For not until the collapse of the old colonial order—either through successful wars of national liberation or by the voluntary or negotiated withdrawal of foreign occupying forces—were local Christian churches free, but also under new pressures, to find their own identity as the people of God in independent nations. They could now begin the process of adapting their ministries and witness to revolutionary political conditions, local cultural contexts, and to the often impoverished economies of the area.

Efforts to "contextualize" the witness of the gospel, or to "inculturate" the faith in local theologies and liturgies, became matters of the highest priority. Local churches were pushed toward greater maturity and self-reliance as positions formerly held by foreign missionaries were nationalized. In some cases, missionaries were denied entry visas by local governments. As noted earlier, the old missionary role was redefined to suit the new situation. Now the classic 19th-century missionary doctrine of the "three-self church"—self-governing, self-supporting, and self-propagating—became a sheer necessity.

In both North and South, the consequences were equally painful. The cry, "Missionary, go home!" was heard with increasing frequency.[11] Local governments passed laws limiting the number of missionaries or the tenure of their service; some countries excluded them altogether. Wholesale indictments were brought against missionaries for "cultural imperialism" and wrongful "proselytism." Efforts were made in some places to outlaw conversions as contrary to local custom, or to prohibit baptisms.

Local churches were sometimes intimidated into giving up evangelistic efforts. In some cases local church budgets were pared so drastically that support for outreach activities was eliminated, and churches were in danger of becoming inward-looking ghettos. Christian communities were in places stigmatized as unwanted minorities, politically disloyal, and dependent entirely on outside money and support. Especially in Asia, the resurgence of ancient ethnic religions in the postcolonial era led many Christians to feel that they were unprotected and did not really belong. Christian communities for their part complained of discriminatory practices by government officials.

Maintaining religious freedom—above all, freedom to do evangelism and make public conversions—became a very delicate issue. The spread of Marxist atheist ideology, with its doctrinaire view of all religion as an "opiate for the masses," into the lands of the two-thirds world would only exacerbate charges that Christians were imperialist "running dogs," guilty of acts of political subversion and promoting cultural alienation. Small wonder that some churches in Africa and other regions began to give serious consideration to a short-term "moratorium" on the sending of missionaries and the receipt of funds from abroad, so that they might develop a deeper sense of their own local identity.

The most extreme form of anticolonial reaction occurred in the People's Republic of China, the area which, prior to 1949, had been the largest single "mission field" for both Protestants and Catholics. In the wake of the Chinese Communist revolutionary victory over the Nationalists in 1949, missionaries were expelled, overseas funds were cut off, and ties with foreign religious organizations were broken. A good many missionaries were tried as criminals, some being imprisoned with life sentences. Under the leadership of the Chinese Patriotic Three-Self Reform Movement, a progressive group within the Chinese Protestant church, the missionary movement of the past was branded as "imperialistic." Chinese Christians were warned to denounce and dissociate themselves resolutely from former Western friends, to be vigilant against imperialism, and to accelerate the development of a

Chinese church cooperating with government and people in the task of socialist reconstruction.

In China this movement of dewesternization led to rapid changes: nationalizing of former mission schools and hospitals, prohibition of all public evangelism, close regulation of church activities by a governmental bureau for religious affairs, elimination of unpatriotic church leaders and pastors, and eventually the adoption of a "postdenominational" expression of Protestantism. In the councils of Western mission agencies, meanwhile, self-searching and self-accusation regarding China went on in the 1950s. Who was responsible for "losing" China, and why had it happened? What were the lessons to be learned from the traumatic China experience? How could these lessons be implemented in other mission areas? The debate over China was a concentrated version of the kind of discussion that took place at high levels in many Western mission agencies in the period following decolonization. In a special way, China symbolized the breakup of the entire old missionary order, and its implications were far-reaching.

The reemergence of the Chinese church from the painful and trying experiences of the "cultural revolution" after 1980, and its viability as a church without Western mission ties, was in many ways the other side of the coin in symbolizing the emergence of a new missionary era.

DECLINE OF CHRISTENDOM

In the West, the breakup of the old missionary order was accompanied by the steady *decline of "Christendom,"* the 1600-year-old entity based on the *corpus Christianum* from the time of Emperor Constantine. Today the West is frankly recognized as having entered a post-Christian cultural era. The effects of the Enlightenment, secularization, science and technology, urban industrial development, and ideological upheaval have cut deeply into the old "value system" with its traditional Christian amalgam of church, government, education, morality, and family life. The most striking evidence of the decline of Christendom has been the spread of atheistic ideology into "Christian Russia" and after the Second World War from the USSR to the traditionally Christian lands of Eastern Europe, and more recently into some postcolonial regions of Asia, Africa, and Latin America. Luther's

East Germany has been transformed into a dedicated Marxist ally, with a steadily dwindling Christian minority population.

In the post-Christendom situation European Christianity confronts the phenomenon of empty churches and nominal church members. Christian identity is increasingly divorced from churchgoing and active practice of the faith, and is becoming a cultural relic. Portions of the urban laboring class appear to be permanently alienated from the life of the church. Young people trek to Asia in search of gurus and religious experiences to satisfy spiritual needs not met by the churches. At times the label "pagan" or "neopagan" is applied to the religious situation in countries like France. Church-state ties, where they still exist, are progressively loosened, and many find them totally anachronistic. Despite vestiges of the old order, such as state collection of church taxes, the traditional rituals of infant Baptism and youth confirmation, and compulsory religious instruction in schools, the Christian cause seems to be that of a dwindling minority. Some socialist societies consciously sponsor secular name-giving ceremonies, youth dedications, and weddings in competition with religious rites. Persons no longer wanting to be identified with the church, for personal convenience or professional advancement, procure "church-leaving" certificates, or have their names removed from church rolls.

THE WEST AS A MISSION FIELD

According to statistics brought to light by the *World Christian Encyclopedia* (1982), massive defections in the West from Christianity to other religions or to no religion occur each year. Over a 12-month period, some 2,765,100 persons in Europe and North America (more than 7500 each day) cease to be practicing Christians.[12] Studies of mainline denominations in the United States have shown that, after two centuries of steady annual growth, many major denominations have stopped growing in membership—they began to decline in the 1960s and continued to do so through the 1970s—and that the growth rates of all others have slowed considerably.[13] Roman Catholics have reported a steep decline in the average number of new parishes since 1950. A disproportionate number of young people under the age of 30 are reportedly dropping out of church participation, and church school enrollments have declined drastically.

By way of illustration, the baptized membership of the Lutheran Church in America declined by 177,130 members from 1962 to 1985, while in the same period the confirmed and communing membership increased slightly. This represents only a 5.5% loss of persons who claimed membership in the church in 1962, but when measured against the 29% growth of the population of the United States during the same period, the loss rises to 34.5%.[14]

A further dramatic illustration of the denomination's failure to conserve its membership is offered by the fact that the same Lutheran Church in America during the decade 1976–1985 removed nearly *one million members* from its rolls, or an average of 97,000 per year, for reasons other than death or transfer. These persons simply "disappeared" without trace, raising serious questions about the adequacy of congregational ministries to inactive members. The places of these million lost persons were taken by approximately one million new adherents, permitting the church to characterize its overall growth as "stable." Yet, serious questions remained as LCA officials reflected on the fact that overall net growth was slight. While some new persons were joining, many others were "leaving through the back door."[15] The average number of adult baptisms, another significant barometer of evangelistic effectiveness, was only about *one per congregation* per year.

The situation in other mainline denominations appears comparable. Little wonder that denominational leaders are deeply worried about the phenomenon of back-door leakage, and the lack of evangelistic motivation. For churches which cannot retain *old* members while at the same time failing to enlist *new* members by evangelism at a consistent rate are doomed to die a slow death.

Current estimates suggest that 95 million Americans are unchurched, and an estimated 40 million children are unbaptized and uncatechized. If these figures are true, the United States ranks alongside most of Europe as a leading mission field, and a prime candidate for reevangelization. The precise missionary status of America remains obscure because of the veneer of cultural Christianity, and the marked preference expressed by Americans to be identified with traditional religious values rather than being stigmatized as "atheists" or "unbelievers." Unchurched Americans view themselves as in some sense *believers,* even if not *belongers* to institutional religious groups.

According to a recent Gallup Poll Religious Survey on "Religiosity in America and the Task of the Churches,"[16] unchurched people say they want to *belong* and are waiting for an invitation to join a local congregation. They claim that they hold conservative or traditional religious views not unlike those held by people who are church members. At the same time they find fault with institutional religion, saying that it has lost its *spiritual* center. They also criticize churches for being too concerned with organization and money, while not being warm and accepting toward outsiders. While such responses are undoubtedly defensive and self-serving, they are not wrong in pointing to evangelistic insensitivity and ineptitude on the part of many local congregations.

EXOTIC NEW RELIGIOUS MOVEMENTS

Americans also manifest a growing preference for *privatized* expressions of religion which accord with the shift to freer and more personalized life-styles.[17] This is another indication of the collapse of Christian orthodoxy, for this attitude provides an "open door" for the cults and new religious movements which have mushroomed in recent decades and which capitalize on the weaknesses of the churches. Rejecting basic beliefs of Judaeo-Christian revelation, these movements with their "new age" philosophies fill a spiritual void with diverse tenets borrowed from Eastern mysticism, the occult, Satan worship, self-realization, human potential, and holistic health and healing. They teach devotees how to meditate, chant, practice yoga, achieve inner peace and detachment, and attain altered states of consciousness. They even offer commercially appealing antidotes to stressful living in the modern world.

While "religiosity in general" appears to be growing at a phenomenal rate—both in the United States and throughout the world—its teachings and practices are syncretistic, often heretical, and at variance with historic Christianity. Claiming to satisfy the psychic and spiritual needs of dropouts from the churches, these movements offer only pseudoreligious experiences and undermine the historic Christian faith by their syncretistic tolerance. They foster the notion that *any* religious belief or practice is "just fine" as long as one holds and practices it sincerely. By deviating from the Christian confession of Jesus Christ as Lord and Savior, the "new age" movements weaken Christian identity. They undercut the church's missionary commitment, and increase the urgency of reevangelizing nominal Christians. Some conservative Christian bodies are doing a creditable job of schooling their members with regard to the subversive character and syncretistic teachings of these "new age" religious alternatives, but most denominations seem content to allow their members to fend for themselves.

MOVEMENT TOWARD GLOBAL COMMUNITY

Another factor which spells the death knell of the Western-dominated missionary enterprise of the 19th century is the movement toward *global human community*. As never before, political and economic changes in the world situation since 1945, combined with advances in communications, have fostered a sense of global human interdependence. With this awareness has come a recurring call for the entire human community—East and West, North and South, rich and poor, developed and developing—to work together for peace, survival, and human development. World organizations such as the United Nations (UN) and its special affiliates for world health, food production, population, economic development, and refugee assistance have all accentuated the need for global planning and sharing of resources. The threat of nuclear holocaust has only intensified hopes and aspirations for common solutions transcending ideological blocs.

Today, every threat to peace, security, or human rights in any part of the world becomes—via the mass media—a global issue. The struggle against racism in South Africa, threatened terrorist actions in the Middle East, violations of human rights in the USSR or in a Latin American country, protests by a religious minority group in India—all of these are quickly escalated to the status of global issues. This is not to imply that such incidents yield to global solutions. Indeed, the world's international peacekeeping organizations have generally not proved competent to deal with conflicts between nations or superpowers, but they still represent the best hope of the human race for maintaining a semblance of peace and security. While the United Nations Organization has come under sharp criticism for its failures and shortcomings, and is often viewed in the United States as a less than neutral sounding board for ventilating hostility by two-thirds world nations against the United States, no one has proposed that it be abolished. It represents the best and most universal forum for global planning and arbitration of disputes available.

The religious and ecclesiastical aspect of the movement toward a global human community is the *ecumenical movement* of the 20th century and its organs for mission, service, dialog, and cooperation. On one hand, the ecumenical movement represents a movement away from old-world domination toward sharing of power and responsibility between older and younger churches in all six continents. On the other, it epitomizes a global Christian response to threats to Christian identity posed by the collapse of colonialism and the demise of Christendom. As W. A. Visser 't Hooft, first General Secretary of the World Council of Churches, once observed:

> Precisely at the time when the world is being unified and a world civilization begins to take shape, the world position of Christianity is undermined and the process of estrangement between Church and world becomes increasingly acute and manifest.[18]

The statement recognizes that the growth of the ecumenical movement is not simply an effort to overcome isolation and forge closer bonds between scattered churches in the world Christian community. Ecumenism summons the churches to deal in a united way with the most urgent issues confronting the churches around the world. Since Edinburgh 1910, the intrinsic relationship between unity in Christ and participation in his mission in and to the world has served as a catalyst to ecumenical effort.

NEW AXIS OF CHRISTIAN COMMUNITY

Not only has the Western-dominated colonial structure of the 19th century given way to a globally organized new human community in the 20th century, but the collapse of the old structure has been attended by the loss of economic vigor and political influence on the part of the former "great powers." Two giant military and economic "superpowers"—each with its own ideology and supporting bloc—now dominate the political scene. The militarily weaker and economically poorer nations, above all, those in the two-thirds world, arrange themselves into regional blocs and interest groups for mutual interest and security. By a strange irony, one superpower is identified as the *defender* and protector of the world's religious interests, especially those of Christianity, while the other superpower is regarded as the *foe* of all religious belief, even though it claims to respect the constitutional right of religious liberty. The irony is further compounded when it is disclosed that that superpower which champions religious freedom and human rights is also the nation that sends out the greatest number of overseas missionaries for service in approximately 200 foreign lands!

Within the world Christian community there has also been a highly significant *shift in the global axis* of Christianity. The *World Christian Encyclopedia* disclosed the astonishing fact that at some point between 1980 and 1985 there were more Christians in the two-thirds world than in Europe and North America combined.[19] Massive defections from church membership in Europe along with increasing losses to other faiths or no faith in North America, when combined with startling Christian growth in the two-thirds world, produced a new situation in which Christians of color and non-European tongues were beginning for the first time to *outnumber* their brothers and sisters of the faith in the North. The consequences of this momentous southward shift in the axis, or balance, of world Christianity have been endlessly discussed.[20] What the long-term effects of the shift will be for theology, churchmanship, worship, cultural identity, or mission outreach cannot now be foreseen. It is generally thought that they will be far-reaching. Unquestionably, the image of Christianity in the 21st century will be much more Asian, African, or Latin American than North American or European.

As far as the global Christian community is concerned, an identity shift has already taken place. The ecumenical movement and the rapid growth of Christian communities in the South has provided the churches with new tools and resources for coping with the agenda of global interdependence. The accelerating growth of churches in Africa and in parts of Asia and Latin America has placed heavy burdens on churches in those regions to provide resources for ministry. Even as churches in the North Atlantic worry about dropouts and the new phenomenon of their minority status, church leaders in two-thirds world nations struggle with such problems as providing adequate pastoral leadership, houses of worship, teachers, educational opportunities, and other necessities for newly formed congregations. In some cases these churches have come to their Western partners to request emergency assistance in the form of theological education by extension programs, materials for rural chapels, or tools for media outreach. The problem for Western mission agencies has been how to foster growth without undermining self-reliance and local initiative.

CHANGES IN GLOBAL CHRISTIAN RELATIONSHIPS

The shift in the axis of Christianity has also brought changes in the style of commitments and relationships. Churches in the South now see themselves not as objects of mission from the West, but as agents of mission in their own right. Some have organized their own mission departments, and recruited and sent out their own missionaries to foreign fields. According to one estimate, more than 16,000 missionaries have been sent out by churches in the two-thirds world, and this number includes an unknown number of missionaries from the South serving in Europe and North America. The home base of mission can now be found in many local churches in Asia, Africa, and Latin America.

Churches of the South also bring their own viewpoints and concerns into the ecumenical movement at the global, regional, and national levels. They demand direct church-to-church relationships in place of their former links with mission agencies. They want to share power over appointments and control over money. They have become effective advocates for the cries of their own people. They have sensitized Western church leaders to the reality of oppressive structures and dependency relationships, as well as the effects of Western support for racist or militaristic regimes. The new ecumenical agenda has for some time been dominated by the theme of *liberation* in both church and society, and a call for the practice of *dialog* in situations of religious pluralism. The conciliar missionary movement, evangelical missions, and the Roman Catholic church have all been deeply affected by the vocal cries and increasing visibility of church leaders from the two-thirds world.

The entry of southern-hemisphere churches into the ecumenical arena also raises new questions about the shape and direction of global mission, and the nature of global partnership. Does the new ecumenical movement of the churches supersede the old missionary movement from the West? Many Western Christians might think that the day of mission is over—and certainly the day of *one-way* mission *is* over—but Christians from the two-thirds world seem eager to play their part in the coming era of global mission. What will that mission look like? How will the world Christian community carry out its task in the framework of interdependence, when faith and initiative are strong on one side but financial resources and technical expertise remain concentrated in the North? Is genuine partnership really possible between churches of unequal strength, resources, and historical background?

The call for self-reliance, cultural identity and mature relationships, recognition of the "dominance-dependence" syndrome, and the "moratorium" discussion—all these have taken place as part of the southward shift in the axis, and the readjustment of relationships within world Christianity. These issues have erupted at a time when the task of world evangelization is far from completed. Just solutions to issues of power sharing and allocation of resources and creative new structures for international Christian witness and service will be a prerequisite for a "new missionary era."

CRISIS OF FAITH IN THE WEST

To this list of developments precipitating the breakup of the "old missionary era" must be added one more—perhaps the most serious of all: the *crisis of faith,* spirit, and theological conviction in the Western world. This was hinted at earlier in our discussion of religious pluralism in the West, and the demise of "Christendom." Lesslie Newbigin, noting the "long-term questioning of the very foundation of faith" and the dissolution of Christendom in the West, wrote:

> A chronic bad conscience has seized the western white man in his relations with the rest of the world so that he fears above everything else the charge of arrogance. . . . A profound crisis of faith within the Western Churches has led to a loss of conviction that there is anything in the Christian faith which is so vital that without it men will perish.[21]

Newbigin traces the roots of this crisis of faith ultimately back to the Enlightenment in Europe. He calls for a far-reaching "missionary encounter" between biblical faith and modern secular culture in which Christian faith neither enters into a synthesis with culture, nor allows itself to be co-opted by it, but attempts to live out a Christian existence while taking modern culture seriously.[22] Newbigin comes to the conclusion that modern Western culture represents the toughest mission field of the world in our day.

The Dutch missiologist Johannes Verkuyl cites multiple causes for the abandonment of missionary commitment in the West:

> . . . the shock caused by the rise of religious pluralism even in the western world; the revival of relativism and skepticism; and some forms of false repentance for the mistakes of mission history, resulting in stagnation, whereas *true* repentance should lead to renewal.[23]

Verkuyl is correct in suggesting that guilt feelings over past associations with imperialism and a sense of having lost moral authority because of complicity in oppressive structures have combined to create doubt about the validity and integrity of Western Christianity. Some critics, including persons within the church, believe that Western Christianity has forfeited its right to preach the gospel to others, especially to persons of other races and cultures. They argue that Christians should limit their role to Christian *presence,* patient listening, quiet identification, and humble *diakonia,* while supporting movements for justice and liberation in the two-thirds world. Some argue that the West should first reevangelize itself before sharing the gospel with the two-thirds world.

These doubts and self-questionings are to some extent legitimate, insofar as they relate to attitudes, methods, and approaches, but they appear to mask a much deeper uncertainty about the ultimate value and truth of Christian faith and the missionary purpose of the church. The Christian mission has in the past shown an ability to deal honestly with abuses and to purify itself of false practices. The fundamental question, as Newbigin's statement implies, is really whether people still *believe* that Christian faith is so vital that it must be shared with others. The *crisis* of Western Christianity has to do not with the *how* but with the *why* of Christian mission. Either God is or is not a sending God. Either the church is sent into the whole world to proclaim the good news, or it is simply an institution for preserving a local cultural tradition. Either it is a missionary church, or it is not the church of Jesus Christ. The crisis of Western Christianity, insofar as it raises questions about the validity of mission activity and evangelism, is a crisis which touches the very foundation of Christian faith and the life of the church. In the West, for the time being, questions about the foundation and goal of mission must take precedence over all other issues.

MISSIONS AS A PROBLEM

"Formerly missions *had* problems," Walter Freytag, dean of German missiologists, is reported to have once said, "but now they have *become* a problem to themselves." Many of the reasons have already been given. Churches in the West have retreated from earlier global mission commitments and hesitated to undertake the work of reevangelizing their own societies and cultures. The Christian West in our day, in contrast to the spiritual climate of a century earlier, appears to have been gripped by a loss of *nerve* which may conceal an even more serious loss of *faith*—some would even speak of massive "apostasy." Strenuous efforts by religious organizations to stem the tide of secularism have done little to alter the overall situation. The old foundations for a strong missionary and evangelistic advance by the churches, still reeling from the collapse of Christendom and the breakup of colonial empires, have crumbled and no longer exist. We have described this as the missionary *crisis* of our age. If there is to be a new era of missionary activity, Christians must deal resolutely with the factors which have caused this crisis.

Mission and evangelism today suffer from lack of clarity and purpose, and from the absence of a clear motivation for witnessing to Jesus Christ and the kingdom. When such clarity of purpose existed, Christians met in great assemblies such as the one at Edinburgh in 1910 to plan the required strategy and to coordinate resources needed for the "unfinished task." Today, when many Christians do not even acknowledge such a task, an even greater need exists. It is to rebuild the foundations and to lay the groundwork for a new era of mission. Not only the world but, above all, the *church* in the West must again become convinced of both the right and the duty—and from these flow also the urgency—of carrying out the Great Commission in our time.

Before 1950, the study of the "theology of mission" in today's sense hardly existed. The discipline was not considered necessary, and much good mission work was carried on without the benefit of serious theological reflection. Some theological issues, e.g., the theological understanding of the church in its mission, the relation between gospel and culture, and the approach to people of other faiths, were reflected on by writers of mission textbooks in terms of their relation to mission practice. But no fundamental consideration was given to the justification and necessity for mission work until that activity was called into question. It was simply assumed that Christians would obey the Great Commission, and that churches had established their right to continue the missionary efforts of past generations.

Some four decades ago, precisely when the world was no longer prepared to concede the right to do missionary work at the ends of the earth, and the missionary enterprise from the West had become a problem to the church, a new discipline called the "theology of mission" came into existence. It replaced what used to be called "mission principles and practice." In this new discipline theological issues became of overriding importance and claimed far more attention than questions of missionary methods and strategy. The theology of mission touched on the very foundation and justification for proclaiming the gospel to those who have never heard it, or refuse to believe it. It also reflected on the total credibility of the life of the church in the modern world. For if one can validly raise the question, Why missions? it will soon be impossible to avoid answering the question, Why the church? Why even the gospel? Why bother to believe in Jesus Christ? Such questions are as urgent for systematic theologians as they are for practitioners of global mission.

Questions like Why go? and Why send? now take precedence over "how to" questions about mission activity. Even when there appears to be agreement on the necessity of the mission of the church, it cannot be assumed that Christians will agree about the "what" of mission. For some who use the phrase "mission of the church" appear to mean by it little more than an affirmation of the church's organizational dynamic. Churches draw up "mission statements" which are often little more than declarations of organizational goals, e.g., how the church as an institution can survive, and even improve its performance. It is not unusual to hear that some particular activity of the church—e.g., its preaching, worship, education, or stewardship—has been designated as "the church's mission." Such loose references to "mission" as designating either the total work of the church or some particularly favored activity are not wrong, but they have the effect of blurring the issue.

The problem with this approach is that "when *everything* is mission, *nothing* is mission." The term "mission" is co-opted for what are essentially ongoing ministries or church maintenance activities. The *essential* mission criterion of outreach into the world, crossing boundaries to bear witness, or proclaiming the gospel to those who have never heard it—above all, "naming the name" of Jesus Christ where it is not known—is easily lost sight of. During the final years of its existence, the International Missionary Council made strenuous (but mostly unsuccessful) efforts to safeguard the categorical *uniqueness* of the missionary calling and of mission work against the tendency to identify these with church work in general (cf. Chapter 3).

For these reasons, it is important to agree not only *that* mission work should be done, but also on *what* it is. To that question we answer that mission consists in activities which are not identical with church work in general, least of all with the maintenance of institutional ministries, however valuable or necessary. *Mission* as applied to the work of the church means the *specific intention* of bearing witness to the gospel of salvation in Jesus Christ at the borderline between faith and unbelief. Mission occurs when the church reaches out beyond its inner life and bears witness to the gospel in the world. The entire life of the church has a missionary purpose, to be sure. But the heart of mission is always making the gospel known where it would not be known without a special and costly act of boundary-crossing witness. This is precisely the point made by the apostle Paul in his reference to the inseparable relationship between *confessing* Christ with the lips, *believing* with the heart, *hearing* with the ears, *proclaiming* the gospel with the mouth, and the *sending out* of proclaimers (Rom. 10:9, 14-15). Such an understanding will protect the specificity of mission within the totality of the church's activities and safeguard its mission from being swallowed up by pressing institutional demands.

In the chapters that follow, we shall note efforts by several Christian communities to express the priority and particularity of mission, and the claims of obedience which it makes upon the life of the churches. We shall also observe these groups struggling with both the advantages and dangers that arise when mission activities are fully *integrated* into the life of the church. Justification for continuing mission activity in our modern skeptical world and a clearer definition of the scope and content of mission today are vital requirements if we wish to rebuild the foundations for mission in the new era. For, with the collapse of the old order, yesterday's answers to today's questions no longer satisfy, and cannot motivate and guide Christians in fulfilling the Great Commission in the new era.

THEOLOGY OF MISSION TODAY

Today there are signs of renewed commitment to the mission task, and growing readiness to tackle the theological issues that stand in the way of a new era of mission by churches in all six continents. The term *mission,* once laden with imperialist overtones and fraught with negative associations, is now beginning to find favor again. The Western missionary, who went from being a 19th-century hero to becoming the stereotypical villain and antihero of 20th-century films and novels, is once again being appreciated for historical contributions. Guilt feelings connected with the end of colonialism and shameful associations stemming from United States participation in the war in Vietnam are giving way to more positive feelings. Churches in the two-thirds world, now active as agents and initiators of mission on their own, have come to see both the missionary and the mission enterprise in a new and more positive light. The discussion about a possible moratorium on the sending of Western missionaries and mission funds to churches of the two-thirds world has helped to clear the air and to promote better understanding between churches in North and South. Despite lingering confusion about the basis and motivation for mission work, and questions about what it is, the atmosphere for discussion today has become more positive. We are in a period of hopeful reconstruction.

The four decades since the impact of the demise of the old missionary order was first felt have been marked by searching, questioning, innovation, and attempts to reformulate crucial theological issues. In the early 1950s the U.S. denominational mission boards related to the National Council of Churches of Christ in the U.S.A., sensing the need for greater clarification about the mission task, engaged in a massive inquiry related to the theological basis and foundation of the mission enterprise.[24] The report of Commission I of the North American inquiry on "The Missionary Obligation of the Church," to which outstanding theologians of the day contributed, was entitled "Why Missions?" The commission's report moved in the direction of a trinitarian understanding of the basis of mission, closely related to the emerging theme of the "mission of God" (*missio Dei*). The North American studies on mission theology were carried out as part of the U.S. and Canadian preparation for the 1952 Willingen meeting of the International Missionary Council, called specifically to deal with burning but as yet unresolved theological issues.[25]

The Willingen meeting proved unable to adopt an agreed statement on "The Missionary Obligation of the Church," but it did succeed in stimulating fruitful reflection on the relationship of the church to missionary obedience, and above all to the mission of God (*missio Dei*). The period between Willingen (1952) and the New Delhi Assembly of the WCC (1961), and particularly the thinking expressed at the Ghana meeting of the IMC (1957), are still strikingly relevant today, and will be reported in Chapter 3.

TRENDS OF THE SIXTIES AND SEVENTIES

The 1960s was a turbulent period for mission theology. In the conciliar missionary movement, it followed the integration of the IMC into the WCC, but in fact pushed mission theology in the direction of an encounter with the secular world. Ecumenical mission theology in this period engaged in radical speculation and innovative thinking about mission which deviated sharply from earlier church-centered missionary thinking in conciliar circles. It assumed that "the world sets the agenda" for the church's mission. This secularizing tendency climaxed at the Uppsala Assembly of the WCC (1968), where "humanization in Christ" (rather than salvation) is taken as the mission aim, and the new "fields" for mission are seen as being the secular world's troubled spots and places of tension. These developments are also described in Chapter 3.

In evangelical mission circles, the 1960s was a time when evangelicals begin to feel growing disenchantment with both the mission theology and program of the conciliar missionary movement. At the Wheaton (1966) and Berlin (1966) conferences, evangelicals drew closer together and laid the groundwork for what would be known in the 1970s as the "Lausanne movement." This new movement made an appeal for a return to clear biblical foundations and for recognition of the priority of evangelism in the church's total missionary effort. These developments are traced in Chapter 5.

For Roman Catholics, the first half of the decade of the 1960s coincided with the epoch-making Second Vatican Council (1962–1965), which initiated decisive changes in the overall orientation and definition of Catholic mission theology. These changes, along with important Catholic regional developments, are described in Chapter 6.

THE MOVEMENT TOWARD CONVERGENCE

The decade of the 1970s, especially after 1974, was by contrast the beginning of a time of convergence, dialog, and mutual exchange between the different viewpoints. We could detect signs of partial reconciliation among the three missionary traditions under study. In 1974 the world's evangelicals held the historic International Congress on World Evangelization at Lausanne, and produced a document known as "The Lausanne Covenant."[26] This has since become both a rallying cry for intensified evangelical mission efforts and a challenge to non-evangelicals. In the same year, 1974, the Roman Bishops' Synod confirmed that "the task of evangelizing all people constitutes the essential mission of the Church," and asked Pope Paul VI to reflect further on the meaning and task of mission in the modern world. In the season of Advent 1975, the Holy Father responded by promulgating one of the truly outstanding mission testimonies of all times, the Apostolic Exhortation *Evangelii Nuntiandi,* "On Evangelization in the Modern World."[27] This document set the tone for all subsequent Catholic mission statements.

Late in 1975, as the World Council of Churches held its Fifth Assembly at Nairobi, the themes of mission and evangelism were given prominent treatment. Assembly statements about "confessing Christ" had a strongly Christocentric, trinitarian, and churchly ring, echoing Eastern Orthodox and Roman Catholic influence, but also responding to evangelical criticisms. Mission and evangelism were again declared to be urgent priority tasks for the church. Nairobi 1975, with its renewed appeal to the tradition of Edinburgh 1910, marks the beginning of a new phase of mission theology in the conciliar missionary movement.

In 1982, not long after the CWME World Conference on Mission and Evangelism held at Melbourne (1980), the new conciliar viewpoint was given further expression in a remarkable document entitled "Mission and Evangelism: An Ecumenical Affirmation."[28] This brief statement is both a *call* to do mission ecumenically and an exposition of seven points of ecumenical *agreement* regarding the focus of global mission today. These recent ecumenical developments, along with the WCC position on dialog, are covered in Chapter 4.

Between 1974 and 1982, therefore, three outstanding documents about the nature and task of mission, all comprehensive in scope, irenic in spirit, and generous in their recognition of the missionary contributions of others, had been laid on the table of the churches for consideration. "The Lausanne Covenant," *Evangelii Nuntiandi,* and "Mission and Evangelism: An Ecumenical Affirmation" point the churches in all six continents toward the fulfillment of their common task. These documents clearly do not eliminate major differences which continue to divide the traditions. They do, however, speak a language of common commitment and help to slow the trend toward further polarization. They also establish a basis of trust for dialog about mission between the different positions. In the case of evangelicals and Roman Catholics, the first phase of a dialog about mission has already taken place (cf. Chapter 6). It will be in the interest of all traditions to continue this dialog for the sake of bearing more effective witness to the gospel in the world.

A NEW GLOBAL CONTEXT FOR MISSION

Mission theology in the late 1980s has entered a period of reconstruction and consensus building. The three principal streams under consideration in this volume, each in its own way, have recommitted themselves to participation in Christ's mission as an essential expression of the life of the church. They have also, each in its own way, set forth appropriate priorities, methods, and approaches for the faithful fulfillment of the task. In the chapters that follow, we shall describe these in greater detail. We shall also survey common issues that are likely to challenge all Christian communities as they carry out their mission in the future.

What will the context for a "new era of mission" be like? It will look remarkably different from the relatively peaceful and stable colonial context of the late 19th century. Here is a probable scenario for the future.

1. Widespread *poverty* and starvation will characterize much of the two-thirds world. The gap between the rich and the poor, between rich and poor nations and within each nation, will widen. Chronic poverty, underdevelopment, inflation, and low productivity will make it difficult

for churches in the poorest two-thirds-world nations to achieve self-reliance. This will limit the ability of churches in those lands to participate in the mutual sharing of personnel and resources for mission. Affluent nations will be called on to continue their efforts in emergency relief and long-term development assistance. Yet, for the most part, churches in the poor lands will be left to solve their own problems.

2. Political *instability* and *authoritarian* political systems on both the right and the left will plague nations of the two-thirds world. These countries, having overthrown colonialism but not finding parliamentary democracy to their liking, will experiment with single-party rule and military dictatorships. *Coups d'état* and short-lived regimes will be the order of the day. In some cases this will impede the progress of Christian mission; for example, it will likely render the continued presence of Western missionaries risky and precarious. In other cases, the local church may actually benefit from political chaos and oppression as a credible countercultural alternative to an existing regime. Oppressive regimes, linked to totalitarian ideologies and using police-state tactics, will produce a growing crop of Christian martyrs.

As local churches become the major or sole protesters against torture and the violation of human rights, they will find their positions untenable unless solidly supported by Christians in influential democratic nations. By virtue of conviction and membership in an international community, Christians living under oppressive regimes will be cast in the role of staunch advocates of human freedom. This will occasionally compel them to make alliances with other opponents of tyranny who do not share their faith convictions.

3. Religious *pluralism,* combined with rampant growth of *fanaticism* and messianic consciousness in some ethnic religions, will result in greater competition between Christianity and the old, established local religions. Rather than simply collapsing before the onslaught of Western culture and Christianity, as the older missionary era had expected, these ancient faiths have undergone revival and developed their own mission consciousness. In many cases they are dedicated to the prevention of further conversions to Christianity; in some cases, they even seek to win back Christian converts to their ancestral faith. This will make Christian witness immensely more difficult. In some cases local churches may be tempted to abandon the evangelistic task; they will need the support and understanding of the global Christian community.

Missionary work will increasingly take place under the sign of the cross, and Christians will have ample opportunity to identify with their Lord. Discipleship will be severely tested. A humble attitude of dialog and a sincere desire to share one's convictions and experiences of Christ will be the best approach to witness. Local mission work under these circumstances will be a real test of the faith and endurance of the Christian community. Religious liberty, wherever it is practiced, will be a real blessing.

4. Despite these inhibiting factors, the *Christian community in the two-thirds world* will continue to grow both in numbers and maturity. By virtue of severe testing and missionary engagement, the quality and vigor of the faith of these Christians is likely to surpass that of Christians in the secular West. In sheer numbers of members, churches of the two-thirds world have already overtaken churches of the declining West.

Heavy demands placed upon limited local resources by growing numbers of converts will require crash programs of leadership training, construction of simple chapels, and increased emphasis on stewardship. Refusal of Western subsidies will require that pastors and church workers live simple lives and forgo amenities of the earlier mission era. Leaders from these young churches, as representatives of rapidly growing communities, will play roles of increasing prominence and their voices will be heard with respect in world church gatherings.

Churches of the two-thirds world, Protestant and Roman Catholic, have already sent out more than 16,000 missionaries to other regions of Asia, Africa, and Latin America and to the West. This number is expected to multiply fourfold by 2000, by which time there may well be more missionaries from the South than from the North! Yet the full missionary potential of these churches will be limited by factors of chronic poverty and political instability. These churches will need resources and support from wealthier churches in the North to continue their active missionary roles, but at the same time they will be reluctant to accept outside help for reasons of local pride and self-reliance.

The relative decline in missionary sending from the West, and the need to reevangelize Western culture, will at last lead to new structural arrangements for the sharing of mission resources between former sending and former receiving churches. Money and personnel for mission will be internationalized by means of international missionary support funds and the composition of international, interracial, and even interdenominational mission teams. More missionaries from the two-thirds world will flow into the West than will go in the opposite direction. Mission will now move "from everywhere to everywhere." With much reluctance, Western churches still nostalgic for the old days will eventually welcome overseas Christian brothers and sisters of darker skins, partly because of the bankruptcy of the Western missionary movement, partly in deference to the principle of partnership. Western churches will necessarily learn to overcome their possessiveness about money, and their need to control events, in order to become genuine collaborators with Christians in other regions in the common missionary task.

5. The *Christian community in the North,* meanwhile, will experience continuing malaise and loss of dynamism before it eventually commits itself to the long-term task of reevangelization. Such a commitment will require massive overhaul of church structures, fundamental reinterpretation of the training and roles of both clergy and laity, and drastic changes in church priorities and self-image. Despite documented losses in numbers and influence, mainline churches will be hesitant to take the leap toward a *missionary* mode of existence, with its call for the practice of authentic discipleship and its rejection of materialistic consumer culture and values; this is so because of the radicality of such demands and the abrupt break with the earlier dominant church mentality that it requires. Yet, here and there small intentional communities of Christians will commit themselves to a sustained missionary engagement with the surrounding society and culture, and their witness will challenge the institutional churches.

The decline of the Christian West will be reflected in the decline in the numbers of missionaries sent out from North America. Their places on the world scene will gradually be taken by missionaries, both Protestant and Catholic, from the churches of the two-thirds world.

From 1910 to 1950 the North American contribution to the world pool of missionaries slowly increased, until North Americans became the majority of the global force, overtaking mission sending from Europe. In 1952, when just under 19,000 Protestant missionaries from the United States were serving overseas, missionaries recruited by boards related to mainline denominations (and therefore related to the

conciliar missionary movement) accounted for fully *half* of all Protestant missionaries sent abroad. By 1979 the total of Protestant missionaries from the United States had increased to nearly 45,000. But
of this total, missionaries related to the Division of Overseas Ministries
of the National Council of Churches of Christ (NCCCUSA) now made
up less than 9% of the total U.S. Protestant missionary force. In the
intervening years the U.S. Protestant missionary force had more than
doubled, but the increase in numbers was now made up of missionaries
sent out by established conservative evangelical mission agencies, such
as the Evangelical Foreign Missions Association and the Interdenominational Foreign Missions Association, whose contribution grew
to 36% of the total, and even more by striking increases in the numbers
sent by "independent" or "unaffiliated" missions, whose missionaries
now constituted nearly 52% of the total.[29] The decline in missionary
sending was most precipitous in the case of the conciliar groups, but
it was offset by the fact that these mission agencies generally worked
closely with growing churches in the two-thirds world, which possessed
their own cadre of indigenous leadership.

In the case of United States Catholics serving as overseas missionaries, a steady increase in numbers is noted after 1956, reaching a peak
of just under 10,000 in 1968, after which the numbers decline once
again to the level of the late 1950s.[30] The Far East and Latin America
have been preferred areas for Catholic sending. The gradual decline
in numbers of Catholic missioners after 1968 is attributable to various
factors, but particularly to the sharp decline in the numbers of new
vocations to missionary service on the part of both men's and women's
religious communities in the years following the Second Vatican Council. An aging process is observed in Catholic missionary orders across
the board. New missionary recruits will come increasingly from Catholic churches of the two-thirds world, and the places of older missionaries under lifetime vows will gradually be taken by Catholic lay
missionaries under contract for defined terms of service.

From available figures it is possible to calculate that missionaries
from the United States representing conciliar Protestantism and Roman
Catholic agencies constituted no more than 20% of the total United
States overseas missionary force in 1980. The overwhelming majority
of United States missionaries were drawn from circles of evangelicalism, fundamentalism, and Pentecostalism. Numbers are obviously not

adequate as indicators of missionary influence, but together with financial commitments they say much about the mission philosophy, goals, and program of United States churches in their mission outreach. The vast increase in the strength of the evangelical missionary movement destines it to play a decisive role in the spread of the gospel around the world. At the same time, North American evangelicals, like their conciliar and Roman Catholic counterparts, will increasingly find their own leadership challenged and ultimately overshadowed by the new wave of missionary agents from churches in the two-thirds world. To play a continuing part, Western missionaries will need to learn supporting roles in relation to these missionaries from the South, who by the 21st century will have taken over the initiative for global mission.

6. Massive *demographic changes* will mark the new missionary area, with the world's population rising to 6.25 billion by 2000. Despite impressive Christian growth in the two-thirds world, no more than 32% (approximately two billion) of the world's total population will then be counted as Christian. This means that the 2.4 billion non-Christians of 1970 will have grown to 4.25 billion non-Christians in 2000! The number of persons adhering to no religion whatever—including atheists and secularists—will have increased from several million in 1900 to one billion in 2000![31] These trends justify mission planning and strategy systematically directed toward unevangelized segments of the world's population.

A startling phenomenon related to world population growth has been the *massive increase* in the number of *large cities*. In 1900, the world had 400 "metropolises," defined as cities of over 100,000 population. Only 20 were "megacities" of over one million population each, and only two (London and New York) were "supercities" of over four million. By 1986 these have mushroomed to 1780 metropolises (over 100,000), 286 megacities (over one million), 46 supercities (over four million) and 14 "supergiants" (over 10 million each). By 2000 the number of megacities (over one million) will reach 433![32] Formidable metropolitan giants like Tokyo, Shanghai, Beijing, Bombay, Calcutta, Jakarta, Sao Paulo, Mexico City, Buenos Aires, and Los Angeles will shape the mission context of the future.

A new urban style of mission along with requisite training for Christian survival in great cities will be demanded. On the one hand, cities with their anonymity and secular atmosphere will offer nearly impenetrable barriers to mission activities. On the other hand, cities with their greater freedom are less likely to be places of persecution, and their cultural pluralism will facilitate the rapid movement of the gospel. It may well be true that mission in the 21st century will be won or lost in the battle for the soul of big cities.

NEW FIELDS OF MISSION

In the new era of global mission, the movement will be from everywhere to everywhere; every country will be a "home base," and every country a "mission field." Each church will both send and receive. Every congregation will be a mission structure, and every Christian a witness for Christ. The Christian mission will relate to the *whole* of life, taking as its *model* the ministry of the Messiah, up to and including the bearing of his cross; as its *content* the proclamation of Christ crucified and risen, along with the entire counsel of God; and as its *goal* the witness to God's kingdom throughout the world by word and deed. The Christian community in all nations will be in some sense a "sacramental" embodiment of the kingdom and a sign of its coming.

Where will the "mission fields" of the new era be found? Only the briefest hints can be given, based on the suggestions of various missionary groups.

The conciliar document *Mission and Evangelism: Ecumenical Affirmations* provides these illustrations of mission fields:

- people who have no opportunity to know the story of Jesus;
- the poor of the earth, to whom Jesus promised the kingdom of God, who constitute the majority of the world's population;
- people struggling for justice, freedom, and liberation, often without the realization of their hopes;
- the marginalized and dropouts of affluent society, searching desperately for comfort and identity in drugs or esoteric cults;
- people who find little meaning, except in the relative security of their affluence;
- many Christians who are nominal in their commitment to Jesus Christ;
- a world where wars and rumors of wars jeopardize the present and future of humankind, and an enormous part of natural resources and people are consumed in the arms race.[33]

The poor of the earth and people of other living faiths are considered to have high priority in the church's missionary witness (cf. Chapter 4).

Evangelicals at Pattaya conducted miniconsultations directed toward the evangelization of a wide variety of peoples: Muslims, refugees, Marxists, traditional religionists, nominal Christians, the urban poor, and others. The Strategy Working Group of the Lausanne Committee for World Evangelization in cooperation with MARC-World Vision is in the process of developing profiles on some 15,000 to 25,000 distinct people groups who are considered to be "unreached" (cf. Chapter 5).

Pope Paul VI in his Apostolic Exhortation *Evangelii Nuntiandi* spoke of a mission task addressed to everyone: to the whole world; to all creation; to the ends of the earth (*EN* 50). He recognized that the church which evangelizes "begins by being evangelized herself" (*EN* 15). The pope stressed the "first evangelization" of those who do not know Jesus Christ (*EN* 51), the importance of renewed proclamation to nominal Christians "living quite outside Christian life" in a dechristianized world (*EN* 52), and also "first proclamation" to sections of humanity which practice non-Christian religions (*EN* 52). He considered that "non-practicing Christians" and atheists were among the most difficult but also most necessary fields for evangelization (*EN* 56). Catholic mission congresses in Latin America and elsewhere have also laid heavy stress on the "preferential option for the poor" and mission through dialog with people of living faiths (cf. Chapter 6).

The Lutheran World Federation (LWF) at its Budapest Assembly (1984), in its discussion on mission in the context of secularization, drew attention to the worldwide *movement of peoples* which has a profound impact on the task of mission. It called for urban team ministries on an ecumenical basis, and multilingual ministry projects among migrants, guest workers, tourists, and other mobile groups. It also called for dialog with scientists, people influencing culture, artists and writers, politicians and trade unionists. It recommended special emphasis on "youth in mission," i.e., both as evangelizers and people to be evangelized. The LWF urged the creation of cross-cultural chaplaincies in international educational centers. The same assembly requested expanded facilities for training laity for dialog with people of other faiths, and the equipping of lay people and clergy for the work of reevangelization.[34]

The overlap and reinforcement in these lists is another striking evidence of growing convergence in the Christian community regarding the tasks to be accomplished. Christian communities in North, South, East, and West need to dialog not only about theological obstacles to missionary cooperation. They should also consult intensively about tasks which demand the highest priority in terms of planning and resources. Local churches will of course define their own mission context and set their own priorities. But international consultations between Christians of different denominational backgrounds, and from all regions, will be a tremendous catalyst to joint mission planning and the ecumenical sharing of resources. Continental mission congresses have proved useful for regional consultation.

Is it reasonable to think that sometime around 2010—or possibly even earlier—another truly representative World Missionary Conference might be held near the crossroads between North and South, bringing together representatives of churches in all six continents for consultation on the "unfinished task"?

MISSION—GOD'S OWN CAUSE

This historical pilgrimage from the old to the new missionary order would not be complete without a reminder that global mission, in the final analysis, is not simply the church's task but is God's own cause. The church is in mission because "God so loved the world that he gave his only Son. . . ." Before the historic mission of the apostles and of the church there was the eternal mission of the Triune God, who initiated the *sending* process in the mystery of the Incarnation out of love for a lost and alienated creation. The most spectacular confirmation of the *present* reality of divine power and sustenance in the mission work of human beings has been the curious surprises which God has wrought in human history. Dramatic instances of God's presence have been seen in the survival and even growth of churches amidst severe persecution, and the revival of Christian faith when it appeared to be dead. Recent examples can be found in the experiences of churches and individual believers in Eastern Europe, Asia, Africa, Latin America, and elsewhere.

We have referred earlier to the tribulation of the Christian community in the People's Republic of China. During the Cultural Revolution of

1966–1976, all places of worship were closed and the practice of religion was systematically eradicated by the Red Guards. Bibles and hymnals were destroyed, houses of worship desecrated, and church leaders were ordered to return to secular work. A large number were humiliated, imprisoned, or held under house arrest. Outwardly, the Chinese church ceased to function.

Beginning in 1979, a few churches were reopened, and public worship was formally allowed. In a mere eight years since 1979 more than 5000 Protestant churches have been opened or reopened, in addition to a great number of meeting points and home worship gatherings. About 300 ministers have been ordained, one-sixth of them women. Ten theological seminaries have been opened with a total enrollment of 500 students. Over two million Bibles and New Testaments have been printed in China, together with 70,000 hymnals and 80,000 copies of a new catechism.[35]

Chinese Christians who likened their condition during the Cultural Revolution to spiritual death have now experienced a powerful resurrection. The dramatic revival of the Chinese Christian community, and its vigorous resurgence today, have taken place without the intervention or assistance of any foreign churches or mission bodies. Even today Chinese Christians jealously safeguard their independence and reject offers of foreign missionaries and imported Bibles. They are quick to attribute the miraculous events of the past decade solely to divine grace. But older Chinese believers know that the crowds which frequent public churches in China's large cities today would not be there except for the patient and faithful sowing of the seed of the gospel by earlier pioneer missionaries from the West. Both the earlier tribulation of the Chinese church, and its resurgence in this decade, are signs that the Triune God does not simply abandon his human flock or "turn over" the work of mission to human agents and instruments, but himself accompanies and oversees it as God's own activity.

The church continues its mission into the new era because it is from start to finish God's own mission.

2

LUTHERAN MISSION IN HISTORICAL PERSPECTIVE

In this chapter we shall examine the Lutheran missionary idea and the rationale for mission within Lutheranism since the Reformation. To do this we shall summarize briefly the major missionary motifs to be found during the Reformation itself—above all, in the thinking of Luther—and in the succeeding periods of Lutheran Orthodoxy, Pietism, the 19th-century confessional revival, and 20th-century ecumenical relations.

Lutheran missionary thinking and participation in mission reflect a history of more than 450 years. Within this history there have been sudden changes and discontinuities. It is not always easy to find the unifying thread. Tracing this history makes one appreciative of the pitfalls involved in attempting to define a valid missionary mandate for the 21st century.

REFORM MOVEMENT WITHIN CATHOLIC CHRISTENDOM

It is now common to observe that Lutheranism originated as a "confessing movement" within Western Roman Catholic Christendom. The Reformation sought to correct the errors of an existing Christendom, not to initiate a new form of Christianity. The preface of the Augsburg

Confession (1530) clearly states that the goal of the Lutheran party was to remove dissensions and misunderstandings about the faith, to further agreement on one Christian truth, and

> to have.all of us embrace and adhere to a single true religion and live together in unity and in one fellowship and church, even as we are all enlisted under one Christ.[1]

Yet, historical circumstances led to the formation of separate Lutheran churches, having definite confessional features, a development which was not anticipated by the reformers. Various reformation and renewal movements led in time to the division of Western Christendom, and these divisions have proved to be irreversible.

Both of these developments—the rise of the Reformation as a confessing movement witnessing to the true gospel and church, and the emergence of Lutheran regional churches in the wake of the Reformation—occurred at a time when Western Christendom had reached its furthest extent of territorial expansion prior to the age of Western exploration and colonialism. The missionary movement within Europe had come to an end, the mission frontiers having long since disappeared from view. The "infidel" Turk loomed as the chief menace to the security of the Holy Roman Empire. In this situation the concerns of the Lutheran Reformation were primarily for the renewal of faith and the reform of the church on the basis of Scripture and evangelical teaching. Although the evangelical understanding of the gospel would later have crucial implications for evangelical missionary activity, world evangelization was for the time being not in the foreground of concern.

The Reformation thus did not originate as a call to greater missionary or evangelistic obedience, as in the case of later 19th-century movements for awakening or revival, but as a movement to bring about reform and renewal of existing Christian life. This helps to explain why the Lutheran response to the call to mission and evangelism has often seemed belated, half-hearted, and less than enthusiastic.

Lutheranism has displayed a real reticence toward embracing mission activity—possibly not greater than other historic confessional traditions taken as a whole, but distinctly so when compared to evangelical movements which arose in the post-Reformation era. Free churches, groups sharing the American frontier experience, and bodies that adopted revivalist methods, among them the Methodists and Baptists, have on the whole taken the missionary concern much more to heart than Lutherans have.

RESTRAINTS ON LUTHERAN MISSION ACTIVITY

Some of the Lutheran restraints have to do with unresolved theological problems, such as the nature of the church and the authority of its ministry. Others are related to the exegesis of key passages of Scripture, such as the Great Commission of Matthew 28. Still others relate to structural problems and matters of church polity. In any case, the meaning of mission and evangelism for Lutherans did not receive a clear formulation in the period of the Reformation. As a consequence, Lutherans face a special challenge in coming to terms with the call to mission.

Missiology today lays a heavy emphasis on the correlation of *theory* and *practice,* and the importance of testing theory by practice. Lutheranism in its history has given rise to various theories and practices of mission, but, taking the period as a whole, there has been no close correlation between its theory and its actual practice of mission.

As an example, during the period of the Reformation there is a rich abundance of hints and suggestions about mission available from Luther's primary writings. However, the authoritative Lutheran confessions make no statement whatever about mission theology or practice. Apart from scattered undertakings, no real mission practice is available for examination until the 18th century. The period of Lutheran Orthodoxy is quite vocal on the false practices of its Roman opponents but presents little in the way of approved mission practice of its own, apart from some scattered state-church undertakings in colonies or among dependent peoples.

When Lutheran missionary practice does begin to evolve in a major way, as under Lutheran Pietism, the underlying theory is not always explained. Another problem is that the practice, when it finally develops, does not necessarily match the original theory. One has only to compare Luther's idea of mission with 19th-century Lutheran practice to note the stark contrast.

LUTHER AND MISSION: A RICH BUT UNTESTED POTENTIAL

Luther's own thought possesses a uniquely missionary structure. Here the enormous untested potential of the Reformation for mission practice can be seen. Here also are revealed some of the contradictions and negations that reached their climax in the period of Lutheran Orthodoxy. In this sketch we can only hint at the reformer's originality as a missionary thinker.

Before plunging into Luther's missionary contribution, we must first quickly dispose of an issue that has clouded Luther's reputation as a missiologist since the 19th century. It was Gustav Warneck (1834–1910), the "father of mission science," who first promoted the view that the Reformation was disappointing from the perspective of missionary thinking, and Luther himself defective in terms of missionary awareness. Warneck was critical of Luther chiefly because the reformer had not issued a call in support of "a regular sending of messengers of the Gospel to non-Christian nations, with the view of Christianizing them."[2]

This deficiency was sometimes rationalized by the explanation that Luther had other pressing tasks at home, or lacked the opportunity to do mission work abroad, or simply believed that the end of the world was so near as to make the effort less than worthwhile.

It is clear that Warneck and his contemporaries, in judging the missionary awareness of the Reformation, had as their major criterion a readiness to support the work of foreign mission societies. This led them to overlook Luther's deeper missionary insights.

Subsequent investigations by Luther scholars have tended to overturn Warneck's premature and one-sided judgment. The wry comment of Werner Elert (1885–1954) is typical: We should not, said Elert, look to Luther for advice on how to run a missionary society. Rather we should be concerned to understand the profoundly missionary structure of Luther's thought and his missionary understanding of gospel and church.[3] Walter Holsten observed that it was now time to grasp the deeper meaning of God's mission as laid bare by the Reformation rather than judging Luther by standards of the 19th-century missionary movement.[4] Indeed, the task of bridging the gap between Luther's sheer theocentric or vertical view of mission and the more society-oriented horizontalist view advocated in the 19th century by neo-Pietist groups remains a challenge to us today.

LUTHER AS THE FATHER OF EVANGELICAL MISSIONS

An early Lutheran mission historian, Gustav Leopold Plitt (1836–1880), made some accurate observations about Luther and mission, but unfortunately they did not penetrate deeply.[5] Plitt conceded Warneck's point that Luther had not actually supported mission society endeavors, but insisted that the reformer had been faithful to the missionary command in a more fundamental way. Since the gospel had fallen into oblivion in Christendom, said Plitt, and since for Luther the Gentiles were those who had never heard the pure Word of God preached in Germany, missionary obedience could only mean preaching the gospel anew. And since the distortion of the gospel message had led to the degeneration of mission into ecclesiastical propaganda, forced conversions, papal crusades and unevangelical methods, Luther's obedience to mission meant reestablishing the church on its one true foundation in Jesus Christ and the gospel.

For Luther, said Plitt, mission was the essential task of the church in every age, but only a church itself grounded in the gospel can do mission. This interpretation, which credits Luther with being the father of genuine church-centered evangelical mission work based on the gospel, is true as far as it goes, but it misses the radicality of Luther's missionary thinking.

GOD'S MISSION AND THE KINGDOM OF GOD

For Luther, mission is always preeminently the work of the Triune God—*missio Dei*—and its goal and outcome are the coming of the kingdom of God.[6] Luther sees the church, along with God's Word and every baptized believer, as crucial divine instruments for mission. Yet nowhere does the reformer make the church the starting point or the final goal of mission, as 19th-century missiology tended to do. It is always *God's own mission* that dominates Luther's thought, and the coming of the *kingdom of God* represents its final culmination.

Luther thus anticipates the present-day line of missiological thinking which takes the kingdom of God, rather than the church, as its key concept. At the same time, he sharply negates the pragmatic, human-istic, and activist notions often associated with "working for the king-dom."

In brief outline, Luther's basic missiological view can be found in the words of his Large Catechism:

> What is the kingdom of God? Answer: Simply what we learned in the Creed, namely, that God sent his Son, Christ our Lord, into the world to redeem and deliver us from the power of the devil and to bring us to himself and rule us as a king of righteousness, life, and salvation against sin, death, and an evil conscience. To this end he also gave his Holy Spirit to teach us this through his holy Word and to enlighten and strength-en us in faith by his power.[7]

The Christian prays "Your kingdom come" not because human faith and prayer make the kingdom come—for God's kingdom comes of itself even without our prayer—but that it may be realized in us and that God's name may be praised through his Word and our holy lives. Listen to Luther again on mission and unity:

> This we ask, both in order that we who have accepted it may remain faithful and grow daily in it and in order that it may gain recognition and followers among other people and advance with power throughout the world. So we pray that, led by the Holy Spirit, many may come into the kingdom of grace and become partakers of salvation, so that we may all remain together eternally in this kingdom which has now made its appearance among us.[8]

Prayer for the kingdom is thus no perfunctory ritual but a spiritual preparation for entrance into, and participation in, the reality and power of God's kingdom. The kingdom is at one and the same time a *present* reality and a *future* expectation; a *personal* experience in the life of faith and a *public* event of cosmic dimensions:

> God's kingdom comes to us in two ways: first, it comes here, in time, through the Word and faith, and secondly, in eternity, it comes through the final revelation. Now we pray for both of these, that it may come to those who are not yet in it, and that it may come by daily growth here and in eternal life hereafter to us who have attained it.[9]

In a summary statement that speaks both of the manner of our participation in God's kingdom and of its ultimate form or manifestation, Luther continues:

> All this is simply to say: "Dear Father, we pray thee, give us thy Word, that the Gospel may be sincerely preached throughout the world and that it may be received by faith and may work and live in us. So we pray that thy kingdom may prevail among us through the Word and the power of the Holy Spirit, that the devil's kingdom may be overthrown and he may have no right or power over us, until finally the devil's kingdom shall be utterly destroyed and sin, death, and hell exterminated, and that we may live forever in perfect righteousness and blessedness.[10]

Luther does not underestimate the power of the adversary to undermine the kingdom or to block the entrance of believers. In the reformer's response to the third petition of the Lord's Prayer, "Your will be done," he adds that all who pray these petitions for the accomplishment of God's will and hold fast to the gospel and faith will suffer furious attacks and assaults from the devil. Satan cannot bear the exposure of his own lies, and like a furious foe "raves and ravages with all his power and might, marshaling all his subjects and even enlisting the world and our flesh as his allies."[11] "For where God's Word is preached, accepted or believed, and bears fruit, there the blessed holy cross will not be far away."[12]

Even so, the purpose of our prayer is not to effect the final victory of the kingdom, which belongs by right to Christ alone, but to enable Christians to emerge unscathed from the conflict:

> What we pray for concerns only ourselves when we ask that what otherwise must be done without us may also be done in us. As God's name must be hallowed and his kingdom must come even without our prayer, so must his will be done and prevail even though the devil and all his host storm and rage furiously against it in their attempt utterly to exterminate the Gospel.[13]

For Luther the final victory of the kingdom is not based on any calculation of the odds, or any frantic call for human cooperation with God to overcome the powers of evil, but solely on confident hope in the ultimate victory wrought by Christ.

THEOCENTRIC MISSIONARY ESCHATOLOGY

The starkly theocentric and eschatological outlines of Luther's missionary thinking have been sketched by Paul Drews (1858–1912), on the basis of an analysis of Luther texts.[14] The triune God is seen as the sole author of mission, bringing the kingdom irresistibly to fulfillment by divine means and according to a divine timetable. According to Drews:

1. The movement of gospel preaching, begun by the apostles, is universal and continues until the last day (Rom. 10:18). No place will finally be without gospel proclamation (Ps. 19:1).

2. The preaching of the gospel to the heathen is substantially completed, but still in progress. Newly discovered lands existed in Luther's day where the gospel had never been preached. Like a stone which makes ripples in the water, gospel proclamation extends further and further, despite persecution, until all who had not previously known of the good news receive it. Before this happens, however, faith may be extinguished in some places, or even turned into heresy.

3. Although the gospel will be preached throughout the whole world, humankind as a whole will not embrace faith in Christ. The devil will simply not allow the conversion of the whole world. "For we must always have the holy cross, with the consequence that the majority will be those who persecute Christians."

Accordingly, continuous proclamation of the gospel is necessary so that some may be saved. Christ's kingdom is still in a state of becoming, it is not an accomplished fact. The universal proclamation of the gospel, not the conversion of the entire world, is Luther's realistic expectation.

4. God needs no special mission agencies to accomplish the divine mission. God is able to make use of persecution, the dispersion of believers, the travels of merchants, the captivity of believing soldiers, or the acts of unbelieving rulers to bring about universal witness. Special mission agencies and missionary agents do not play a necessary role in the mission of God.

5. No clear dividing line can be drawn between "Christendom" and the "non-Christian world." Christendom is populated by what Luther calls "Christian Turks," i.e., nominal believers. The human condition before God—what makes people "heathen"—is everywhere the same. It consists of unbelief and idolatry.

Drews' principal conclusion was that the institutionalization of missions in the 19th-century sense was simply not required by Luther's theocentric view. The coming of the kingdom depended solely on God's sovereign power and freedom, working through the Word and the Holy Spirit, and using such agents as God chose for the purpose. The triune God was engaging the devil in fierce combat for the souls of humans, and God's kingdom of grace and righteousness would ultimately triumph over the devil's kingdom of sin and death.

In this cosmic context, said Drews, planned global witness to "evangelize the world in this generation" or a strategy to fill the world with rapidly growing churches did not correspond to Luther's sober eschatological expectation. Luther had a deep aversion toward mass movements, like Nikolaus Ludwig Graf von Zinzendorf (1700–1760) two centuries later, holding that true believers, because of the demand of the cross, would always remain a minority.

Moreover, Luther believed regressions from the faith would occur. When people failed to hold the gospel in respect, teach it to their children, and show gratitude for it through lively faith and sincere good works, God would withdraw the gospel from them and give it to others. Again and again he chided the German nation for its unbelief, citing the ancient Near East, North Africa, and the Mediterranean basin as places where the Christian community had once thrived, but no longer.

No people had a permanent claim on the possession of the gospel. Each generation must believe for itself, and therefore evangelization has to be a continuous process. Luther's references to the phenomenon of nominal Christians in his day shows that he clearly anticipated today's task of reevangelization in the West.

MISSIONARY AGENTS, PRINCIPLES, AND METHODS

Drews exposed with radical sharpness the theocentric and eschatological dimensions of Luther's missionary thinking. Yet his pessimistic conclusion—that God is the author of mission and there is little to be done, humanly speaking—did less than justice to Luther's statements about missionary agency. More recent studies of Luther and mission seek to counteract the impression of sheer divine initiative by pointing to the earthly agents employed in the mission of God.[15] They establish the centrality of the church in mission, and the duty of each baptized believer to witness as need or opportunity arises.

For Luther, the missionary witness of each Christian is a self-evident matter. The Bible contains countless examples of faithful witness by God's servants from the patriarchs onward. The urgency arises from the fact that all people without exception require the message of both law and gospel and must hear it.

Thus Abraham, when he went to Egypt, could not be silent about God's grace. So also Jacob, Joseph, Daniel, and Jonah proclaimed God's Word. The Ethiopian eunuch, converted by Philip, utilized the prerogative conferred by Baptism to evangelize others.

In two sermons from 1523 Luther commented at length on the meaning of being anointed to God's "royal priesthood" (1 Peter 2:9) through Baptism:

> It belongs to the work of a priest that he is God's messenger and has a command from God to proclaim his Word. The "wonderful deed," that is, the miracle which God has performed in bringing you from darkness into light, is to be preached, and that is the highest priestly office. And your preaching is to be done in such a way that one person proclaims to another the mighty deed of God: how you were redeemed from sin, hell, death, and all misery through him and called to eternal life. Thus you shall also instruct other people in how they too can come to such light. For everything is to be done to the end that you recognize what God has done for you and accordingly allow it to become the most pressing thing for you, so that you proclaim it publicly and call everyone to the light to which you were called.[16]

Luther cannot doubt that every Christian has God's Word and is anointed to the priestly office. He draws these consequences:

> If it is so, that you have God's Word and are anointed by him, then you are also responsible to confess, teach, and spread that word [he cites 2 Cor. 4:13; Ps. 116:10; Ps. 51:15]. Thus it is doubly certain that a Christian has not merely the right and power to teach God's Word, but is responsible to do so on pain of incurring the loss of his soul and God's disfavor. But you ask: Yes, how? Don't you yourself teach that when one is not called, one should not preach? Answer: Here you must place the Christian in two kinds of situations. First, when one is in the place where there are

no other Christians, one needs no other call than that of a Christian, inwardly called of God and anointed; there one is responsible to preach to erring heathen or non-Christians, and to teach the gospel out of brotherly love, even when no one has called you to that.[17]

For this, says Luther, is precisely what St. Stephen did, who had no apostolic office, as well as Philip the Deacon, and Apollos. For in such cases official letters of authorization from prince or bishop are not needed.

"Necessity breaks all laws and has no law. Love is responsible to help where no one else is available to help." In the other case, where many Christians come together sharing the same baptismal authority, one should wait to be invited by one's fellow believers before giving testimony.[18]

THE CHURCH'S MISSIONARY NATURE

In a beautiful passage from the Large Catechism, Luther explains his conception of the church's missionary role:

He [the Holy Spirit] has a unique community in the world. It is the mother that begets and bears every Christian through the Word of God. The Holy Spirit reveals and preaches that Word, and by it he illumines and kindles hearts so that they grasp and accept it, cling to it, and persevere in it. . . . I believe that there is on earth a little holy flock or community of pure saints under one head, Christ. It is called together by the Holy Spirit in one faith, mind, and understanding. It possesses a variety of gifts, yet is united in love without sect or schism. . . . Until the last day the Holy Spirit remains with the holy community or Christian people. Through it he gathers us, using it to teach and preach the Word. By it he creates and increases sanctification, causing it daily to grow and become strong in the faith and in the fruits of the Spirit.[19]

This is consistent with Luther's belief that "God's Word is never without God's people." The dynamic *word,* energized by the Spirit, has power to encircle the earth and engender faith anywhere. The missionary *church* which results from gospel preaching also sends forth the gospel into the world. Each baptized *believer*—the lay priest living in the world—witnesses through her or his calling. This is Luther's informal missionary *triad*—Word, church, and believer—which makes it possible for the mission of God to dispense with special missionary agents.

It is important to note that while this view recognizes the central importance of the Christian community in mission, it is a far cry from the "church-centric" missionary view, according to which the church is both the starting point and the goal of mission. For Luther, the church is never more than an instrumentality in a mission which from first to last remains God's own cause.

LUTHER ON PROPAGANDA, CULTURE, AND RELIGION

Other studies of Luther's missionary thought have drawn attention to the fact that the reformer's well-known emphasis on *justification by faith* and his distinction between *law and gospel* lead to a crucial observation: God's mission is not to be identified with human *propaganda*. Adolph Schlatter (1852–1938) hailed the doctrine of justification by faith as the formative motif in all evangelical missionary activity, and freedom from legalism as its missiological corollary.[20] Heinrich Frick (1893–1952) and Paul Althaus (1888–1966), following Martin Kähler (1835–1912), saw in Luther's legacy a warning against missionary imperialism in its various forms—political, cultural, or ecclesiastical—and a continuous call to reflect on purity of motives.[21]

Karl Holl (1866–1926), in a 1924 study on "Luther and Mission," found lively impulses and correct guidelines for mission practice latent in Luther's theology. While commenting on Luther's understanding of the church as essentially missionary in nature, and lay priesthood as missionary engagement, Holl also observed the reformer's sensitive view of customs and cultures which allowed no slavish transference of European standards and values to mission areas. Local customs and folkways had to be given their rightful place. Converting people from idolatry to faith in the living God had nothing to do with imposing legalistic ecclesiastical or ritual regulations!

The missionary's task was to declare the gospel in such a manner that true religion was awakened as a response of faith, thanksgiving, and praise to God. The effect of Holl's study was to draw out from Luther's thought practical principles for missionary methodology and contextualizing the gospel in a local setting.[22]

Luther's keen interest in reforming the existing mission practice of his day, mainly as applied to Jews and Muslims living within the empire, is reflected in a sermon preached on the text of Matt. 23:15. Jesus is quoted as saying that the net effect of proselyting missions by the Pharisees of his day, as they traversed land and sea to make a single proselyte, was to make their converts "twice as much children of hell" as they themselves. Luther pursues this homiletical opportunity with tremendous gusto, lashing first the Pharisees for their imposition of circumcision on God-fearing pagans, and for binding converts to temple worship in Jerusalem. He comments that Jonah at Nineveh, Daniel in Babylon, and Joseph in Egypt taught nothing but the knowledge of the true God and the renunciation of idolatry, and imposed no legalistic requirements.

Luther then attacks legalistic Roman missionary practices, decrying the fact that when Jews were baptized they were subsequently required to subscribe to Roman articles of faith and the pope's decretals. Condemning the arrogance and presumption which underlie such practices, he hints that Jews and Muslims have no real motive or incentive to become Christians. The complexity of Christian doctrine, the scandal of Christian divisions, and the lack of a living model of Christian discipleship and community are for Luther major disincentives to conversion.[23]

MISSION THEOLOGY OF THE CROSS

Luther's mission theology, as seen here, is always a "theology of the cross," and thereby a theology of missionary servanthood that rejects propaganda as a substitute for the gospel, along with legalism which negates evangelical freedom. The well-known missionary tendency toward triumphalism, which finds expression in maximizing numbers of converts and exalting one's own religious superiority, is undercut by Luther's consistent application of the teaching of justification by faith alone, grace alone, Christ alone. Luther's central focus on the crucified Christ, and his fundamental view of *simul justus et peccator* (justified while yet a sinner) as foundations for missionary witness, will also have implications for relations with people of other faiths.

Luther's theological attitude toward the value and significance of other religions for Christians comes to expression in two monumental treatises composed by the reformer in 1529 to deal with the Turkish menace then threatening the Holy Roman Empire.[24] During the last 20 years of his life we find him increasingly preoccupied with Islam, and seeking to grasp it both theologically and empirically. His view of Muslims is at once nuanced and discriminating, both laudatory and condemnatory. While making surprisingly affirmative statements about Muslim virtues, Luther ultimately rejects Islam as a whole. For him the ultimate criterion for judging a religion is not its ability to produce outward religiosity or moral virtue but the extent to which it confesses or denies the Second Article of the Creed. "For on this article everything depends," says Luther. All other arguments are overwhelmed by his Christocentric adherence; in the end one can only be saved by faith in the merit of Christ, not by pious works.

LUTHER ON ISLAM

As early as 1518 Luther had expressed opposition to "Holy Wars" (crusades) being promoted by the Roman curia against the Turk. The pope as the world's leading preacher had no business promoting such wars, for the church's calling was to fight the enemy with "other weapons and swords" than military. Moreover, Luther viewed the Turk as the "rod of God's anger" to punish Christians and bring about repentance. This interest prompted Luther to investigate the Koran and to comment on the teachings of the prophet Muhammad. Luther is aware that Islam respects Jesus as a prophet, but rejects him as God's Son. He concludes that Muhammad is "a destroyer of our Lord Christ and his kingdom." Still, he is deeply impressed by reports of Muslim virtue.

Muslims are faithful and friendly and careful to tell the truth. Islamic "priests" are earnest, brave, and intensely pious. Corporate prayers are characterized by discipline, quietness, and formal austerity such as cannot be found in evangelical churches. Muslims drink no wine, do not gorge themselves as the Germans do, do not dress frivolously, build simple homes, and live disciplined and obedient lives toward their rulers.

A Christian soldier taken into Turkish captivity would be hard-pressed to maintain his faith; even a Christian cleric would be likely to succumb to the intensity of Muslim religious commitment. Luther recommends that those who have the misfortune to be taken captive should repeat the Lord's Prayer, the Ten Commandments, and the Creed day and night, and pray that God would keep them steadfast in the faith. By so adorning the gospel and lifting up the name of Jesus Christ, the Christian might even win the admiration of his captors.

Given his view that Islam is a system of outward religiosity, rituals, and works-righteousness, and that it cannot save, it is surprising how doggedly Luther pursued the task of theologically critiquing the Koran and commending its study to other Christians. In 1530 he wrote a preface to a Latin book on Turkish customs and mores, and in 1542 he brought out his own version of a "confutation" of the Koran prepared by a Dominican. In 1543 he interceded with the authorities of Basel to permit the publication of the Koran in that city, arguing that in the hands of preachers the Koran would confirm the truth of Christian faith. One must know the Koran, he felt, in order to be able to refute it. It does not appear that Luther had the opportunity of engaging in serious interreligious dialog.[25]

Luther's response to the challenge of religious pluralism was thus to take it very seriously indeed, and to examine it minutely on the basis of documents and eyewitness reports. In the end, theological interest in the Koran takes precedence over all other possible approaches. The Koran is studied with a view to refuting its claims. The response of believing Christians cannot be that of pretended neutrality, intellectual tolerance, or religious relativism. Luther's single-minded dismissal of all claims except the claims of Christ becomes a source of profound challenge to all contemporary practitioners of interreligious dialog.

IN RETROSPECT: LUTHER AS MISSIOLOGIST

Our survey has shown Luther to be a creative and original missionary thinker, firmly grounded in the biblical worldview, and surprisingly contemporary in some respects. The mission of God contrasts sharply with humanistic missionary attitudes of later periods, saturated in personal piety and vulnerable to pressures of cultural imperialism and Western expansion. Mission for Luther occurs in all six continents, wherever the people of God are present and the Word is proclaimed. No polarity of "senders" and "receivers" exists, and no "dominance-dependence" syndrome develops.

"Integration" of church and mission is unnecessary, because "disintegration" has never taken place. Witness in unity is the normal expectation. Laypeople are in the forefront of missionary encounter.

Cultural integrity is upheld, and the study of other faiths is commended. Unevangelical methods and approaches are condemned. The Bible as a textbook for mission seems deceptively simple and relevant as read through the eyes of Martin Luther the missiologist.

On the other hand, Luther's theocentric and biblical concept of mission cannot easily be translated into organizational terms. The praxis belongs to the triune God; it cannot easily be given institutional expression. It is certainly not measurable in terms of statistical growth, numbers of missionaries, impact on society, or other facts reported in annual reports. Its ultimate significance is grasped only in faith, and its final vindication is eschatological. Moreover, in Luther's own day, the grand design of *missio Dei* came to no clear expression. Religious freedom scarcely existed. Lay priesthood made good homiletical sense but, in practice, the implications of Baptism for the witness and service of all believers remained to be worked out. The ecumenical situation fell far short of witness in unity. The abolition of special missionary orders by Lutherans further deprived them of the traditional Catholic means and instruments of evangelization. Accordingly, the "rich but untested potential" of Luther and the reformation for mission practice comes down to the present, not as definitive guidance, but certainly as inspiration and challenge for missiology today. It also becomes a valuable "benchmark" for testing today's missiological axioms.

LUTHERAN ORTHODOXY: SAYING NO TO MISSION

In the period that followed the Lutheran Reformation, that of 17th-century scholastic Orthodoxy, Lutheran missionary thinking profoundly changed. Luther's biblically based conviction about the proclamation of the gospel of the whole creation and his confidence in the ultimate triumph of God's kingdom gave way to dogmatic hairsplitting and ecclesiastical retrenchment. In the period of Orthodoxy, Lutheranism erected formidable dogmatic barriers to mission work by evangelical churches.

On the one hand, Luther's theocentric emphasis was maintained: mission *is* the work of the triune God. On the other hand, Orthodoxy now affirmed much more dogmatically than Luther had that mission is *not* the task of human agents except in the closely controlled circumstances where the *ius reformandi* applied, viz., that evangelical princes are responsible for evangelizing their non-Christian subjects. Under the privilege known as *cuius regio, eius religio,* each ruler had the right to determine the religious allegiance of his subjects. In accordance with this proviso, Lutheran princes—especially from Sweden and Denmark—carried out territorial missions in their overseas possessions, sending chaplains to preach the gospel to both Christians and non-Christians

Under this territorial policy, however, missionary responsibility ceased when one went beyond the territories ruled by an evangelical prince, whether at home or abroad.

To make matters worse, Lutheran Orthodoxy, in a nervous and defensive reaction against its critics, went so far as to maintain that the evangelistic mandate of the Great Commission was no longer valid, and that the apostolate established by Jesus Christ was now defunct. Lutheranism now went on record as saying no to world evangelization—not categorically, but practically speaking—and buttressed its refusal on exegetical and dogmatic grounds. It can hardly be doubted that this refusal has left its permanent mark on Lutheran missionary thinking.

For Lutheran Orthodoxy, the crux of the issue had to do with establishing the Lutheran claim to be apostolic. Roman Catholic critics, such as the Jesuit controversial theologian Robert Bellarmine (1542–1621), had maintained that Lutherans could not lay claim to various marks of the true church, among them apostolicity and catholicity, because Lutherans did not engage in missions overseas and their churches were not to be found in all parts of the earth. Catholics also reproached Lutherans with being too timid and cowardly to undertake hazardous missions to the heathen, as Jesuits and others had done.

In his reply to these charges, the great theologian of Lutheran Orthodoxy, Johann Gerhard (1582–1637), stated that the extent and numbers of believers were not marks of the true church.[26] The only necessary mark was the true and catholic faith determined by adherence to the rule and norm of the Holy Scriptures. In this sense, said Gerhard, Lutherans were truly "catholic," but Roman Catholics were not.

Nor would Gerhard concede that the Roman Catholic church was apostolic, since its missionary agents struck him as "pseudoapostolic" and "anti-Christian." The Lutherans laid claim to true apostolicity in view of their pure apostolic doctrine based on the Scriptures.

Gerhard thus neatly separated the missionary activity of the church from its claims to apostolicity and catholicity. In the polemic of Lutheran Orthodoxy against the Catholic Counter-Reformation, the Lutheran church could claim for itself the marks of the true church without actually supporting a missionary apostolate.

EXPIRATION OF THE GREAT COMMISSION

Still more fateful for Lutheran missionary attitudes was Gerhard's contention that since "immediate divine vocation" had ceased and was no longer to be found in the church since the time of Christ, the Great Commission had no continuing validity in its original form. It had been intended for the original apostles, but the apostolate had expired in its original sense, and the apostles had no real successors.

Once again, the orthodox position over against Rome was dictated by polemical necessity. The gifts and powers of the apostolate, said Gerhard, now devolved corporately upon the church and were mediated through regular ecclesiastical calls to settled parochial ministries. No theological basis existed for a call to preach the gospel to distant heathen.

Moreover, as Gerhard and his contemporaries believed, the task of mission preaching had been essentially completed by the apostles. Thus Gerhard, seeking to counter the claims of the Roman Catholic church to apostolic succession through the see of Peter and the bishops, denied the validity of the missionary mandate of the Great Commission. Only that part of the Lord's commission that related to Baptism and the teaching office remained valid.[27]

In 1651, in response to an inquiry by a Lutheran layman, the Lutheran Theological Faculty at Wittenberg delivered a classical "opinion" about mission activity which expressed the Lutheran Orthodox attitude in the middle of the 17th century. It contained three points:

1. The apostolate had been a "personal privilege" of the apostles which did not devolve on their successors. It would be absurd to maintain that the Great Commission was still in effect, for in that case all ministers of Christ would be duty bound to go to the heathen.

2. No one is excused before God on account of ignorance, for those

persons—or their ancestors—who do not believe in Christ are presumed to have rejected the gospel. God is not obligated to give them a second chance. Nor are European Christians responsible for the ultimate fate of unbelievers abroad.

3. Rulers have the right and duty to propagate the gospel in their own territories. This they have faithfully done.[28]

Under this interpretation, mission work aiming at the universal proclamation of the gospel becomes theologically unnecessary—except in the restricted territorial sense—and even open to suspicion.

The ultimate in theological sterility occurred when Lutheran Orthodoxy, through the Lutheran orthodox theologian Johann Ursinus (1608–1667), condemned Justinian Weltz (1621–1668), a Lutheran layman of noble birth, as a heretic and fanatic. Weltz had challenged the orthodox view of mission work as unscriptural and immoral. He denounced Orthodoxy's position that the apostles had no successors, claiming that the Great Commission retained unqualified validity.

Weltz attacked the view that Christians were not responsible for the fate of the heathen, arguing that Christian compassion obligated believers to reevangelize nonbelievers, even if their ancestors had once been evangelized by the apostles.

Weltz insisted that God would hold Christians responsible for the ultimate fate of the heathen and called on his fellow Christians to send student volunteer evangelists to preach the gospel to the heathen. The evangelical members of the Imperial Diet meeting in 1664 declared his scheme "impracticable," while a leading theologian pronounced it fanatical and satanic!

Weltz, a Lutheran voice crying in the wilderness, became a martyr to orthodox intransigence.[29]

In these depressing utterances of Lutheran Orthodoxy we see an ironic reflection of the theocentric missionary attitude of the Reformation. The mission belonged to God, Weltz was told, and God needed no human helpers. By nullifying the primitive apostolate, Orthodoxy denied itself any theologically acceptable outlet for the genuine missionary impulses which it felt. In denying the validity of the Great Commission, it encumbered itself with guilt and then went to great lengths to justify itself. Weltz proposed a new solution to the problem of mission agency in the form of an evangelical sending society and volunteer missionary agents, but Orthodoxy remained too captive to its viewpoint to give any recognition to these.

Defensive about its own integrity and engaged in a worsening polemic encounter with its opponents, Lutheranism was forced to adopt positions which were dubious and self-serving, and which later Lutherans would have to repudiate in deference to Scripture. Luther's view of *missio Dei* was put to the test, but the orthodox fruit was barren.

LUTHERAN PIETISM: OVERCOMING THE NEGATION

In the period immediately before Pietism, Lutherans raised almost insuperable obstacles to the development of a positive missionary tradition. They rejected the validity of the Great Commission and further undermined the call to mission by arguing that European Christians had no responsibility for evangelizing non-Christians. They denied to regional churches any authority to preach the gospel to non-Christians, except within their own territorial boundaries, and forbade the creation of a distinctively missionary office. What missionary concern they had was concentrated on the "regular calling" of ministers to existing congregations; they made no parallel provision for a "regular sending" to nonbelievers, apart from those occasionally ministered to by chaplains in overseas territories. They made the lay priesthood of the baptized a virtual dead letter.

While keeping Luther's vision of mission as God's own work, they carefully cordoned off the eschatological horizon in the reformer's view, according to which gospel proclamation would continue to the ends of the earth and to the last day. They succeeded in domesticating the *missio Dei* within the ecclesiastical boundaries of Christendom.

Only a deep and powerful movement of renewal, attended by the Spirit, could have overcome these negative forces. Pietism was a massive effort to continue and deepen the work of the Reformation on Lutheran soil. Pietists believed that they were inaugurating a "second reformation"—not unlike the Puritans in England—with the aim of restoring primitive Christianity. Luther had completed the task of reforming doctrine; the pietists had as their goal the reformation of life. It was inevitable that mission and evangelism, along with church renewal and Christian unity, should have been in the forefront of their concern.

CHRISTIANITY AS PRACTICE, NOT THEORY

Philip Jakob Spener (1635–1705), the "father of Pietism," set forth new tasks and goals which prepared the ground for the missionary impulse. In his programmatic essay, *Pia Desideria* (1675),[30] Spener proposed a more extensive use of the Scriptures by individuals and groups, diligent exercise of the spiritual priesthood of the laity, the view that Christianity consists more of *practice (praxis pietatis)* than of theory, reform in theological education; and an emphasis on edification rather than erudition in sermons and religious education. Spener's warm evangelical spirit, his irenic attitude toward other confessions, and his support of lay study-groups *(collegia pietatis)* and the wider distribution of the Bible deeply influenced the rising generation of Lutheran pietists.[31]

It was at the new University of Halle, however, that the translation of pietist impulses into concrete missionary action took place, under the influence of August Hermann Francke (1663–1727).[32] The achievements of Halle pietism, under Francke's leadership, in initiating evangelical *foreign* mission work in South India through Bartholomaeus Ziegenbalg (1682–1719) at Tranquebar (1706), and *diaspora* ministry through Henry Melchior Muhlenberg (1711–1787) in Pennsylvania (1742), are of tremendous significance for Lutheran missions.

1. Pietism reaffirmed the Great Commission as universally valid and quietly set aside Orthodoxy's theological objections. Christians must accept responsibility for proclaiming the gospel to all persons everywhere.

2. Pietism overcame the structural problem of missions that had plagued Orthodoxy by creating voluntary missionary societies, modeled on the *collegia pietatis,* and transcending the territorial restrictions and limitations of regional churches.

3. Pietism solved the problem of missionary office or agency by recruiting suitable persons with a "testifying spirit" and sending them out to cross frontiers and preach the gospel to the whole creation.

Francke told the South India missionaries to model their life and behavior as closely as possible on the life of St. Paul and the apostles in the book of Acts. While the status and credentials of these missionaries in the home churches might have been disputed, overseas they functioned as emissaries of the kingdom, preaching the gospel, baptizing converts, and planting local churches.

4. Pietists for the first time gave Lutherans a body of missionary experience from which concrete lessons of practice and methodology could be derived. At home they mastered the skills of recruiting, training, sending, funding, and promoting mission work. In the mission areas their representatives compiled grammars and dictionaries; translated the Bible, catechism, and hymnody; ordained native workers; built churches; organized congregations; conducted dialog with non-Christians; and kept careful records.

5. Pietists recognized that the eschatological scope of the Great Commission transcended boundaries of nations and confessions and demanded a worldwide partnership of churches in all lands. In India an unprecedented three-way program of cooperation in mission, involving Lutherans, Anglicans, and Reformed groups, and drawing support from Germany, Denmark, and Great Britain, broke new ground. In subordinating national and denominational interests to the greater interests of the kingdom, they anticipated the modern ecumenical movement.

STRENGTHS AND WEAKNESSES

Lutheran Pietism broke through the dogmatic denial and bureaucratic controls of Orthodoxy to reaffirm the Great Commission. It embraced *missio Dei* as an authorization to go forth and witness, and it provided Lutheranism with a new motivation, agency, and strategy.

At the same time, certain debits must be noted. With the missions of Pietism there began a subtle and gradual displacement of divine initiative by human organization and planning. It was inevitable that mission activity, like other activities in the age of the Enlightenment, should undergo a gradual secularization of outlook, however much the matter of human autonomy remained concealed behind pious expressions. For, when human beings assume responsibility for what was heretofore considered God's own exclusive enterprise, it becomes more difficult to say when people are acting in response to God's call or are simply doing God's work for him.

In emphasizing regeneration by the Spirit more than justification by faith as the basis of mission work, pietists may have promoted a type of spiritual elitism that differed from the Reformation's emphasis on the church as the witnessing community, on baptismal ordination, and on the lay priesthood as normal instruments of God's mission.

In making mission work the special concern of spiritually regenerated groups and individuals, rather than the task of the entire church, pietists contributed to a divorce between church and mission which still formally exists in many European regional churches. Even in those churches where mission has been "integrated" into the life of the church, mission work is generally seen as the cause of special-interest groups. Pietism activated many laypersons in mission, but it did not establish a genuine universal priesthood based on Baptism.

Nor was Pietism exempt from the temptation to paternalism and Western dominance. Its standards of perfection could not be readily attained by Christians in Asia and Africa, and self-reliant churches were slow to arise. A narrow, judgmental attitude toward other cultures sometimes opened the door to the danger of confusing Western moral standards with evangelical and biblical ones.

Moreover, the tendency to concentrate on the personal moral and spiritual regeneration of converts may have led to a reductionist "one kingdom" concern with personal faith and salvation, and contributed to the neglect of human justice and the combating of social evils.

To its credit, Pietism grasped anew the universal application of the Great Commission, breaking down Orthodoxy's territorial frontiers, but then limited the scope of that commission largely to the salvation and nurture of individuals.

THE CONFESSIONAL REVIVAL: LUTHERAN MISSIONS IN THE 19th CENTURY

In its late period, Lutheran Pietism, which had done so much to promote foreign missions in India and diaspora mission in North America, lost both its sense of clear confessional identity and its missionary ardor. It became a victim of the rationalistic philosophy of the Enlightenment and the forces of secularization. Yet out of the womb of Pietism and the remnants of Moravianism there sprang the Evangelical Awakening of the late 18th century which gave rise to fresh movements for renewal and new impulses to mission. In 1780, for example, the German *Christentumsgesellschaft* (Christendom Society) sponsored common efforts by like-minded Christians to build the kingdom of God on an ecumenical basis without respect to confessional differences.

After 1800 Lutherans and other evangelical Christians began coming together on a regional basis to give renewed expression to their mission concern, appealing now to common scriptural teachings rather than to the particular confessions. Through the Basel (1815), Rhenish (1826), and North German (1836) mission societies, Lutherans and other evangelical Christians, however divided they may have been at home, pledged themselves to planting overseas "a church of the future" which would transcend the confessional distinctions of Christendom. Their emphasis lay on the kingdom that dawns as a result of the worldwide proclamation of the gospel. They anticipated the emergence of local Christian communities which would not be precise replicas of the confessional churches of Christendom, but rather Spirit-directed communities adapting to their local context.

This unique position, claiming its basis in the Great Commission given by the Lord on the Mount of Olives, ran into sharp opposition and was later shipwrecked on the rock of confessional resurgence.[33] But it could claim to have recovered something of Luther's biblical understanding of *missio Dei* as the universal proclamation of the gospel to the ends of the earth, while not necessarily adhering to the reformer's theocentric and eschatological point of view.

It also owed something to Zinzendorf's vision of the dawning of an inclusive fellowship of Christian believers from all confessions, the so-called Unitas Fratrum, brought together in the last days under the action of the Spirit.

CONFESSIONAL RESURGENCE

The positive spirit of interconfessional cooperation in renewal activities and mission was not to last. It was suddenly dissipated by a quite powerful but unexpected resurgence of loyalty among Lutherans to the confessional standards of the reformation era. The new confessional attitudes were wedded to the missionary zeal of the older Pietism, forming a unique blend of churchly confessional pietism. Unlike the earlier Pietism, which had maintained an irenic orientation toward other Protestants, this new blend of churchly pietism, joined to a deepened confessional consciousness, caused Lutherans to draw apart from other Protestants.

Believing that their own confessional teachings were closer to bib-lical truth than those of other churches, and that they were somehow the "purest" of visible churches, many Lutherans began to break off ecumenical ties formed under the influence of the Awakening. They withdraw from participation in united mission societies, and formed purely Lutheran ones such as those at Leipzig (1836) and Neuendet-telsau (1841, 1849). In America, too, Lutherans were becoming more confessionally conscious, and this new attitude found expression in missionary outreach. The first American Lutheran pastor to be sent as a foreign missionary to India, Father C. F. Heyer, expressed a desire to go out under the auspices of a Lutheran mission society and "not to be beholden to other denominations."

The new Lutheran societies in Europe and America had as their aim the propagation of the pure Lutheran confessional teachings in their fullness, based on the foundation of the Scriptures. As these societies arose, Lutheran interest in promoting the supraconfessional kingdom of God receded in favor of the new goal of planting churches with a clear Lutheran identity in Asia, Africa, and North and South America.

The causes of this movement of Lutheran separation from other evangelical Christians are complex and varied, and belong now largely to the past. Lutheranism in the mid-19th century was undergoing a process of reclaiming its own identity some three centuries after the Reformation. Many Lutherans felt that the theology and piety of the Evangelical Awakening, despite its appeal to the Scriptures, did not express the distinctiveness of the Lutheran understanding of gospel, sacraments, ministry, and church as taught in the confessions. In Amer-ica the movement had its counterpart in a struggle during the 1850s to overthrow the platform of "American Lutheranism," which was seek-ing to modify the teachings and practices of Lutheranism along Puritan-evangelical lines, while being moderately inclined to the use of reviv-alist measures.[34] Lutherans in America responded by decisively re-jecting what they considered to be a compromised or watered-down form of Lutheranism.

Increasingly, Lutherans were willing to engage in fellowship and cooperative relations only with other Lutherans. Ecumenical awareness was at a low ebb. Lutherans did not deny the unity of the church, as confessed in the creeds, but they considered such unity to be purely invisible and not attainable on earth.

REACTION AGAINST UNIONISM

Still another factor promoting Lutheran solidarity was the reaction against abortive state-sponsored efforts to bring about inclusive evangelical church unions in Prussia and elsewhere. These tended to make Lutherans—above all, those connected with the Lutheran Church–Missouri Synod—suspicious of efforts towards *unionism*.

A growing worldwide Lutheran confessional movement now arose which embraced large regional churches in Germany and Scandinavia, some small minority churches in Europe, along with independent free churches founded by mission or immigration in Asia, Africa, Oceania, and North and South America. The Lutheran World Federation (1947) in the 20th century is the global organizational expression of this 19th-century movement of Lutheran unity and solidarity.

Lutheran mission activity in the 19th century, combining evangelism and church planting with confessional separatism, held both positive and negative consequences for the future. On the positive side, Lutheran confessional missions took the church principle seriously and founded churches overseas with full spiritual authority, including Word, sacraments, indigenous ministry, and the "three-self" marks (self-government, self-support, and self-propagation). These local churches were set on the road toward autonomy and self-reliance, and encouraged to be active in missionary activity among their own people. In the sending countries, Lutheran missions advocated the view that mission work wàs the task of the home church and its local congregations, not merely of interested persons and groups. Confessional Lutherans supported the principle of integrating church and mission, though in Europe (in contrast to North America) they were unable to overcome the traditional structural separation between church and mission.

Appealing to Luther's practice of fostering local folk traditions, these missions encouraged their daughter churches to express their own unique cultural identity through local language, kinship ties, and social customs. Ecclesiologically, Lutherans supported church-mission "integration," while culturally they encouraged "contextualization." Overall, they made a Lutheran contribution to world mission and evangelism in all six continents.

On the negative side, there are damaging criticisms.[35] Luther's theocentric view of mission as God's own action through Word, church, and baptized believer was now virtually abandoned in favor of a horizontal view which saw mission activity as the work of organized societies with professional agents. Moreover, due to the emphasis on confessional separatism, Lutheran missions were sometimes tempted to make confessional propaganda for Lutheranism, or deflected from evangelism into the partisan conflicts of the sending countries. The Lutheran confessions were more often seen as defensive shields and protective fences around growing Lutheran communities, not as ecumenical testimonies to the faith of the one holy catholic and apostolic church. Few ecumenical incentives existed.

Lutherans at this time saw themselves as a particular visible church—indeed as the truest among existing visible churches—defending the confessions against attack or compromise. Unionism was deeply suspect, and any kind of positive relationship between mission and unity was excluded, except as it concerned solidarity among Lutherans.

In this situation there was no preparation of young Lutheran churches for participation in the ecumenical movement, soon to burst upon the scene. Nor was the slightest hint given of a possible future form of unity crossing the denominational lines of the West.

Lutherans in the 19th century were challenged to participate in the mission of God, but their energies were consumed in the task of planting local Lutheran churches affiliated with mother churches or societies in the West. According to the church-centered view of mission, as developed in Germany by Gustav Warneck and shared by most Lutherans, "mission is the road from [sending] church to [emerging] church." This church-centered emphasis, when combined with confessional exclusiveness, succeeded in largely eliminating the wider ecumenical and eschatological horizons of mission. The kingdom of God was reduced to a strategy by which Lutheran mission agencies planted Lutheran churches around the world. Questions were seldom asked at this time about the relationship of these churches to the kingdom of God. Their very existence appeared to be its own justification, and no further discussion of mission goals was required.

Lutheran missions in the period of the confessional revival, while most certainly preaching the gospel to non-Christians, placed major emphasis on spreading and conserving a particular historical tradition of Christendom, rather than being open to new tasks and initiatives.

With the entry of Lutherans into the ecumenical movement, all this would change.

LUTHERAN MISSIONS IN THE ECUMENICAL ERA

In the 20th century, especially after two world wars, Lutheran missionary thinking and practice entered a period of significant change in response to the world situation and as a result of Lutheran participation in the ecumenical movement. Lutherans too were deeply affected by developments referred to in the previous chapter: the end of colonialism, the collapse of Christendom, and the growth of a Christian world community in all six continents. Secularization, urbanization, and technological change called for new responses. Ideological conflict and the spread of communism took their toll; East Germany—Luther's home territory—and a number of eastern European countries containing Lutheran minority churches now became atheistic Marxist revolutionary states. In the two-thirds world, meanwhile, many young Lutheran churches arising from the 19th-century missionary movement from the West were caught up in efforts to shake off colonial attitudes, practice self-reliance, and promote development among their own peoples. Others struggled to achieve new identities in the struggle against left- or right-wing totalitarian movements, in the encounter with apartheid in Southern Africa, or in their relationships with dominant non-Christian religious communities.

The world missionary situation confronting Lutheranism in the middle of the 20th century was thus vastly different from the one in which Lutherans had grown to become a worldwide community by mission and emigration a century earlier. Gone were the protective umbrella of Western colonialism under which mission work had prospered, and the conceit of Western superiority in culture and civilization. Lutheran churches in Europe and North America now faced grave doubts about their own adequacy, and experienced alienation and declining numbers. Increasingly, Lutherans began to question the missionary movement from the West, the imposition of Western values on the two-thirds world, and even the validity of evangelizing and converting non-Christians. Some Western church leaders felt the time had come to reevangelize their own nominal Christian populations. Further, sharp differences in political systems now tended to polarize Lutherans in East and West, while misunderstandings and tensions over power, relationships, and resources often divided Lutherans in North and South. It was certainly true for Lutherans, as for others, that mission work suffered from unresolved theological problems, and that the failure to deal with these sometimes resulted in confusion in practice.

Despite the factors making for fragmentation and loss of initiative, the positive new elements in the situation were not to be underestimated. Lutheranism, as never before, had become a world community of churches found on all six continents. With the organization of the Lutheran World Federation in 1947 it had created its own instrument for fellowship and consultation among the churches, common study, joint missionary action, and witness and service before the world.[36] The purpose of the LWF, as stated in the original constitution adopted at Lund in 1947, was set forth in boldly missionary terms: "to bear united witness before the world to the Gospel of Jesus Christ as the power of God for salvation."[37] Other purposes included the cultivation of unity of faith and confession among Lutherans, promotion of fellowship and cooperation in study, fostering Lutheran participation in ecumenical movements, developing united approaches to mission and educational work, and supporting Lutheran groups in need of spiritual or material aid.

The Lutheran response to the new missionary situation of the 20th century was greatly strengthened by the overcoming of isolation among Lutheran groups, and by the availability of common instruments for consultation and developing common policies and strategies on a six-continent basis. At the same time, Lutheran participation in the post-Edinburgh movement of missionary cooperation—as represented by the International Missionary Council (1921), in the work of all of the organs of the World Council of Churches (1948), and, after 1965, in bilateral conversations and relations with the post-Vatican II Roman Catholic church—had the effect of rescuing Lutherans from their 19th-century confessional exclusivism and placing them in the mainstream of the new missionary and ecumenical movements.

LUTHERAN MISSIONARY COOPERATION

The roots of Lutheran cooperation and solidarity can be traced back to two catastrophic world wars in which Lutherans found themselves on opposite sides. During the First and Second World Wars, fellowship and contact between Lutherans was disrupted by hostilities between opposing forces. Unusual acts of reconciliation and mutual assistance were required to restore these relationships. In both wars, German overseas missions (along with those of some other countries) were "orphaned" due to the fortunes of war; German missionaries were interned or repatriated; and local Christian communities were cut off from support. The international Lutheran effort to "save" these orphaned German missions for the Lutheran church—by placing them under temporary trusteeship arrangements and providing for aid and supervision by Lutheran mission agencies from the United States, Canada, Sweden, and Australia—was a providential factor in generating Lutheran global solidarity. Similar efforts to rehabilitate war-devastated German churches, to assist in the work of relief and reconstruction in European Lutheran minority churches, and to facilitate the relocation of millions of refugees contributed to the growing desire on the part of Lutherans to manifest their growing sense of unity in faith and life.[38]

In 1923 an intermediate expression of Lutheran solidarity, the Lutheran World Convention (LWC), was formed in Eisenach, Germany, primarily for consultation, fellowship, and study among Lutherans. In 1947 the Lutheran World Federation (LWF) was organized at Lund, Sweden, as a free association of Lutheran churches but with a strong executive arm, and a permanent secretariat located in Geneva, Switzerland.

One of the actions of the first LWF assembly was to authorize the formation of a Commission on World Missions (CWM), later provided with its own departmental staff (DWM). Annual meetings of the Commission on World Missions, beginning in 1949, had the character of a "Lutheran world mission parliament" in which key policy issues were examined and debated. They brought together representatives of Lutheran mission agencies in the West and church leaders from the two-thirds world. The Commission sought to carry out the Lund Assembly's instructions that a "unified approach" be developed by the Lutheran church in its mission, and that mission become the task of the church in every nation and of every local congregation and believer. Lund had recommended that Lutheran churches and mission agencies consult together, coordinate policies, and pool resources in cases where several groups of Lutherans worked in a single area. Aid should be given with the purpose of building self-supporting, self-governing, and self-propagating churches, a single national church in each land, "so that an indigenous, self-supporting Lutheran church may carry forward in a unified way the work of the kingdom in that area."

> The sovereignty and equality of voice and responsibility of all churches, younger and older, should be achieved as soon as possible and should be fully recognized. There should also be a recognition of our interdependence upon each other.[39]

Thus, Lutheran churches and missions around the world were encouraged to engage in mutual consultation, practice internationalization, share resources, and manifest interdependence, thereby bearing "united witness before the world to the Gospel of Jesus Christ as the power of God for salvation." To isolated and weak churches these opportunities for fellowship and cooperation in mission were a source of immense encouragement and strength.

RELEVANT LWF ASSEMBLY STATEMENTS

From time to time the Lutheran World Federation in its assemblies adopted official statements which, while not directed specifically to mission theology or practice, had ground-breaking significance for the wider understanding of Lutheran mission. Two such statements were adopted at the LWF Sixth Assembly (Dar-es-Salaam, 1977) on the practical application and implementation of confessional integrity in the life of the church, and on justice as an integral aspect of the church's mission.

The statement on "Confessional Integrity" was drafted at the Sixth Assembly in the context of a heated debate over how to banish the influence and practice of apartheid from the life of LWF member churches, including those located in southern Africa. The statement began by noting that Lutheran churches are "confessional churches" whose unity and mutual recognition are based upon acknowledgment of the Word of God and the normative character of Lutheran confessional writings. It went on:

> Confessional subscription is more than a formal acknowledgment of doctrine. Churches which have signed the confessions of the church thereby commit themselves to show through their daily witness and service that

the gospel has empowered them to live as the people of God. They also commit themselves to accept in their worship and at the table of the Lord the brothers and sisters who belong to other churches that accept the same confessional understanding.[40]

The situation in southern Africa constituted a *status confessionis* for Lutheran churches, and demanded a public expression of church teaching.

> This means that on the basis of faith, and in order to manifest the unity of the church, churches would publicly and unequivocally reject the existing Apartheid system.[41]

The consequences of this decisive assembly resolution were not merely to condemn apartheid and to make intercommunion between black and white congregations a test of confessional integrity. The statement also committed Lutheran member churches "to withstand alien principles" which threaten to undermine faith and to destroy unity in doctrine, witness, and practice. Lutherans were also challenged to show through their daily witness and service that the gospel has empowered them to *live* as the people of God. Confessional loyalty, far from having a purely formal character, was being redefined in living, existential terms.

Another statement from the LWF Sixth Assembly dealt with "Socio-Political Functions and Responsibilities of Lutheran Churches," and spoke especially of the need for Lutheran solidarity in the struggle against injustice and oppression.

> The churches cannot withdraw from their responsibility as a part of the society in which they live. They must find a way between the extremes of complete adaptation to their surroundings and a complete withdrawal from them. . . . Therefore, they must find in each society a way of critical engagement that expresses their dependence on God and their solidarity with the world, but that does not at the same time serve worldly powers in an idolatrous way.

Although the Lutheran "two kingdoms" doctrine had suffered from misinterpretation and misapplication, it had special relevance:

> the doctrine clearly intends not only to affirm God's sovereignty over the whole creation but also to direct the church to witness and Christians

to participate in the structures by which their daily life is organized, as a form of responsible care for the creation, mutual service to the neighbor and to all humankind, and involvement in the struggles for greater freedom and justice for all.

The key paragraph which then follows has vital significance for the character of Lutheran missionary witness:

> *Advocacy for justice is an essential, integral part of the mission of the church.* It belongs inherently to the proclamation of the word. Justice under the law of God is a witness to the universal sovereignty of God's law over all his creation.[42]

With this statement the LWF went on record as saying that advocacy of justice was an *essential*—not an occasional or incidental—aspect of the mission of the church. Missionary proclamation, so said the assembly, included not only the saving message of grace and salvation through Jesus Christ (gospel), but also the divine condemnation of injustice, oppression, and idolatry (law). No proclamation of the kingdom of God was complete without a witness both to God's wrath and to God's salvation. Christians were bidden to involve themselves in the struggle for human justice, not as a *substitute* for proclaiming the gospel, but as an indispensable accompaniment to it.

CURRENT MISSIOLOGICAL DIRECTIONS

Where is Lutheran missiology moving? In an effort to answer this question we shall cite six indications of current missiological trends in Lutheranism. These trends can be seen in intra-Lutheran discussions, and in Lutheran comment on ecumenical developments. Some of these trends will be further evident in the chapters that follow.

In some cases, the new trends correct older ones, as in the current reaction against 19th-century church-centered framework for missionary thinking and practice. In other cases, as with the effort to recover the *missio Dei* line of thinking, we may detect a return to the missionary legacy of Luther and the Reformation.

No such thing as a "normative" Lutheran missiological pattern exists, since the Lutheran confessions have not spoken on the subject of mission theology and practice. But Lutherans have sought in a variety of contexts to clarify their missionary thinking in response to the missiological challenges of the 20th century.[43] These changes, taken together, constitute an "updating" of the Lutheran missiological agenda.

1. *The kingdom of God as the goal of mission*

Lutherans are now in wide agreement that the kingdom of God, understood in terms of its biblical meaning, must be taken as the key term in thinking about world mission. As the triune God is the author of mission, the kingdom of God must be seen as its final goal or consummation.

Jesus came proclaiming the kingdom, and in his messianic ministry embodied it through acts of healing, redemption, and reconciliation. The church is neither the *ground* of God's mission nor its *goal;* hence the church-centered framework favored by 19th-century Lutheran mission thinkers must be set aside as theologically inadequate. Mission is more than a process of reproducing churches. It is a witness to the fullness of the promise of God's kingdom. It is also a participation with Christ in the ongoing struggle between the kingdom of God and the powers of darkness and evil in this world.

The final victory of God's kingdom is eschatological, and remains for the present an object of faith and hope. Christians are encouraged by signs of the kingdom breaking into the present, and they are commanded by their Lord to work and pray for its coming.

The meaning of the kingdom for the church's missionary obedience today, and the issue of appropriate methods, tactics, and resources, must be carefully studied on the basis of the witness of Scripture, and in relation to the contexts and challenges posed by the world situation. This remains a crucial missiological task for today.

2. *The church as instrument of God's mission*

The church derives its mission and sending authority from its Lord, Jesus Christ. Its integrity as church and its faithfulness to its mission both depend on the church's closeness to, and union with, Christ. Only the Word and sacraments constitute the indispensable basis for the church; all else is provisional.

As the body of Christ, the church is called in faith to conform to the way of the cross and the pattern of the Servant. Christ remains the Lord of mission, and continually calls and empowers the church for its mission through the Holy Spirit. The church has the character of a divine instrument witnessing to the coming of the kingdom and preparing for it. As the body of Christ, the church also foreshadows the presence of the kingdom. As an instrument of the kingdom, the church is always aware of its own *provisional* character, and continually open to being renewed and restructured for its missionary task. The church seeks not its own enhancement or enlargement but only the consummation willed by God, and manifested in Christ, for the world and for creation. Its constant concern must be to seek the divinely willed expression of the kingdom under the conditions of history.

3. *The calling to mission and unity*

The decision to return to Luther's *missio Dei* understanding of mission, designating the kingdom of God as goal, with the church as an instrument, and setting aside the 19th-century church-centered framework, has profound ecumenical implications. For one thing, the policy of confessional exclusivism—under which Lutherans aimed to reproduce purely Lutheran churches around the world—cannot be maintained.

The newer concept of Lutheranism as a confessing movement within the one holy catholic church militates against confessional exclusivism. The significance of the confessions in the life of the church is once again grasped in the Reformation sense of being testimonies to the truth of the prophetic and apostolic Scriptures which are to be believed and confessed by all Christians.

For Lutherans, this means an obligation to use their confessions not as *barriers* to fellowship with other Christians, but as an *encouragement and inspiration* for ecumenical witness. As the LWF Second Assembly at Hannover put it:

> The Lutheran church is therefore called to use its confession in the service of all churches. This does not mean using it as a law of faith, but it does mean proclaiming it as a clear and true exposition of the Gospel truth which will invite others to confess the same Christ at their place and time and in their language.[44]

With regard to the planting of new churches, no concise guidelines emerge, due to the multiplicity of existing denominational programs and structures, but there are clear implications. The Lutheran church receives the call to mission from its Lord not in isolation but as part of the one holy catholic and apostolic church. It affirms "one Lord, one faith, one baptism" (Eph. 4:5) and one Table of the Lord. It is bound in unity with all who are baptized and confess the name of Christ to strive for unity in witness and fellowship.

This means that in pioneer situations where no other churches exist, Lutherans will work in a representative capacity on behalf of the whole church of Christ, avoiding denominational propaganda and teaching the essentials of apostolic tradition. In situations where other churches exist, Lutherans will seek to undergird the ecumenical witness to the gospel, engage in efforts to remove obstacles to unity, and generally exalt the Lordship of Jesus Christ and the cause of God's kingdom over sectarian partisanship.

The call to be one in Christ, and to do mission in unity, poses far-reaching questions for the ultimate validity of denominational structures. It reinforces earlier statements about the provisional character of all church structures in the light of the *eschaton* and in view of the church's missionary witness to the coming kingdom and the final consummation.

4. *"Salvation history" as a valid paradigm*

Over against some current tendencies to collapse "sacred history" into secular history, to discover "God's presence" in contemporary events, to view all religions as "ways of salvation," or to see in contemporary revolutionary movements evidences of God's salvation in Jesus Christ, Lutherans reject the notion that salvation can be universalized.

God's saving intention for the whole world is *uniquely* manifested in the revelation given to Jewish lawgivers, prophets, and patriarchs, incarnated in the life, death, and resurrection of Jesus Christ, witnessed to by the apostles and the church, and recorded in the prophetic and apostolic Scriptures of the Old Testament and the New Testament.

Therefore all hopes and expectations for deliverance or liberation through messianic leaders, revolutionary movements, or religious systems can have no ultimate validity as expressions of God's eschatological salvation. This does not exclude the possibility that such movements may offer genuine hope or meaning in the short term for the human situation. They represent *penultimate* hopes and possibilities alongside the Christian's *ultimate* hope of salvation and the kingdom through God's action in Christ.

Put in another way, the term *missio Dei* should not be used indiscriminately to refer to contemporary revolutionary movements or promises of justice or peace, but must be reserved for God's saving action in Jesus Christ. The kingdom remains uniquely God's gift to the world in Christ, and is not the product of an evolutionary process of development nor of a revolutionary act. This is certainly not to imply that movements for justice and peace are contrary to the will of God, for God does indeed will them. Lutherans understand such movements to be expressions of God's providential will which mandates peace and justice for the entire creation. They are to be judged by the criterion of God's universal law and righteousness. But they are not to be identified with the movement of the kingdom which comes by grace through faith in Jesus Christ, and which invites the response of obedient discipleship.

With regard to other living faiths and ideologies making salvific claims, Lutherans hold much the same view. The teachings and practices of other religions are not regarded as "ways of salvation," or as expressions of God's kingdom in Jesus Christ, however much they may embody elements of personal nobility, religious insight, and piety. We have already noted Luther's *dialectical* view of other faiths (Islam in particular) according to which the reformer tended to see them as outstanding examples of moral achievement, devotion, and personal sacrifice, but ultimately lacking in the one thing needful: the knowledge of salvation through Jesus Christ. In the final analysis, other religions are no more than systems of self-salvation. Everything depends, said Luther, on the Second Article!

This deeply felt motivation to extol Jesus Christ as the sole source of salvation—and as the central theme of salvation history—has special implications for the Lutheran understanding and practice of dialog. To understand what dialog is and to practice it properly, one must see it in relation to the next point: justification by grace through faith.

5. *Justification by grace through faith as the Word of proclamation*

God's act in freely forgiving sinners for Christ's sake, and accepting them despite their unworthiness as joint heirs with Christ of God's kingdom, is the heart of the gospel message. It also says a good deal about the nature of Christian mission, including the practice of dialog.

God is a God who lovingly condescends in Christ to meet us in our human condition, and whose infinite capacity for grace precedes any merit or moral improvement on our part. God stoops to our weakness because that is God's nature, and because God desires out of compassion to seek and to save the lost. In responding to the Great Commission, the church identifies with the passionate heart of the Creator.

Through the *external Word* of gospel proclamation we hear the good news of salvation addressed to us, and by grace, through faith, we are enabled by the Spirit to lay hold of the gospel promises. As this occurs, God makes of us "new creatures." We become witnesses to the new creation in Christ Jesus.

This gospel message must be addressed, without exception, to *every* human being. Proclaimed from faith to faith, it remains the power of God for salvation to all who believe. Baptism and the Lord's Supper are the same "word made visible." God's power accompanies Word and sacraments and makes them efficacious. The power of the external Word does not depend on human oratory or persuasiveness, but rests on God's own promise and presence. This continues to be a source of comfort and encouragement.

Humans, whether ordained ministers or lay believers, can proclaim the message with confidence, for they are merely agents of God's own Word. When the gospel has done its work in the life of a new believer, that person becomes a joyous witness to the gospel's power. In this way God continuously renews the church.

The Christian witnesses to Christ not out of a conviction of sinless perfection, but as a *redeemed sinner;* not boasting of new-found moral superiority, but wanting to share the gift of life with other human beings. No other attitude is possible in dialog than that of grateful humility and Christlike identification. The motive for Christian witness to non-Christian neighbors is not the expectation of "making converts" but rather the desire to extol Christ as the hope of salvation.

In this doctrine of justification by faith the church is reminded of its priority task, and one which no other institution can carry out: to proclaim the gospel to the lost creation (Rom. 10:14). Concern for the unevangelized is, or ought to be, a mark of faith. In the comprehensive mission task of the church, telling the good news has priority.

6. *The correlation of creation and redemption in mission practice*

Creation waits with eager longing to be set free from bondage to decay, and to obtain the glorious liberty of the children of God (Rom. 8:19-21). Work for peace and justice, and care for the resources of the earth belong to the Christian's obligation to love the neighbor. But the creation cannot set itself free by its own efforts, nor can the dedication of human beings alone transform fallen nature or restore it to a state of sinless perfection.

Yet the kingdom of God, coming as a free gift in Jesus Christ, and reconciling humans to their Creator and to one another, becomes the starting point and motivation for the Christian's participation in the renewal of the earth. The kingdom, as set forth in the life and teachings of Jesus Christ, and realized in the reconciliation of sinners, becomes on the one hand an essential precondition for the Christian's loving service. On the other, the kingdom reveals God's demand of righteousness under the law, and helps to define the scope and goal of the Christian's obedient participation in the renewal of the earth, i.e., "a new earth in which righteousness dwells."

By the same faith which enables the believer to lay hold of the promises of salvation, the Christian is also given strength to work purposefully in the secular realm for peace and justice, and to struggle against evil and oppression, fully recognizing the ambiguity of all human actions and decisions, and remembering that only God's kingdom is ultimate. Working for peace and caring for the earth are good works springing from a faithful heart. The Christian's vocation is to serve God both in the present age and in the age to come. The Christian knows that the same God who is active through gospel and sacraments to redeem the world is also working through divine law and justice to preserve the earth and to maintain it as a place of human habitation.

The careful distinction between law and gospel, and between the two kinds of God's action in creation and redemption, will save the Christian from naive dependence on utopian schemes for world peace and justice. Christians do not underestimate the power of sin and evil! At the same time, this distinction will realistically equip Christians for creative participation as God's collaborators in the care of the earth and its preservation for all generations to come.

7. The necessary relation between justification and justice

The importance for Lutherans of clarifying the relationship between justification and justice is already implied in the two preceding points. One and the same God works through the gospel of salvation to free sinners from guilt and condemnation, and calls them to serve their neighbor in the world through faith active in love. One and the same human creature responds to the gospel invitation in faith and as a committed disciple of Christ strives to fulfill the whole counsel of God.

We have already noted that according to a current Lutheran understanding, "advocacy for justice is an essential, integral part of the mission of the church." Lutherans have not always held this view, and are still seeking to reach a more adequate theological understanding of the relationship between the two divine gifts of justice and justification. Can the mandate to practice justice be grounded in the gospel of justification by faith? Is the heritage of the Reformation relevant and useful in the struggle for justice?

Especially since the rise of "liberation theology" in Latin America, and in light of the struggle against apartheid in southern Africa, as well as the earlier struggle against Nazi tyranny, Lutherans have had reason to seek a more compelling formulation of the relationship. Some have adhered to the classical point of departure in the confessions according to which a careful distinction between gospel and law, and between justification and justice, is required. Others have been so moved by the concrete experiences of oppressed classes, races, and women, and by their actions to overcome all remaining vestiges of oppression, as to search for new kinds of formulations which more positively express the interdependence of justification and justice.

A recent statement from a conference of "Lutheran Theologians of the Americas" puts the matter as follows:

> The God who justifies us in Christ calls us to do justice. In the midst of economic dependence, militarism, poverty and other structures of death, we discern the signs of the kingdom of God among the oppressed and the impoverished struggling for life and liberation. Here it is impossible for Christians to be neutral. All who proclaim the word of God must also identify and challenge the forces of death and destruction which defy the kingdom of God. We affirm our Lutheran understanding of Christian vocation to direct us to serve the neighbor and to engage in the struggle for the transformation of society. God is at work to overcome

the demonic forces which breed suffering and death in our personal lives, in the church, and in society.[45]

In the struggle against the demonic forces which resist the coming of the kingdom, say these theologians, Christians may not be neutral. As followers of Christ they will employ the spiritual weapons of faith, prayer, and identification with the cross of Christ. As citizens of this world, they will also make use of all available weapons of civil justice, human rights, and protection under law, not excluding the right of political organization and public demonstration. For they are called to be children of God in both kingdoms.

In attempting to state the proper theological relationship between evangelization and Christian responsibility for society within the total context of God's kingdom, Lutherans face the same kind of dilemmas that challenge evangelicals as they attempt to define the relation between evangelism and social responsibility, and which Catholics also face in trying to relate "integral liberation" through Jesus Christ to secular movements for liberation. All seek to gain new light from the Scriptures as they reinterpret their historic convictions. The intense pressures felt by local churches, and the rigorous demands of mission practice in today's world, inevitably call for new theological answers to undergird the continuing mission mandate.

A LUTHERAN MISSIONARY UPDATING

It would be an exaggeration to speak of a "revolution" in Lutheran missionary thinking within the past generation. Yet it would not be wrong to speak of a modest *aggiornamento*—an "updating"—in Lutheran missionary awareness. This updating is most evident in the growing Lutheran *ecumenical* engagement, and in the commitment to *justice*. The far-reaching consequences for Lutheran missionary practice have already been suggested.

In the discussion of issues related to gospel and culture, Lutherans have not had a great deal to say, perhaps because the matter of inculturating the gospel and contextualizing faith in a local Christian community has not historically posed a major problem for them. In this area Lutherans need to do further theological work. With regard to the crucial area of relations with people of other faiths, an adequate Lutheran response still needs working out in detail. In view of the wide divergence of viewpoints held across the ecumenical spectrum, a Lutheran theological assessment of other faiths becomes urgently necessary—as succeeding chapters will demonstrate. It is also essential for a correct approach to interfaith dialog. As they go about the work of updating their own agenda, Lutherans will benefit greatly from considering the missionary reflections of other Christians.

3

ECUMENICAL MISSIONARY THINKING IN ITS RECENT DEVELOPMENT

Ecumenical thinking in the conciliar tradition contains a rich and indispensable legacy of missionary thinking, planning, and strategy. It represents the evolving vision of individuals and representatives of mission agencies and their creative efforts over the years to discern the outline and shape of God's larger intention for the missionary obedience of Christians. We have already traced the roots of the expanded missionary movement from the West in the massive outpouring of student missionary volunteers in the 1880s and 1890s, the holding of the first great world conference on missionary planning and strategy at Edinburgh (1910), and the subsequent formation of the International Missionary Council (IMC, 1921) as a permanent organ of missionary planning and consultation. IMC meetings held at Jerusalem (1928) and Tambaram-Madras (1938) were important occasions for mission leaders—at that time chiefly from Western churches and mission agencies—to consult together, share ideas, and occasionally to launch joint efforts. In the reports of these conferences we can see the emergence of an ecumenical tradition of missionary thinking.

In this chapter we shall examine the course of ecumenical thinking about mission theology and policy during the past 40 years, concentrating on the new missionary situation existing after World War II.

Ecumenical missionary thinking in this period becomes increasingly international in character, representing the interaction of church leaders from all six continents, above all, the two-thirds world. Radical changes in mission philosophy can be observed, along with conflicts and tensions between the principal agents, reflecting the turbulence of the new missionary situation. Three main stages can be identified in the ecumenical development of mission thinking since 1948. The first stage, roughly from 1948 to 1961, is characterized by an emphasis on *the church as the agent of God's mission*. The concept of *missio Dei* begins to gain acceptance in ecumenical circles. The second stage, from 1961 to 1975, is marked by a shift toward *the world as the locus for God's mission*, with a marked displacement of the church from its earlier place of centrality. The mission of God is now given a distinctly new and different connotation. These years represent a particularly troubled period for ecumenical missionary thinking, and one which produces a disquieting response from the side of Lutheranism. The final period, from 1975 to the present, is notable for its reaction against the one-sided worldly orientation of the previous period. The church is once again affirmed as a valid instrument in the mission of God, Christology is given a more central role, and ecumenical mission is seen as moving toward a synthesis between the previously opposed viewpoints.

"PARTNERSHIP IN OBEDIENCE": THE CALL AND VISION OF UNIVERSAL MISSION

At the Whitby, Canada, meeting of the IMC (1947) delegates from older and younger churches in North and South could rejoice that their fellowship in the gospel had been able to survive the "testing of war" and "the years of separation" and had emerged in an even deeper "vision of the reality and fullness of the universal church."[1] They marveled at the spiritual unity that bound together the body of Christ, as illustrated by united international Christian action to preserve orphaned churches and missions—twice within a single generation.[2] In spite of menacing obstacles, they felt obliged to renew the call and vision of a universal mission as the supranational task of all churches:

> But above all earthly circumstances stands unchanged the command of Christ to preach the Gospel to every creature. This command has not yet been fulfilled by the Church. It cannot be fulfilled unless all the

forces of all the churches, older and younger alike, are gathered in a common loyalty, inspired by a common task and mobilized in a common service. The situation is one of extreme urgency.[3]

All churches, whether "older" or "younger" (Whitby recognized that such terms were becoming obsolete) were under an obligation to prepare themselves for a global partnership in evangelism by deepening their spiritual life, fostering an ecumenical awareness, promoting the missionary spirit, mobilizing and training laity for service, and developing a sense of stewardship. Older and younger churches were urged to become partners in establishing "pioneer work in all those parts of the world in which the Gospel has not yet been preached and where the Church has not yet taken root."[4] Partnership in obedience was understood to embrace wide areas: training and use of personnel, finance, and policy formation. Self-support and progress toward self-reliance were urgent priorities in view of the unfinished evangelistic task. The grace of receiving and the grace of giving were alike necessary.

At Whitby, the Great Commission, reinterpreted for the times, was understood to mean:

> All churches alike are committed to the total evangelistic task, which in our day includes the proclamation of the Gospel to those who have never heard it, the conversion of nominal church members, the recovery of those vast areas in the lands of the older churches which have fallen away from the Church, and the Christianization of those parts of man's life which have not yet acknowledged the lordship of Christ. Though emphases differ, the task is essentially the same in every land. The older churches have still much to contribute to the life of the younger, but it is equally true that the older churches need for the fulfillment of their task the help of the rich spiritual resources which are being developed in the younger churches.[5]

In a remarkable way, Whitby anticipated almost every positive development in later ecumenical mission policy, including reevangelization and "six continent mission."

"THE MISSIONARY OBLIGATION OF THE CHURCH": A NEW THEOLOGICAL BASIS

At Willingen, Federal Republic of Germany (1952), the IMC once again took up the task of reformulating the missionary mandate and revising traditional missionary policies.[6] Prior to Willingen, mission study-groups in North America and elsewhere had worked intensively on draft statements dealing with the theological basis of world mission. Meeting at Willingen, mission leaders believed that they faced "a world in which other faiths or revolutionary power confront us in the full tide of victory"[7]— an obvious reference to the success of the Maoist liberation struggle in China. Yet the Christian response was being weakened by both lack of unity and a certain hesitancy and mobility. "In too many parts of the world the churches give the impression of being on the defensive, struggling to conserve their resources amidst the storm, instead of advancing into new areas of need in the name of the Saviour of the world."[8]

Speaking of the church's single calling to mission and unity, Willingen said that "the calling of the Church is to be one family in Him and to make known to the whole world, in word and deed, His Gospel of the Kingdom."[9] It reformulated the definition of local church autonomy and independence by substituting for the usual marks—self-government, self-support, and self-propagation—the deeper tests of being "a worshipping, witnessing, suffering and expectant community."[10] This represented a significant advance over the old "three-self" formula of church independence. The essential function of mission agencies in the West was "to keep before all Christians the obligation to preach the Gospel to every creature"; in relation to younger churches it was to cooperate "in pioneer undertakings and new advances."[11]

Missionary vocation was stated to be the task of the whole church, of every Christian, and of every baptized believer. Only in that context could it be considered the specific task of "foreign missionaries."[12] These statements all underlined the need for new missionary concepts and initiatives.

Major interest at Willingen centered in the conference's effort to reformulate the theological basis of mission, using the now common, but then new, term *missio Dei* (God's mission) as a key concept.[13] The conference proved unequal to the task. The Dutch missiologist, Johannes Hoekendijk, had issued a sharp challenge to all "church-centered" missionary thinking by arguing that it revolved around an illegitimate center. When the church is taken as the starting point and goal of mission, Hoekendijk said, evangelism degenerates into a process of planting institutional churches and making propaganda for a denomination. The true context for mission, he believed, was the *world,* not the *church.* The correct sequence was kingdom–gospel–apostolate–world. The church had no fixed place in this sequence but simply "happened" in the act of the apostolate. That is, it was not to be understood substantively but in terms of its apostolic function. Proclamation of the gospel and erecting signs of the kingdom were its sole justification.[14] The church, said Hoekendijk, must be understood as an instrument of God's redemptive action and a means of establishing *shalom* in this world through integrated acts of proclamation, demonstration, and community living *(kerygma, diakonia, koinonia).*[15] It must abandon all pretense of being a permanent institution.

Others at Willingen resisted Hoekendijk's reductionist emphasis, insisting that the church as a "foretaste of the kingdom" and as an instrument of God's purpose was more than an apostolic function. Still others argued for a stronger emphasis on the eschatological dimension of mission, and a clearer statement of how the kingdom of God has *already* come in Jesus Christ, but has *not yet* come in its fullness. This failure to resolve important theological differences led the conference to issue a compromise statement that was not acceptable to all.[16]

A Lutheran observer of trends in the theology of mission, Wilhelm Andersen, expressed his own dissatisfaction with the results of Willingen in these words:

> A theological redefinition of the basis of the Christian missionary enterprise cannot be worked out within the limits of the phrase "the missionary obligation of the church". . . . If it is our purpose to formulate a theology of missions, it is not the Church which should be the starting point of our investigation, and our thought must not remain confined within the boundaries and limits of the Church. Theologically, we must dig deeper; we must trace out the originating impulse in faith in the Triune God; from that standpoint alone can we see the missionary enterprise synoptically in its relationship to the Kingdom of God and in its relationship to the world.[17]

Andersen's comments showed the impact which the critique of church-centered thinking, linked especially with the work of Hoekendijk, had begun to make upon Lutheranism.

The final Willingen statement on missionary obligation, significantly entitled "The Missionary Calling of the Church," wavered uncertainly between Trinitarianism, Christocentrism, and church-centrism.[18] It appeared mostly to reject any criticism of church-centered missionary thinking. In parallel statements which harmonized unresolved differences the statement said:

> The missionary movement of which we are a part has its source in the Triune God Himself. Out of the depths of His love for us, the Father has sent forth his own beloved Son to reconcile all things to Himself, that we and all men might, through the Spirit, be made one in Him with the Father in that perfect love which is the very nature of God. . . .
>
> We who have been chosen in Christ, reconciled to God through Him, made members of His Body, sharers in His Spirit, and heirs through hope of His Kingdom, are by these very facts committed to full participation in His redeeming mission. There is no participation in Christ without participation in His mission to the world. That by which the Church receives its existence is that by which it is also given its world mission. "As the Father hath sent me, even so send I you."
>
> God sends forth the Church to carry out His work to the ends of the earth, to all nations, and to the end of time. The Church is sent to every inhabited area of the world. . . . The Church is sent to every social, political and religious community of mankind. . . . The Church is sent to proclaim Christ's reign in every moment and every situation. . . . The Church is thus compelled. . . not merely to build up its life where it is and as it is, but also to go forth to the ends of the earth, to all nations, and to the completion of time.[19]

The Willingen statement briefly referred to the church as being in the world and identifying itself with the world, as its Lord had done. The church's solidarity with the world was for the purpose of more effectively communicating the gospel. In an eschatological note, the statement bids Christians to "discern the signs of the times" and to proclaim "the hidden reign of our crucified and ascended Lord" by way of preparing the whole earth for the day of his coming.[20] Yet, overall, the statement appears to reinforce the then dominant view that the church is the agent of God's mission, and that closer integration between church and mission is the way to promote mission in unity. At Willingen the claims of the *world* to be the locus of God's mission were for the time being pushed aside. A decade later, these claims would return to claim their due.

"THE CHRISTIAN MISSION AT THIS HOUR": QUESTIONS ON THE WAY TO INTEGRATION

The Ghana Meeting of the IMC (1957-1958) is usually considered the transitional meeting in which issues were discussed and final recommendations were hammered out leading to the integration of the IMC into the WCC at New Delhi (1961). The fact is often overlooked that the Ghana assembly asked searching questions about the shape and direction of the ecumenical world-mission enterprise on the eve of integration. Many of these questions are still relevant today.

In relation to the underlying theme of the assembly, "What is the distinctive task of the Christian world mission at this hour?" Ghana was searching for honest practical answers to unanswered questions about the framework and scope of world mission. "Do we believe in the Christian world mission in the sense that it is a mission in which Christians throughout the world should participate?"[21] If so, the far-reaching implications that followed had to be taken seriously: "Are we in danger of making the conception and practice of mission so broad and diffuse that it loses its distinctive character and 'cutting edge'? Or are we, on the other hand, in danger of limiting it in such a way that our practice fails to express the fullness of the Gospel or to meet the real needs of men today?"[22]

To the first question, Ghana replied with a resounding yes. It called for proof of the assembly's acceptance of "one Church sent to the world in obedience to Christ" by renunciation of such categories as "sending and receiving countries," "older and younger churches."[23] Ghana sought to move beyond slogans of partnership to implementation of actual methods of reciprocal living and working together in obedience to Christ.

Underlying the second question appears to be the nagging fear that in broadening the base of mission and opting for church-mission integration, one might run the danger of blunting the categorical uniqueness of the mission imperative to cross frontiers and proclaim the gospel to all humankind. John Mackay warned of the danger of the church becoming "an absolute, an idol, an end in itself without regard to its true nature and honourable mission as the servant of Jesus Christ." Walter Freytag, under the catchword of "the lost directness," spoke of the multiplication of interchurch aid, including material and financial help, without any corresponding increase in missionary effectiveness.[24]

The editor of the Ghana report, citing the danger of introversion, put the matter this way:

> If the recognition that the base for the Christian world mission is now world-wide means that in practice what comes to be taken for mission becomes simply a going to and fro within the orbit of the Christian community, then the Christian minority will have ceased to penetrate the world's life and will be taking refuge in a Christian ghetto.[25]

The section reports suggested that some of the frontiers to be crossed in the act of "new pioneering" were those between the church and other living faiths, and between the church and its society or nation.

Although the integration of the IMC into the WCC was a foregone conclusion at Ghana, in view of the draft plan of integration presented to the assembly by the Joint Committee of the World Council of Churches and the International Missionary Council,[26] the prointegration arguments were nevertheless not totally convincing to all present. Those favoring integration argued that it was the appropriate outcome of inevitable trends; that theologically mission and unity belonged together; that integration would put mission at the heart of the ecumenical movement; and that there was no justification for the continued existence of two separate world bodies with overlapping membership and participation.[27]

Others argued with equal conviction on the opposite side that mission was a task best carried out by voluntary agencies, and that integration into church structures would have the effect of stifling initiative and quenching the spirit. Without disputing that mission and unity belonged together, they said that the real issue was an organizational one and that this fact was being obscured by theological slogans. Church history provided ample evidence that mission can be fulfilled *without* unity. It might even be argued that *only* in mission shall we be able to understand the nature of the unity which God wills for his church.[28]

In its resolutions approving integration the Ghana assembly took note of the concerns of those who feared that integration might mean "the loss of missionary vision and thrust," and recommended that member councils not eligible for membership in the WCC be given the privilege of affiliate membership in the new Commission on World Mission and Evangelism.[29]

In a post-Ghana reflection on the meaning of the statement that "mission belongs to the very *esse* of the church," Erik W. Nielsen attempted to synthesize the positive and negative elements in the integration debate:

> Perhaps one may say that what is involved is *both* a widening of the missionary perspective or dimension *and* a concentration; a realization of the fact that Mission is not just a special type of activity which can be identified and circumscribed within a mission board or a special Division of Mission, but is something which has to do with the very existence of the Church, with its very *raison d'etre*, with its not being for itself but for the world, to the ends of the world and the end of time, that every element of the Church's life and existence is part of this "sentness" to proclaim the Cross and Resurrection to and in the world, whether it has to do with the Christian witness in the sphere of politics, of social-economic questions, of health and education or anything else. . . .
>
>   In every aspect of this existence there must be the missionary dimension and call. And yet at the same time as the perspective is widened there is need for concentration. We have not said that everything that the Church does is Mission, but we have said that in the very existence of the Church, and therefore in everything that the Church says and is and does, there must be a "missionary perspective."[30]

Nielsen believed that the new Division for World Mission and Evangelism could become just such a "point of concentration" within the WCC where such activities as Faith and Order and Inter-Church Aid would all be brought into a sharper missionary focus. His notion of a "point of concentration" was intended to maintain the unique missionary thrust within the integrated ecumenical structure, and to answer the criticisms of those who said that "when everything is mission, nothing is mission."

Nielsen's words were inspired, in part, by the penetrating address given by Walter Freytag, the Hamburg missiologist, at Ghana. Freytag, who had spoken of the frustration and limitation Western missions felt due to the loss of directness and the "endangered image," recognized that "now. . . uniqueness is no more."[31]

Freytag went on to list the possible responses available to Western missions. The first, he said, is to do nothing. The second is to "try to escape to the beginning, looking for new unevangelized fields."[32] But if escapism is motivated by a desire to escape from the reality of cooperating with young churches, it could be a form of disobedience. The proper response, in his judgment, was to go forward in faithful obedience, accepting the new situation and learning to concentrate on the real priorities. Such concentration, in Freytag's opinion, had rather little to do with organizational mechanisms, but rested on theological insights and on the application of theological and missiological criteria to the task. Freytag went on:

> Does God not make us free for the more difficult but essential task, to concentrate on the message of Christ Himself, which means on the message of the Cross?. . . Mission means taking part in the action of God, in fulfilling His plan for the coming of His Kingdom by bringing about obedience of the faith in Jesus Christ our Lord among the nations. In that context missions as empirical organizations or institutions (there is no obedience possible without becoming concrete in such human form) are one indispensable member in the varieties of services of the churches. Their task consists in being sent to proclaim the Gospel outside the Church, to gather into one the children of God who are scattered abroad. . . . That means that this service has to remind every Church that it cannot be the Church in limiting itself within its own area, that it is called to take part in the responsibility of God's outgoing into the whole world, that it has the Gospel because it is meant for the nations of the earth, and that the Church has its life towards that end, the goal of God in the coming again of Christ.[33]

As Christians live in the obedience of faith, said Freytag, they become part of God's own missionary action. In Freytag's words one could hear an echo of Luther's own *missio Dei* concept.

"ONE BODY, ONE GOSPEL, ONE WORLD":
THE IMC LEGACY TO THE WCC

Following the Ghana meeting and just prior to the formal act of integration that made the IMC part of the WCC, the IMC issued a document summarizing Whitby's thoughts on partnership and the unfinished task, Willingen's theological reflections, and Ghana's probing questions about the future. Written by Lesslie Newbigin, then General Secretary of the IMC, but later to become the first Director of the WCC Division of World Mission and Evangelism, *One Body, One*

Gospel, One World[34] was an eloquent rationale for integration but also a forceful statement of the IMC's concern for a point of missionary concentration within the new structure. Newbigin recognized the hesitancy and loss of momentum in the missionary movement, and took note of the profound changes in the Christian world community brought about by the rise of independent churches in the two-thirds world. He decried ecumenism without mission, but equally rejected any retreat to 19th-century colonial missionary attitudes and practices. His vision of the future was that of "the whole Church, with one Gospel of reconciliation for the whole world."[35]

A new beginning, said the IMC position paper, called for a profound act of repentance on all sides. On the side of the mission agencies, penitence was needed for past triumphal images, paternalistic attitudes, and economic and political dominance. The dangerous dichotomy between "sending" and "receiving" churches, tending to equate *mission* with *power,* had to be renounced.[36] On the side of the churches, penitence was due for fostering the concept of the church as a "receptacle" for the mission activity of others, rather than a body in mission, and for treating lay people as mere recipients of the ministry of others. The churches must undergo a very deep repentance and learn again what it means that "the Church *is* a mission" and that "the Church's mission is none other than the carrying on of the mission of Christ Himself."[37]

Newbigin traced the following principles for action:[38] *(a) The church is the mission:* The entire membership of the church, not merely a few professionals, must know that commitment to Christ is commitment to his mission. *(b) The home base is everywhere:* "It is the duty and privilege of every part of the church everywhere to be involved not only in the missionary task at its own door, but also in some other part of the total worldwide task."[39] Christendom discovers a mission task on its own doorstep. *(c) Mission is in partnership:* Responsibility for evangelizing an area rests primarily with the church in that area, but not exclusively. No local church should say to an outside mission agency, "We do not need your help," yet "such help can only be rightly given if it is so given as to respect the integrity of the church in the area as truly the Body of Christ in that place."[40] A reversal of roles between former givers and former receivers is needed to break down past stereotypes. *(d) Mission and interchurch aid:* Despite the overlapping interests of world mission and interchurch aid and the inseparability of witness and service, the categorical uniqueness of such terms as "mission" and "missionary," Newbigin believed, should not be abandoned. This brings us to the heart of his argument: the point of missionary concentration.

The most passionate words in *One Body, One Gospel, One World* seek to locate, define, and validate the specifically missionary task within the total life of the worldwide fellowship of churches. Making this point was clearly vital for the success of integration. Mission is wider than evangelism, said Newbigin, and it can no longer be equated with simply crossing geographical frontiers. *"The differentium lies in the crossing of the frontier between faith in Christ as Lord and unbelief."* [41] Accordingly, the meaning of the term "missionary" must be redefined to suit the new global context: "He who is sent to make Christ known and obeyed as Lord among those who do not so know and obey Him is a missionary, whether his journey is long or short. The missionary frontier runs through every land where there are communities living without the knowledge of Christ as Lord." [42]

The geographical dimension of frontier crossing is not thereby eliminated—it still remains—but the missionary task at every person's doorstep is now accentuated. The church is involved in the missionary task at its own door, but also shares in the total worldwide task. Newbigin emphasized Erik Nielsen's earlier point at Ghana about a necessary "point of concentration": "Because the Church *is* the mission there is a missionary dimension of everything that the Church does. But not everything that the Church does has a missionary intention. And unless there is in the life of the Church a point of concentration for the missionary intention, the missionary dimension which is proper to the whole life of the Church will be lost." [43]

In that sense, deeds of service and interchurch aid activities can be regarded as mission in the narrower sense when they are part of an action of the church in going out beyond the frontiers of its own life to bear witness to Christ as Lord among those who do not know him, and when the overall intention is that people are brought from unbelief to faith. By means of such arguments, the IMC, in its final days before integration, sought to safeguard the uniqueness of the missionary vocation within the total life of the churches and the ecumenical movement.

NEW DELHI: AN ENDING AND A NEW BEGINNING

On November 19, 1961, in a solemn act of integration at New Delhi, the World Council of Churches was declared the legal successor of the International Missionary Council.[44] The WCC General Secretary, Dr. Visser 't Hooft, gave it as his opinion that because of integration "we are. . . forced to rethink the meaning of the missionary and apostolic calling of the Church in every land."[45] Shortly after his election as first Director of the new WCC Division of World Mission and Evangelism, Lesslie Newbigin spoke of the changes integration would bring. Past forms of missionary activity "must be held constantly open to the new insights that God may have to give us in the wider fellowship," he said, while at the same time churches will be forced to acknowledge "that the missionary task is no less central to the life of the Church than the pursuit of renewal and unity."[46] The WCC Constitution authorized the creation of a Commission on World Mission and Evangelism (CWME) with the following aim: "to further the proclamation to the whole world of the Gospel of Jesus Christ to the end that men may believe in him and be saved."[47] Some of the key functions of the CWME were seen to be:

- to keep before the churches their calling and privilege to engage in constant prayer for the missionary and evangelistic work of the church;
- to remind the churches of the range and character of the unfinished evangelistic task and to deepen their sense of missionary obligation; and
- to deepen evangelistic and missionary concern in the whole life and work of the World Council of Churches.[48]

Other mentioned functions were to stimulate biblical and theological study on the missionary task, and to foster cooperation and united action in evangelization. This "aim" of the CWME remained unchanged until the Fifth Assembly of the WCC at Nairobi (1975), when it was revised as follows: "to assist the Christian community in the proclamation of the gospel of Jesus Christ, by word and deed, to the whole world and to the end that all may believe in him and be saved."[49]

The Bangkok Assembly of the CWME (1973) agreed to make the CWME a subunit of the new WCC Program Unit on Faith and Witness.

References to "the unfinished evangelistic" task were deleted, and the functions and activities of the CWME were now expressed as follows:

> *(a)* to assist the churches and councils and groups in common reflection on the content and meaning of the Gospel and the manner of its proclamation and witness;
>
> *(b)* to promote and carry out biblical and theological studies on the nature of the Christian life and witness, as demand arises from the life of the member churches in their encounter with the contemporary world, and from the concerns of the various branches of the ecumenical movement; and
>
> *(c)* to help churches, mission agencies and groups to discern the range and character of the ongoing evangelistic task and the opportunities and priorities for mission in different cultural and social circumstances; to encourage them to attempt new forms of mission and to plan and share their resources for joint action in each place, and on a wider scale, in such ways as will manifest more fully the unity of the church.[50]

A number of other functions and activities were also specified.

INTEGRATION IN RETROSPECT

Integration was the overriding concern of ecumenical missions in the period from Willingen to New Delhi. Inevitably, this compelled the mission enterprise to focus on its wider church relationships. Great hopes and expectations were held out, and warnings were overruled. The missionary movement was expected to benefit from the greater support it would receive from the churches; the churches for their part would be enriched by the blessings that would come from having the missionary concern at the heart of their life. This meant, on one side, a broadening, and on the other, a deepening. Theologically, the decision seemed right and necessary, despite some apprehensions about the practical outworking of the change. The future could not be foreseen.

The decision to integrate was by no means trivial or inconsequential. It went far beyond structure. Missionary activity was now drawn into the orbit of ecumenical policy formation, priority setting, and allocation of resources. Meanwhile, the entire agenda of the world church in all six continents suddenly seemed to invade the serene world of mission with its former priority of completing the unfinished task. The 1973 Bangkok meeting of the CWME moved to eliminate any reference to the "unfinished evangelistic task," possibly on the assumption that the task itself was a never-ending one. Certainly the task was now enormously broadened, and constantly changing. The difficulty of maintaining a missionary "point of concentration" within the total life of the church became transparent, despite continuing efforts to promote education for mission in the local parish.

The distinction between a specific missionary *intention* and a broader missionary *dimension,* and the claim that crossing the frontier between faith and unbelief constituted the unique *differentium* of mission activity, proved incapable of being maintained in practice. The older and narrower definition of mission was imperiled by a growing tendency to label virtually everything the church does—above all, its urgent priority tasks—its "mission." The more specific missionary understanding of the old IMC with its well-defined functional parameters was absorbed into the WCC's increasingly holistic definition of mission. Without question, a broadening of the missionary concept took place, but no corresponding embrace of the missionary "point of concentration" on the part of the churches was discernible in the short term. From the viewpoint of this observer, the actual benefits flowing from the act of integration did not appear to match the promises. Some of the consequences, moreover, were potentially disastrous for mission work in the ensuing period.

ECUMENICAL MISSION AT STAGE TWO: THE WORLD AS THE LOCUS FOR GOD'S MISSION

No sooner had the act of integration been completed than the WCC began to reflect an ironic shift away from the post-Willingen view of the church as the agent of God's mission toward a more secular paradigm. The church-centered missionary framework, sharply criticized at Willingen by Hoekendijk but not overthrown, now came to be steadily displaced in the years after New Delhi by the concept of the *world* as the locus of God's mission. The new direction was concisely summarized in the phrase, "The world sets the [church's] agenda." The church as the base for mission did not of course disappear—the WCC was, after all, a movement of churches—but it did come under attack. The radical criticism of church-centered missionary activity—focused on negative or obsolete aspects of congregations, institutions, and church structures—stood in ironic contrast to the support the WCC received from its community of churches, and this incongruity in the years between 1968 and 1975 led to a crisis of identity. It also led to considerable alienation of support in missionary circles formerly related to the IMC.

This development had not been anticipated in the debate over integration, but the deeper causes were already present in the pre–New Delhi discussions. Willingen had failed to resolve certain deeper theological issues, such as Christology, eschatology, and the nature of the kingdom, and these returned to claim their due. *Missio Dei* continued to be the dominant motif in this later period, but it was now reinterpreted more in the sense of God's presence in secular history rather than in the traditional sense of "salvation history." Whereas at Willingen the theological mandate had been so understood as to make the church the principal vehicle of God's mission, after New Delhi the church was increasingly relegated to a marginal or "ex-centric" position. Integration itself contributed to this trend by opening the door to a broader worldly agenda.

In view of the multiplication of issues and programs, the hope expressed at Ghana that an effective point of concentration for the activity of frontier crossing could be maintained proved difficult. An example of this was the section on "Witness" at New Delhi, which surveyed the evangelistic situation around the world.[51] It gave special attention to the roles of laity and clergy in witnessing and called for the "reshaping of the witnessing community." From this came the impetus that led the WCC to authorize a study on "The Missionary Structure of the Congregation"[52] between New Delhi and Uppsala. This study was to have an unexpectedly heavy influence on the development of ecumenical mission theology in the post–New Delhi period. Based mainly on Western theological trends and sociological analysis, and reflecting the troubled cultural milieu of this period, this study would decisively divert the attention of the churches from the practice of church-mission integration toward a world-oriented understanding of mission.

"WITNESS IN SIX CONTINENTS": MISSION IN THE SECULAR WORLD

The meeting of the integrated Commission on World Mission and Evangelism at Mexico City (1963) illustrated the interaction between mission and evangelism concerns and the convergence of programs relating to overseas mission and home mission.[53] Special sections were devoted to witnessing to persons of other faiths, witnessing to people in the secular world, the witness of the congregation in its neighborhood, and the witness of the church across national and confessional boundaries. Committee sessions heard reports on education for mission and evangelism, on lay people abroad in mission, and on the training of missionaries, as well as Joint Action for Mission, theological education, Christian literature, and urban and industrial evangelism. The meeting is remembered for its ringing affirmation that "this missionary movement now involves Christians in all six continents" and must express "the common witness of the whole Church, bringing the whole Gospel to the whole world."[54]

From a missiological standpoint, the deeper significance of the Mexico City meeting stemmed from the fact that it initiated a sustained inquiry into Christian witness to people of other faiths, and Christian witness in the secular world. The conference recognized the ambiguity of the secularization process, opening up as it did possibilities for both human freedom and human enslavement. Although unable itself to discern a clear vision of the task, the conference went on record with a statement setting the direction for mission in a secular world:

> Christian witness participates in the common agony and hope which men experience in the process of secularization. It should articulate questions and answers from within the modern world and take up the points of decision which God himself has provided through secularization. Thus we can come to deeper understanding of the presence of Jesus Christ in the world and communicate the Gospel. . . . The Christian message to man in the secular world is not only the proclamation of a transcendent God who reigns as the Lord of nature, but also the proclamation of God as the Lord of world history who became a man in Christ. His divinity has become visible in his true humanity, as he emptied himself to be one of us so that men might fulfill the tasks to which they were ordained in creation.[55]

Further references to the humanness of Jesus Christ, the kingdom of God as the destiny of humankind as a whole, and the principle that "mission has to take place *from within this world*"[56] foreshadow the theological interpretation underlying the study of the Missionary Structure of the Congregation.

THE MISSIONARY STRUCTURE OF THE CONGREGATION

The period between Mexico City (1963) and the Fourth Assembly of the WCC at Uppsala (1968) was one of intense reflection on the meaning of mission. In general it carried forward Mexico City's concern that mission should be seen as the common witness of Christians in all six continents, and that the implications of mission in a secular world be explored more fully. During this period the WCC Program Unit on Faith and Witness added a subunit on "Dialog with Men of Living Faiths and Ideologies." In 1966 a major WCC-sponsored World Conference on Church and Society was held in Geneva. In 1967 Philip Potter led the Central Committee in a major review of the WCC's contribution to the churches in the area of evangelism.

But clearly the dominant missiological event of this period was the publication of two reports on the "Missionary Structure of the Congregation" and some related working papers.[57] *The Church for Others* and *The Church for the World*, the reports of the European and North American working groups on the quest for new missionary structures, decisively influenced the shape of the Section II Report of the Uppsala Assembly ("Renewal in Mission").[58] They helped to sharpen the controversy over the meaning of mission, and provoked reaction to WCC statements and programs, both within the WCC and on the part of evangelicals outside the WCC.

The starting point for the missionary structure study was the conviction expressed at New Delhi that "one of the main hindrances in the pursuit of the evangelistic calling of the Church lies in the traditional structure of the local congregation."[59] The Department on Studies in Evangelism was authorized to make a comprehensive study of the following questions:

> To what degree does the existing structure of our local congregation affect its witness? Does it enable and encourage members of the congregation to go out into the world and live out the Gospel? If not, what changes in structure are needed?[60]

The questions posed for study and the initial guidelines showed that the original intent of the inquiry had been to seek ways of renewing and reforming church structures so as to make them more missionary minded. It was foreseen that relationships between church, gospel and kingdom of God would need to be clarified. Before the ecclesiological self-study was finished, however, it would touch on the very center of the gospel and the foundation of the church's missionary proclamation.

The Western European Working Group met five times between 1962 and 1965 before submitting its final report in 1966.[61] Its main concern was to develop a "new theological understanding of mission and its relation to the world and to the Church."[62] The North American Working Group, employing an "action-reflection" model, collected "parables of missionary action" that offered clues for mission strategy, especially in metropolitan areas.[63] The reports and essays are for the most part exploratory, experimental, and deliberately provocative— designed to open up new possibilities. It must be added that they do not now, and did not then, represent official positions of the World Council of Churches. Intended mainly for study and reflection by the member churches, they were nevertheless symbolic of missiological trends of the period.

The interim report on the "Missionary Structure of the Congregation," as presented in 1965 to the WCC Central Committee, was non-controversial in its findings and warmly received.[64] It spoke of a "truly missionary congregation" as a "community for others," fulfilling its calling by being present as a servant people in a world for whose sake Christ gave himself in full obedience. The quest for authentic missionary structures, which conform to a life of genuine Christian obedience and are suitable for discipleship in modern society, is the fruit of renewal through obedience to God's Word. For the most part, traditional congregational structures were viewed as no longer appropriate for the complex forms of human life in the modern world, and hence they should be either reformed or abandoned.

The report presented the following findings as points of consensus:

1. Every structure must serve God's own missionary purpose and action, as revealed in Jesus Christ. This applies to its worship, its service, its message, and its polity.
2. Church structures must be as flexible as is demanded by the character of God's own action in the world.

3. All church structures are temporary, and none are strictly normative, including the local congregation and parish.

4. New forms of missionary presence are emerging in recognition of special "charismata" the church has been given, e.g., in industrial communities and house-churches.

5. New congregational structures need official recognition as legitimate forms of missionary presence, entitled to offer and receive the Word and sacrament.

6. Churches in new localities must be adapted to the actual life in the area.

7. The local parish is a "gathering of ministries rather than a collectivity of individuals and families. . .; ministry is a corporate, not merely an individual task."[65]

The task of the future, the report continued, was to move out into changing forms of life without losing continuity of faith, and to maintain the true marks of the church without falling into static conservatism. These references to "continuity of faith" and maintaining the "true marks of the church" suggest that the central committee's interest in the study lay in the area of church renewal for mission in the modern world.

The really controversial part of the missionary structure report was that dealing with its underlying theological presuppositions, which went considerably beyond ecclesiological renewal. The theological interpretation of mission in the Western European Working Group's report overthrew the church-centered view of mission—and with it the basis of church-mission integration. It substituted for it a new definition of mission and a new understanding of the relationship between God, church and world. Hoekendijk and others now proposed a model of mission that was widely accepted by the two working groups on either side of the Atlantic, and which was incorporated into both reports.[66] The mission of God, said *The Church for Others,* must be distinguished from present mission activities which are "historically determined answers of the churches to challenges in the past." These could be understood as "transitory forms of obedience to the *missio Dei*" that are relative and dispensable today.[67] Missions aimed at conversion of individuals and the planting of churches must be examined in relation to the mission of God, one of the working papers said. It must be seriously questioned whether "God's ultimate plan is to incorporate all people into the church."[68] Remarks such as these, even though expressing only views of individual scholars rather than official viewpoints of the WCC, nevertheless tended to identify the WCC in public thinking with a radically new and unhistorical understanding of mission.

Hoekendijk's own view was that the original meaning of the term "apostle" had been wrongly applied to the geographical expansion of the church and to a hierarchical understanding of church authority. Mission, he believed, had been perverted into a spatial concept, and more recently equated with a movement across frontiers.[69] The true sense of "mission" and "apostolate," however, could only be understood in the functional sense of serving as the agent of the messianic kingdom, and helping to inaugurate the messianic pattern of *shalom*. Missionary service was acceptance of the form of messianic life and participation in the mission of the Messiah, i.e., "to announce. . . and perform the decisive redeeming act of God in the last days and in a universal context. . ., thus inaugurating the new order of the Spirit by establishing the Kingdom, offering 'peace and salvation.' "[70] *Shalom* summarized the gifts of the messianic era and included "all aspects of the restored and cured human condition: righteousness, truth, fellowship, communication, peace, etc."[71]

A necessary consequence of this view, said Hoekendijk, was that the church was displaced from its central position in the divine economy of salvation. The church is a function of the apostolate, the servant of *missio Dei*, which is at work beyond the church but embraces both church and world. The church serves the *missio Dei* in the world by pointing to God at work in world history and naming him there.[72]

For Hoekendijk, it appeared, *missio Dei* had become identified with a process of historical transformation whereby humankind would gradually achieve the goals of the messianic kingdom through the processes of secular history. Secularization was rendering religious categories and institutions obsolete. "Our knowledge of God in Jesus Christ leads us to affirm that God is working his purpose out in the midst of the world and its historical processes."[73] The older view that God reveals himself primarily to the church, and only to the world through the church, must now be questioned. The new sequence should read: God–world–church. "God's primary relationship is to the world, and it is the world and not the Church that is the focus of God's plan. . . . The

Church lives through God's dealings with the world."[74] Accordingly, "the Church exists for the world. . . . The Church lives in order that the world may know its true being. . . . Its centre lies outside itself; it must live 'excentredly.' "[75] The message and structure of the churches must be reformulated in relation to the variety of actual realities amid which the churches live. "Hence it is the world that must be allowed to provide the agenda for the churches."[76] Hoekendijk's reflections went far beyond the challenge to church parochialism and self-sufficiency; they implied a quite new, unhistorical, and methodologically unclear model for Christian mission.

The North American report affirmed that the church has no mission of its own, but is called to participate in God's mission. It saw God's redemptive mission as culminating "in the coming of Christ, the true man, the head of the new humanity," and lifted up "humanization" as the goal of mission. *Humanization,* it stated, best communicates the meaning of the messianic goal in our period of history.[77] The concern of the missionary congregation must be to point to the humanity in Christ as the goal of mission. "Missionary structures are those which demonstrate that they are expendable in the interest of humanizing society."[78] The theme of "humanization" would again be taken up at the Uppsala assembly in its section on mission.

"SOURCES FOR CHANGE": THE LUTHERAN RESPONSE TO THE MISSIONARY STRUCTURE STUDY

The new missionary paradigm of the mission structure study—with its leading motif of "messianic shalom" in the Western European report and of "humanization" in the North American version—did not go unchallenged. Not only the radical devaluation of church and mission structures, but even more the underlying theological assumptions came under attack. The most thorough and documented response came from the Lutheran World Federation's Commission on Stewardship and Evangelism, and was published as *Sources for Change.*[79] The LWF Commission recognized the searching criticisms and provocative structural proposals of the ecumenical study. Yet it found them one-sided in both method and result.[80] Three broad areas for criticism were identified by the LWF in the WCC missionary structure reports: (1) the lack of emphasis on the inner renewal of human beings, based on the new birth in Jesus Christ as an event in the life of individuals; (2) the question of whether traditional congregational and parish structures might not be renewed through spiritual nurture and education for mission, rather than being simply discarded on account of obsoleteness or ineffectiveness; and (3) the study's "new vision" of the mission of God in the world, now viewed as a single historical process "in which the world is inevitably moving towards the one purpose of perfect reconciliation and harmony under the will of God."[81]

The Lutheran commission was greatly aided in its response by an incisive survey and evaluation of the missionary structure reports by Dr. Werner Krusche (German Democratic Republic).[82] Krusche agreed with the premise of the ecumenical study that "the world is rightly taken as the point of departure."[83] The church's understanding of church and gospel grows, said Krusche, as it goes into the world with the gospel. This is in keeping with the Reformation understanding of the world as God's creation and the locus of the Christian's vocation and sanctification. But the biblical understanding of "world" was not sufficiently accounted for, said Krusche, by the theological premise that "through the death and resurrection of Jesus Christ all men already belong to the new mankind, even if they are not yet aware of it."[84]

This thesis, said Krusche, is contrary to the New Testament and shortcuts the reality of divine judgment and the necessity of faith, Baptism, and conversion:

> For nowhere in the New Testament does it say that everyone, as a result of the salvatory death of Jesus Christ which took place for all, already belongs to the new mankind, i.e., is without judgment, and that this must merely be confirmed by baptism. It is rather the uniform witness of the New Testament that one is a new creature, i.e., that one is a part of the new mankind, when one is "in Christ." This being in Christ, as a fellowship of existence with Him, the risen crucified one, and as integration into His body always (and only then) becomes a reality in baptism grasped through faith.[85]

The world to which the church owes its service is a lost and fallen world

> in which God initiated the redeeming counteraction by sending His Son, who with His death and resurrection broke through the law of death

which was ruling and ruining this world and who gives life in the form of freedom from the compulsion to self-assertion and self-justification.[86]

Krusche disputed not simply the new view of mission, but also the new sequence of God–world–church in the ecumenical study:

> Only God's saving acts in the world should be described as missionary. The *missio Dei* must be comprehended in a precise way as the sending of the Son into the world for its *salvation* and as the sending of the Church into the world with the saving Gospel.[87]

Hence the use of the concept *missio Dei* to designate God's total action with the world in history could not be justified; it applied only to God's redeeming activity through the gospel:

> If the concept of *missio Dei* is strictly conceived as the sending of the Son (and of the Spirit) into the world, then the order God–church–world is justified, as long as it is kept in mind that God acts in the world in a *saving* way exclusively through the Gospel proclaimed by the Church.[88]

The exclusive content of *missio Dei* will then be the gospel of God's justification of sinners, the gift of reconciliation with God, and the new life in fellowship with him under his Lordship. Krusche went on:

> The Church can fail to give the world many things, but it cannot fail to give the world the Gospel, for passing it on is the only purpose for the Church's existence.[89]

Thus the Lutheran response reaffirmed the historic mission of the church, which takes place in the form of the proclamation of God's great deeds, leads to Baptism and service in this world (attacking the misery of the world in all its forms), and signals the salvation of the kingdom.

Personal salvation cannot, Krusche believed, be pushed into a secondary place in favor of the theme of "world formation." For gospel mission takes place through the cooperation of proclamation and service. Churches were reminded of the dialectic of justification and new obedience in Christ, of both proclaiming and doing the will of God.[90] *Shalom,* if used as a concept, should properly include not merely *temporal* well-being, but also *eternal* salvation. It could not be realized apart from the restoration of the broken fellowship between human beings and God, and it was finally and completely expressed only in the resurrection of the dead.[91] Mission was therefore a critical event confronting humankind with a decision to accept or reject the offer of the gospel. A church that did not seek to "win" human beings for Christ and "integrate" them into his congregation would be disobedient to the *missio Dei*.[92]

Moreover, the Lutheran response went on, while the church lives in solidarity with the whole of humankind, this should not lead to a minimization of the reality of evil. The gospel itself draws the borderlines between church and world.[93] The church knows that its witness and service have ultimate meaning and achieve their goal only in the light of the resurrection of the dead and the second coming of Christ. Christians are liberated to self-sacrificing service for others and joint action with non-Christians, but they know from the gospel that the new world will not be brought about by their deeds, but rather by the deed of him who raises the dead.[94]

Therefore Christians are warned not to be deceived by utopian enthusiasm or by pseudomessianic movements. Living in repentance, the church must undergo radical self-examination and be open to correction and experimentation in the light of the gospel.[95]

The Lutheran response to the WCC missionary structure studies was, in effect, to reaffirm the continuing validity of gospel proclamation, with justification by faith as its heart, along with the task of making disciples and gathering them into churches. The intense debate triggered by the WCC's studies on the Missionary Structure of the Congregation sharply reveals the conflicting trends in mission theology during the 1960s.

THE WORLD COUNCIL OF CHURCHES AND EVANGELISM: "THE ECUMENICAL THEME PAR EXCELLENCE"

During this period the WCC Division of World Mission and Evangelism undertook a far-reaching review of the WCC's role in evangelism, which was presented to the Central Committee in 1967. DWME Director Philip Potter, showing sensitivity to the charge that evangelism was a "neglected vocation" in the life of the World Council, examined three questions: "Is evangelism at the heart of the life and work of the

WCC? What does the WCC mean when it speaks of evangelism? What is to be done to manifest more evidently the central concern of the WCC and its member churches for evangelism?"[96]

Potter noted the intense interest that groups in Europe and North America had shown in the study of the missionary structure of the congregation, but then added that for some curious reason the study had not been taken seriously in Asia, Africa, and Latin America.[97] Very likely this was because churches in the two-thirds world saw the debate over missionary structures as a Western argument which did not fit into their own frame of reference. Much of what Potter reported, and the statements he quoted, reflected the discussion on evangelism from Amsterdam to New Delhi, and bore little trace of the new model of mission set forth in the missionary structure reports. From the 1959 WCC study document entitled "A Theological Reflection on the Work of Evangelism" Potter cited the following statement on evangelism:

> The commission given to the whole Church to be obeyed at all times is: "You shall be my witnesses." It is a false differentiation to speak of the Church in its congregational expression on the one hand and its evangelistic mission on the other. The truth is not that the Church has a mission to the world but that it is God's mission to the world. It bears the Gospel of Jesus Christ and lives by its calling to belong to his continuing ministry.[98]

On the goal of evangelism, Potter quoted with approval a statement from the 1954 Advisory Commission on "Christ—The Hope of the World," which described the church's mission as:

> participation in the work of God which takes place between the coming of Jesus Christ to inaugurate God's Kingdom on earth, and His coming again in glory to bring that Kingdom to its consummation. . . . Our work until His coming again is but the result of our share in the work which he is doing all the time and everywhere. The Church's mission is thus the most important thing that is happening in history. And yet because the mission of the Church points beyond history to the close of the age, it has this significance too, that it is itself among the signs that the end of history has begun. The hope of our calling is set towards the hope of His coming.[99]

Potter referred to such statements as those above as pointing to emphases in the ecumenical discussion on which there is consensus. Yet it is clear that his quotations, based largely on earlier WCC statements, did not take into account the harsh critique of church-centrism and the dubious theological impulses from the missionary structure study.

"ALL THINGS NEW: RENEWAL IN MISSION"

The WCC Fourth Assembly in Uppsala (1968) climaxed a tumultuous period in the life of the organization. No assembly before or after had been so preoccupied with "the revolutionary ferment of our time" and with "the most radical contemporary rebellions against all 'establishments,' civil and religious." [100] The winds of change, which had reached hurricane force by 1968, provided a special context for the assembly theme, "Behold, I make all things new." Uppsala marked a milestone in ecumenical missionary thinking, and climaxed the development of *missio Dei* based on the *world* as the locus of God's mission.

In the report of Section II, "Renewal in Mission," traditional references to mission and to the IMC's theology of integration were quietly deleted in favor of a Christological statement of the mission mandate which took "humanization" in Jesus Christ as its theological keyword. The humanization theme, adapted from the North American report on "The Church for the World," [101] now appears in the concrete sense of "the invitation to men to grow up into their full humanity in the new man, Jesus Christ." [102] The term "humanization" is stripped of philosophical connotations and detached from the notion of humanization as part of a historical world process. Significantly, the final section draft contains scarcely a trace of any reference to the theological work of the Western European Working Group for the missionary structure study, no mention of *shalom* as the goal of mission, and no reference to the sequence "God–world–church" as defining the proper relationship between church and world. [103] Thus "Renewal in Mission," though influenced by the studies of missionary structure, is theologically much less radical than the work which preceded it, and appears to embody a number of compromises. The radical worldliness of the Uppsala report on mission is found instead in its strategic proposals.

Section II describes the mission of God "as the gift of a new creation which is a radical renewal of the old." [104] There follows a catechetical statement about Jesus Christ—incarnate, crucified, and risen—as the "new man" totally available for others, who by his death restores all people to sonship and by his resurrection inaugurates the new creation. The new birth in Christ by faith through the Spirit results in a change in attitudes and relationships: "For there is no turning to God which does not at the same time bring a man face to face with his fellow men in a new way."[105]

In a plenary address at Uppsala the veteran ecumenist, Visser 't Hooft, pleaded for an understanding of the gospel in its fullness, one which he hoped would reconcile the *vertical* concern about God's saving action in the life of individuals with the *horizontal* emphasis on human relationships in the world:

> A Christianity which has lost its vertical dimension has lost its salt and is not only insipid in itself, but useless for the world. But a Christianity which would use the vertical preoccupation as a means to escape from its responsibility for and in the common life of man is a denial of the incarnation, of God's love manifested in Christ. The whole secret of the Christian faith is that it is man-centered because it is God-centered. We cannot speak of Christ as the man for others without speaking of him as the man who came from God and who lived for God.[106]

The former WCC general secretary charged that neglect of responsibility for the needy anywhere was a form of *heresy* as great as denying a key article of faith![107] In this holistic sense of concern for the whole human being, Uppsala could speak of evangelism as bringing about occasions for people to respond to Jesus Christ.

Other parts of the section report dealt with the renewal of structures for mission.[108] It is here that the secular focus of the Uppsala mission statement becomes evident. The church in mission is the church for others, the report said. However, the fields for mission are no longer exotic places in foreign lands, but rather localities in the *secular* world where there is human need, growth, tension, decision-making responsibility, and conflict. By way of illustration Uppsala referred to power centers, revolutionary movements, the university in change, urbanization and industrialization, suburbia and rural life, relations between developed and developing countries, and even the *churches* themselves.[109]

The new criteria for determining mission priorities would expose the church to loss of prestige and financial support. One of them pointed forward to Melbourne: "Do they place the church alongside the poor, the defenseless, the abused, the forgotten, the bored?"[110] Restructuring the church at all levels and mobilizing the people of God for mission were encouraged. The Mexico City vision of mission in six continents was again evoked. In the end, the Uppsala statement on mission received approval "not because anyone is completely happy with it but because everyone can find something, sometimes a great deal, that is very good."[111]

Uppsala foreshadowed the growing rift with evangelicals, epitomized in Donald MacGavran's question, "Will Uppsala betray the two billion?"[112] It also anticipated the debate on mission priorities in the 1970s. For ecumenical missionary thinking, Uppsala's significance lay in the fact that it consolidated the emphasis on mission in the *secular* world and the focus on the *world* as the arena for mission, a focus that began shortly after New Delhi.

"SALVATION TODAY": THE TWO-THIRDS WORLD SPEAKS OUT

In the mind of its planners, the purpose of the Bangkok Assembly of the CWME (1973) was to explore the theological keyword in the CWME aim—*salvation*—and to do this in dialog with the hopes and struggles of people in the contemporary world.[113] A three-year preparatory process included regional study groups on "Salvation Today" and the collection of modern "salvation testimonies" drawn from various cultures, religions, and social systems.[114]

In actual fact, however, both the timing and location of the meeting changed its character into one whose real dynamics lay in the struggle between delegates from North and South over issues of power sharing in the ecumenical movement, and in the debate over church identity. The moratorium proposal was then emerging as a burning issue. Whereas Uppsala had been marked by a climate of "old world" unrest, Bangkok was a two-thirds world meeting at which church leaders from Asia and Africa freely spoke their minds. The theological effort made at Bangkok to give contemporary expression to "salvation" proved inconclusive, and gave rise to widespread criticism. This was partly due to the fact that the conference had no clear biblical exposition of salvation as a working basis, and partly to the conference committee's practice of associating biblical salvation more or less indiscriminately with salvific themes and personalities in contemporary social and political movements and in other religions.[115] Moreover, as it turned out, the real underlying theme to emerge from the conference was not so much "Salvation Today" as it was "Liberation in Christ"—liberation from various forms of captivity.

Still, Bangkok did succeed in producing a useful statement on "Salvation Today." Its "Letter to the Churches" spoke of salvation in Christ which is "simple and comprehensive" and frees "the whole of human reality. . . from all that keeps it in slavery."[116] The Uppsala emphasis on integrating the vertical and horizontal dimensions and reconciling the tension between personal salvation and social responsibility was fully incorporated into the key statement of Section II at Bangkok, "Salvation and Social Justice." Citing the messianic manifesto of Jesus at Nazareth (Luke 4:18), the report declared:

Through Christ men and women are liberated and empowered with all their energies and possibilities to participate in his Messianic work. . . . The salvation which Christ brought, and in which we participate, offers a comprehensive wholeness in this divided life. . . . It is a salvation of the soul and the body, of the individual and society, mankind and the "groaning creation". . . . As evil works both in personal life and in exploitative social structures which humiliate mankind, so God's justice manifests itself both in the justification of the sinner and in social and political justice. We have to overcome the dichotomies in our thinking between soul and body, personal and society, humankind and creation. Therefore we see the struggles for economic justice, political freedom and cultural renewal as elements in the total liberation of the world through the mission of God. This liberation is finally fulfilled when "death is swallowed up in victory". . . . This comprehensive notion of salvation demands of the whole people of God a matching comprehensive approach to their participation in salvation.[117]

The churches must be liberated from their captivity to interests of class, race, and nation in order to initiate action for liberation in the world. "Mission under these conditions should be conceived of particularly in terms of what is required in obedience to Christ the Liberator."[118] Commitment to justice should be seen as a top priority for mission agencies, which must be especially careful not to give support to oppressive structures. In discussions on the work of specialized programs (urban industrial mission, rural mission) and international agencies (theological education, Christian literature, Christian Medical Commission), the basic concern was that "the message—or Good News—of liberation is to be heard among the disadvantaged, the oppressed, the exploited, the weak, the poor and the disabled." This meant *identification* with such persons and *participation* in the struggle against powers and structures that enslave them.[119]

The anger and resentment of churches from the two-thirds world against Western dominance exploded in the discussions on Sections I ("Culture and Identity") and III ("Churches Renewed in Mission"). "Can I be black and Christian? Can I become a Christian and keep my identity?" Citing the problem of cultural alienation experienced by Christians in Africa and Asia, the report on cultural identity continued:

> Culture shapes the human voice that answers the voice of Christ. Many Christians who have received the Gospel through Western agencies ask the question "Is it really I who answers Christ? Is it not another person instead of me?". . . How can we responsibly answer the voice of Christ instead of copying foreign models of conversion—imposed, not truly accepted? We refuse merely to be raw materials used by other people to achieve their own salvation. The one faith must be made at home in every context, yet it cannot be completely identical with it. Therefore there will be a rich diversity. . . . Racial and cultural identity are divine gifts and human achievements to be taken up into Christian identity.[120]

Bangkok was not simply pleading for a fuller recognition of cultural pluralism within the ecumenical movement. It was saying in no uncertain terms that the European model of Christianity was dead, and with it all Western claims to cultural dominance in the two-thirds world. Asian and African Christians were no longer willing to be regarded as second-class Christians or as wards of a missionary Christianity.

The North-South debate also erupted as an ecclesiological issue in the discussions on patterns of partnership relations in Section III. "Partnership in Mission" had been on the agenda of every ecumenical conference since Edinburgh, but it had remained an "empty slogan" because the actual dynamics of church-to-church relationships were distorted by "economic inequalities" so as to "perpetuate relationships of dominance and dependence." The very idea of power, the report said, was alien to a true understanding of the church. It must give way to "a mature relationship between churches" based on "mutual commitment to participate in Christ's mission in the world." [121]

The assembly recognized the potentially destructive effects of the abuse of power within the ecumenical movement, as well as the unresolved dilemma of how to structure partnership between "the powerful and the powerless" without compromising the integrity or identity of either. [122] Bangkok could only plead for more equitable power sharing and for the restructuring of relationships in such a way as to reduce the gulf between senders and receivers. It recommended the widest possible discussion of the moratorium proposal "as a possible strategy of mission in certain areas." [123]

The real significance of Bangkok is that it marked the emergence of the liberation theme as the dominant motif in ecumenical mission—to be taken up again at Melbourne—and the transition from Western mission agency dominance to two-thirds world leadership in the CWME. At the close of the assembly the newly elected DWME Director, Emilio Castro, could say, "We have seen the end of one missionary era; we are beginning a new one in which the idea of world mission will be fundamental." [124]

The old distinction between the foreign-mission enterprise and home mission had ended, said Castro. The mission of the churches *in* the United States could now be of potentially greater importance to the world than the sending of missionaries *from* that country. The missionary situation in Sweden was becoming the responsibility of Christian churches in Africa, Asia, and Latin America. Western countries now needed the help of former "mission churches" in dealing with the challenge of secularism. The church was appearing in a multiplicity of new identities around the world. In the new era of world mission, a moratorium on the sending of personnel and funds could not be advocated as a general principle but only as a specific solution in a given time and place. "Never should it [a moratorium] constitute the abandonment of our missionary mandate. . . . It must be a moratorium *for* mission, never moratorium *of* mission." [125]

Bangkok was an important phase in the readjustment of relationships between missionary partners, but it was too preoccupied with the internal problems of churches and their relationships within the ecumenical movement to do much about mission in the world. Its theological work was generally a disappointment. It did clarify issues of church identity and strengthen the resolve of some weaker churches to take steps toward greater self-reliance and church autonomy. It also demonstrated that world mission, understood as the practice of interdependent partnership between roughly equal partners, would have to wait until more churches moved out of a state of dependence toward greater self-reliance and self-identity as churches.

4

"CONFESSING CHRIST TODAY": CONSOLIDATION AND RECONCILIATION IN ECUMENICAL MISSION

After the tumult and divisive debates of Uppsala, the Fifth Assembly of the World Council of Churches (Nairobi, Kenya, 1975) on the theme "Jesus Christ Frees and Unites" was judged to be one of "consolidation and reconciliation."[1] Evangelism figured prominently and was highlighted in the report of the moderator, M. M. Thomas, to the opening assembly,[2] in the plenary address by Bishop Mortimer Arias,[3] and in the report of Section I, "Confessing Christ Today."[4] The prominence of the evangelistic theme and the treatment it was given were surprising in view of developments which took place between New Delhi and Uppsala. The earlier preoccupation with mission in the secular world, and the sharp critique of churchly structures were no longer so prominent. In their place, Nairobi provided a churchly, confessional, and trinitarian statement on mission. Nairobi marks the beginning of a new phase in the development of ecumenical mission theology, as seen in the attempt to reconcile "churchly" and "worldly" approaches to mission.

What accounts for the new view, and for the concentrated attention to evangelism? In the first place, the WCC assembly met on the continent of Africa, where African member churches were experiencing unprecedented growth. The All Africa Conference of Churches (AACC), one of the assembly hosts, had given particular attention to the evangelization of frontier situations at the AACC meeting in Lusaka, Zambia (1974).[5] Also in 1974, the WCC Commission on World Mission and Evangelism had been instrumental in convening a consultation of Orthodox theologians on the subject of "Confessing Christ Today" in Bucharest, Romania. This consultation helped to make the Orthodox contribution to the development of mission theology in the ecumenical movement more explicit. It contributed directly to the draft of Section I at Nairobi.[6] In July 1974 the International Congress on World Evangelization brought together 4000 persons of evangelical persuasion at Lausanne, Switzerland, to consider strategies and programs for completing the Great Commission.[7] Finally, in October 1974 the Third General Assembly of the Synod of Bishops met in Rome to consider "Evangelization in the Modern World." The Synod reaffirmed "that the mandate to evangelize all people constitutes the essential mission of the church."[8] Philip Potter, WCC general secretary, was invited to address the Roman Synod on the main theme.[9]

Thus the Nairobi Assembly met at a time when the churches of Africa, the Orthodox theologians, the evangelical world, and the Roman bishops were all giving attention to the meaning and practice of evangelism. Nairobi not merely reflected these antecedents, but also sought to build bridges toward other Christian movements in relation to the missionary and evangelistic task.

In his WCC moderator's address at Nairobi, M. M. Thomas of India struck a note of ecumenical convergence around the theme of evangelism. He believed that he saw a "striking. . . theological convergence between the work of the 1973 Bangkok Assembly (CWME) and the 1974 Lausanne Congress, the Roman Bishops' Synod and the Orthodox Consultation":

Firstly, in their emphasis on the whole gospel for the whole man in the whole world; secondly, in their effort to relate evangelism to the identity of the Church and to its growth, renewal and unity; and thirdly, in their affirmation of the realities of the contemporary world, especially the renascence of cultures and religions, and the dynamics of service, development and justice in society.[10]

In this new equation, the reaffirmation of the *church* as the bearer of divine salvation stands out in marked contrast to WCC statements before and after Uppsala. Thomas declared without hesitation that Bangkok, Lausanne, and Rome had reached a consensus with regard to salvation at three points: "the affirmation of its comprehensive nature, the recognition of the eschatological basis for historical action, and the understanding of the Church as the sign and bearer of salvation in the world." [11]

Thomas seemed sensitive to the charge that WCC programs for social and political justice reflected a "social utopianism which denies the fact of sin and affirms a self-redemptive humanism." [12] Lutherans had brought such charges during the debates on missionary structure, and now some Orthodox critics of the WCC complained that the council had not placed its thinking on the social content of salvation solidly enough within the perspective of "the ultimate goal of salvation, . . . the eternal life of God." [13] Thomas' reply was that precisely our hope in the coming kingdom of God in Jesus Christ "provides us with an incentive to participate in efforts to build a more human social order in the perspective of the Kingdom of God." [14]

The discussion indicated that, despite the narrowing of the range of disagreement, important differences continued on the meaning of evangelism, especially with regard to social action and dialog with persons of other faiths.

In his ringing address on evangelism, Bishop Mortimer Arias attempted to restate the WCC's commitment to evangelism as an *essential, primary, and permanent* task. [15] Arias' speech clearly illustrates the third stage of development in ecumenical missionary thinking, viz., the reconciliation between "churchly" and "worldly" positions. Advocating what he called a "holistic or integral approach," Arias proposed his own list of convergences: between mission and unity, word and deed, "naming the name" and action for justice. "We are not seeking unity *per se*, but rather, as in the prayer of Jesus, '*that the world may believe*.' " [16] Appealing to the vision behind the act of integration at New Delhi, he declared that its purpose had been to give expression to the theme: "the whole church with one gospel for the whole world." Then, harking back again to the tradition of the IMC and the solemn commitments made at New Delhi, he called on the WCC to confess its institutional sins:

We have not always been faithful to our recognized calling; we have not always given priority to what ought to be our priorities; we have not always been worthy of our predecessors from Edinburgh 1910 to Mexico 1963; and we have not always fulfilled the hopes which gave rise to the WCC and its merging with the IMC.[17]

Arias' indictment of the WCC for failing to live up to its evangelistic mandate was tempered with praise for the essential correctness of its position on evangelism. Speaking of the WCC's work with migrants and refugees, its protests against social injustice, violence, and racism, and its search for justice and reconciliation, Arias added: "All this is mission, and it can be an integral part of true evangelism in the world today."[18] The holistic approach includes "announcement, prophetic denouncement, personal and community witness, the call to repentance, to conversion and to incorporation in the Christian Church, and participation in the struggle for a more just and human life."[19] With this challenge, blending penitence with encouragement, Arias sought to reinsert evangelism at the center of the WCC's concern.

An evangelical representative associated with the Lausanne Congress, John R. W. Stott, welcomed Arias' eloquent plea for evangelism but also observed that it was "not typical of recent ecumenical utterances."[20] Stott believed that the WCC needed to recover five things: (1) recognition of the lostness of humans; (2) confidence in the truth, relevance, and power of the gospel of God; (3) conviction about the uniqueness of Jesus Christ; (4) a sense of urgency about evangelism (in the narrow or specific meaning of the term); and (5) a personal experience of Jesus Christ. He pleaded that evangelical and ecumenical leaders take steps to overcome "the wide gap of confidence and credibility which exists today."[21]

Without question, the WCC at Nairobi was making efforts to promote reconciliation, overcome polarization, and build bridges toward evangelicals, Romans Catholics, and the Orthodox. According to one veteran observer, the Nairobi Assembly, with the report on "Confessing Christ Today" as its centerpiece, "has probably saved the World Council of Churches from disintegration."[22]

Section I begins on a reassuring confessional note, at once Christological and trinitarian:

We boldly confess Christ alone as Saviour and Lord. We confidently trust in the power of the gospel to free and unite. . . . We have been

led by the Holy Spirit to confess Jesus Christ as our Divine Confessor
. . . . His name is above every name.[23]

In a series of carefully crafted both/and statements, the report sets forth
the comprehensive and dialectical nature of evangelism:

> Through the power of the cross, Christ promises God's righteousness
> and commands true justice. As the royal priesthood, Christians are there-
> fore called to engage in both evangelism and social action. We are com-
> missioned to proclaim the gospel of Christ to the ends of the earth. . .
> [and] to struggle to realize God's will for peace, justice and freedom
> throughout society. . . . Christians witness in word and deed to the in-
> breaking reign of God. . . . Christ's decisive battle has been won at
> Easter. . . . Yet we must still battle daily.[24]

Other Nairobi subsections dealt with cultural identity, structures that
hinder confession, and eucharistic community. Noting "our hesitations
about explicitly confessing our faith before others," the report went on
to issue a bold "call to confess and proclaim" the "whole gospel" for
the "whole person" in the "whole world" by the "whole church."
The call to evangelism was a call to repentance, renewal, and unity.
Strikingly, a reference to the church's "unfinished mission" now reap-
pears:

> Yet, even imperfect and broken, we are called to put ourselves humbly
> and gladly at the service of the unfinished mission. We are commissioned
> to carry the gospel to the whole world and to allow it to permeate all
> realms of human life.[25]

The repeated emphasis on *wholeness*—in some ways the new ecumenical trademark—is familiar. The *world* as the locus of God's mission has not disappeared. But what may be most significant about
Nairobi is that here the WCC once again quietly embraces the New
Delhi theology of integration, which held that the church or Christian
community is the proper and primary instrument of God's mission in
the world. What this would mean for mission practice, and for relations
between conciliar Christians and other groups, remained to be seen.

MELBOURNE CONFERENCE 1980: "YOUR KINGDOM COME"

The World Council of Churches CWME Melbourne Conference of
1980 ranks as one of the most important and best prepared conferences

on mission and evangelism held in recent years.[26] Its chosen theme, the kingdom of God, is the central theme of most current missiology.[27] The special advantage of the kingdom theme is that it is equally adapted to a discussion of the church's relation to the missionary task, and to reflection on the worldly context of mission. As the coordinate term for expressing the goal of *missio Dei,* the kingdom theme is ideally suited for dealing with the unfinished theological agenda of the Willingen Conference (1952), where such issues as the relation between church and kingdom, eschatology, and Christology were not treated with finality. Melbourne continued the movement observed at the Nairobi Assembly of the WCC (1975) to reconcile churchly mission with mission in and to the world.

The plan of the Melbourne Conference was to deal with key issues related to the kingdom under four sectional topics: (I) "Good News to the Poor," (II) "The Kingdom of God and Human Struggles," (III) "The Church Witnesses to the Kingdom," and (IV) "Christ—Crucified and Risen—Challenges Human Power."[28] Documentation for the conference was outstanding, including six preconference issues of the *International Review of Mission,* plus two follow-up issues, and a twelve-issue series of occasional papers on aspects of the kingdom.[29] In the plenary addresses, Bible studies, worship, and intercessions, the idea of the kingdom held a prominent place.[30]

Melbourne also reflected the effort begun at Nairobi (1975) to link the CWME more directly with the great missionary tradition coming from Edinburgh (1910) as well as with the spirituality of the student missionary movement. This linkage was apparent in WCC General Secretary Philip Potter's opening address:

> The World Council of Churches is proud to be the inheritor of the great missionary movement which launched the decisive stage of the ecumenical movement at Edinburgh 1910.[31]

Potter added:

> The missionary movement and the world missionary conferences have always been based on worship, prayer and Bible study in the presence and hope of the kingdom.[32]

Such statements were not without significance in view of charges by evangelicals that the ecumenical movement had forfeited its claim to

be the successor to the Edinburgh tradition. While Potter's remarks do not necessarily imply a repudiation of any mission statements produced under the aegis of the WCC from New Delhi to Nairobi, they can be understood as part of an effort to project a different, and for the most part a more positive, missionary image.

Soritua Nababan, Indonesian Moderator of the CWME, urged delegates at Melbourne "to pray confidently, for the kingdom is already in our midst" and yet also to "pray expectantly, for the kingdom in all its fullness is yet to come."[33] Nababan felt that polarizing debates on the meaning of mission weakened the church's witness in the world, and sapped its zeal and enthusiasm for mission. Bible study leader Krister Stendahl explained that the Lord's Prayer was "a sustained cry for the coming of the kingdom." As participants learned to pray that prayer with renewed zeal and purpose, he believed, "we shall be lifted into God's agenda by the very Spirit in which Jesus taught us so to pray."[34] Similarly, Ernst Käsemann, in a passionate biblical exposition of the kingdom theme, commented:

> Christians and church communities are credible only as long as people hear issuing from them the passionate cry, "Your kingdom come!"[35]

Careful efforts were made to sustain the mood of prayer for the coming of God's kingdom through worship and intercession. Despite these efforts, the atmosphere of hope and expectancy was sometimes dissipated by intense theological debates, moralistic attacks on forces of evil, and strategic planning to transform both church and world. This alternation between waiting for God's kingdom and actively engaging in the work of God's kingdom seems to belong to the dialectic of the church's participation in *missio Dei*.

Melbourne continued and deepened the unfinished Bangkok (1973) discussion on liberation. At Bangkok, liberation was expressed in the cry of churches from the two-thirds world for freedom for cultural identity, and in the call for a redistribution of power between churches in the North and South. At Melbourne, the liberation debate erupted as the challenge to the churches to come to terms with the universal human phenomena of poverty and powerlessness among the world's poor. What was the missionary significance of the fact that most Christians were wealthy and privileged, while the majority of those who

had not heard the gospel were poor and oppressed? Who were the poor, and what was their special claim upon the kingdom of God? What were the contemporary missionary implications of Jesus' identification with the poor, and of his messianic manifesto given at Nazareth (Luke 4:18-19)? While the kingdom was the main theme, focus on the poor and the church's response to the poor became the dynamic factor in the theological discussions and strategy proposals. It was no mere coincidence that the CWME Melbourne conference followed closely on the heels of the Latin American Roman Catholic Bishops Third General Conference at Puebla, Mexico (1979), at which the church's "preferential option for the poor" was reaffirmed.

Section I: Good News to the Poor[36]

> In the perspective of the kingdom, God has a preference for the poor. Jesus announced at the beginning of his ministry, drawing upon the word given to the prophet Isaiah, "The Spirit of the Lord is upon me, because he has anointed me to preach good news to the poor. . ." (Luke 4:18) [I.1].

Throughout the history of Israel God had shown his preference for the poor, the section report stated, and now the church must express this continuing concern for the poor to whom Jesus has granted the blessings of his kingdom.

> To the poor this challenge means the profound assurance that God is with them and for them. To the rich it means a profound repentance and renunciation [I.4].

The poor received the promise that God has come to their rescue, while the rich were called to renounce the security of wealth and material possessions, to give up wealth as a power of exploitation, and to turn from indifference to the poor toward solidarity with the oppressed.

Unable to agree on the identity of "the poor" in the world today, Melbourne wisely resisted the temptation either to equate "material poverty" with "spiritual poverty" (cf. Luke 6:20 and Matt. 5:3) or to oppose the two.[37] The poor are those who have been deprived of the basic "necessities of life," but they equally include those who, while "possessing material and cultural riches still do not live in a state of

well-being" but suffer from "malaise, anomie and self-destructive be-
haviour" [I.7].

> The Gospel of the kingdom is addressed to whole people in all of their
> life relationships. God is working for the total liberation of the whole
> of human life [I.6].

Accordingly, the churches discover a particular missionary and evangelistic task in bringing the gospel to the poor, no matter what their
identity:

> The Church of Jesus Christ is called to preach Good News to the poor,
> even as its Lord has in his ministry announced the kingdom of God to
> them. The churches cannot neglect this evangelistic task. Most of the
> world's people are poor and they wait for a witness to the Gospel that
> will really be "Good News." . . . Mission that is conscious of the king-
> dom will be concerned for liberation, not oppression; justice, not ex-
> ploitation; fulness, not deprivation; freedom, not slavery; health, not
> disease; life, not death [I.16].

Melbourne could find a few bright places, e.g., in the *base communities* of Latin America, where the poor were proclaiming the good
news to each other. It also knew of instances where wealthy churches
had shown understanding for the plight of the poor by working for a
just society. But it knew of far more instances where churches were
"indifferent to the situation of the poor or—far worse—actively allied
with those forces that have made them poor" [I.18]. In many countries
the churches were identified with the *status quo*, alienated from the
poor by middle class values, and "full of satisfied, complacent people
who are not willing to look at the Lazarus on their doorstep" [I.18].
Proclaiming the good news to the poor is thus a call to develop an
authentic ecclesial life-style consistent with the message of Jesus
Christ. Melbourne issued four specific recommendations:

  (a) to become churches in solidarity with the poor;

  (b) to join the struggle against the powers of exploitation and im-
poverishment;

  (c) to establish a new relationship with the poor inside the churches;

  (d) to pray and work for the kingdom of God [I.20].

Section II: The Kingdom of God and Human Struggles[38]

This section reflects the CWME's ongoing concern for mission in the secular world and in relation to other faiths and ideologies. It provides a theological rationale for relating the vertical and horizontal dimensions of the kingdom, the church's dual role as proclaimer of the gospel and participant in human struggles, and the dialectic of divine justice in history alongside the justification of sinners by grace through faith for eternity.

The section report recognized the hesitation felt by churches in many places about how to witness in circumstances where churches may feel overwhelmed by powers working in opposition to the kingdom of God [II.1-2]. In such circumstances churches may be tempted to "avoid confrontation with the struggles of this world on the grounds that the kingdom of God is not 'of this world' " [II.3]. But the hope that we have in Christ challenges Christians to involvement.

> It is our conviction that the churches are called to return to and renew the hope they have in Jesus Christ, instead of succumbing to despair and passivity, so as to be able to join forces with all those who hope. . . . They are called to remember and present to God the struggles of this world and intercede on behalf of the world. This should lead the churches to be more sharply aware of their real relationship to the ongoing struggles of humankind and to examine their own structural relations and ideological conformity to the principalities and powers of this world [II.3-4].

As they do this, Christians expect no utopia on earth, but maintain a sober and critical distinction between the ultimate hope of the kingdom which transcends history and their presence in the midst of human struggles to bring about greater justice and liberation here and now:

> In their witness to the kingdom of God in words and deeds the churches must dare to be present at the bleeding points of humanity and thus near those who suffer evil, even taking the risk of being counted among the wicked. The royal reign of God appears on earth as the kingdom of the crucified Jesus, which places his disciples with him under the cross. Without losing sight of the ultimate hope of the kingdom of God or giving up their own critical attitude, the churches must dare to be present in the midst of human struggles for penultimate solutions [II.4].

The specific task of the churches, according to the theological section, is to "disclose the final revelation of God himself in Jesus Christ" and to "establish such visible signs of the kingdom of God as to offer new hope to all those who long for a more human world" [II.5]. This means witnessing to hope for the whole creation in the life, death, and resurrection of Christ, and turning human minds to Christ as Lord of the kingdom.

What this means concretely is spelled out in five areas illustrating human struggles facing the churches today. Underlying all the suggestions is the sense that the churches must struggle to evangelize themselves in order to become instruments of the kingdom. This means returning to an understanding of the gospel as both the proclamation of a *message* to the world and as the proclamation of a *way of life* [II.8]. Churches can be true to their missionary task of bringing the gospel to the world only as they allow the gospel to challenge their own life-styles and structures.

In countries struggling for liberation and self-determination, churches should take the side of the poor and the oppressed [II.12]; where liberation has already occurred, they should participate actively in building a new society, rejecting any uncritical relationship with the government [II.10]. In relation to struggles for human rights, they should protest unjust economic systems, becoming advocates of the voiceless, and opposing escalating militarism and doctrines of national security [II.14-18]. Participation in struggles for human rights is seen as a "central element in the total mission of the church to proclaim by word and act the crucified and risen Christ" [II.19]. In places of strong institutional religious revival, churches should seek meeting points for dialog and cooperation with people of other faiths [II.22]. In Eastern socialist countries, Christians should maintain the hope of eschatological salvation and lift up such virtues as compassion, reconciliation, love, and forgiveness [II.26]. In Western consumer-oriented societies, Christians need to witness against false goals such as acquisitiveness and overconsumption [II.29]. The crucified and risen Christ is the "judge of shallow life-styles and invites the churches to repentance and new life" [II.30].

Section III: The Church Witnesses to the Kingdom[39]

The Melbourne section dealing with the church contains many traditional elements: proclamation and conversion, community, healing,

common witness, and eucharistic fellowship. Its most astonishing theological statement is: "The whole church of God, in every place and time, is a *sacrament of the kingdom* which came in the person of Jesus Christ and will come in its fulness when he returns to glory" [III.1; emphasis added]. Here we find one of the clearest affirmations of the new status given to the church as the instrument of divine mission, especially in the post-Nairobi period. Eucharistic worship is singled out for special attention.

Proclamation of the gospel is a distinct and indispensable witness to the kingdom, says the report:

> The story of God in Christ is the heart of all evangelism, and this story has to be told, for the life of the present church never fully reveals the love and holiness and power of God in Christ [III.2].

Proclamation is the responsibility of the whole church and of every member. The credibility of the church's proclamation of the gospel will depend on the authenticity of the church's total witness, as measured by the fact that *(a)* it is a truly worshiping community; *(b)* it welcomes outsiders; *(c)* its members offer their service in both church and society; and *(d)* it is ready to move like a pilgrim into new situations and across new frontiers [III.6].

> The proclamation of the Good News is a continual necessity and all people, believers and unbelievers, are challenged to hear and respond since conversion is never finished [III.7].

Proclamation is understood holistically, and demands communication in deed and word, in teaching, learning, and serving. Proclamation expects conversion under the action of the Holy Spirit: a transfer of loyalty to God's kingdom through faith in Jesus Christ and a leaving behind of old securities [III.9-10].

Despite the distance between the ideal church as "sacrament of the kingdom" and the reality of the local congregation, Melbourne did not rule out the possibility that renewal for mission could occur through the institutional church [III.12]. Along with "base Christian communities," which are a "gift of God" offering renewal to the poor, it commended house churches, prayer groups, retreats, monastic communities, and groups practicing new life-styles. The church's participation in healing—especially healing of the whole person—"is a sign

of the kingdom's arrival" [III.17]. The quest for visible unity, and the development of united mission strategies that overcome the disruptiveness of division, are further evidences of the growth of the kingdom:

> We believe that unless the pilgrimage route leads the churches to visible unity, in the one God we preach and worship, the one Christ crucified for us all, the one Holy Spirit who creates us anew, and the one kingdom, the mission entrusted to us in this world will always be rightly questioned [III.24].

Through the Eucharist, Christians deepen their communion with Christ and are also called to participation in the Lord's own sacrificial ministry. The Eucharist is "pilgrim bread" which gives life to Christians so that they may be formed in the image of Christ and so become effective witnesses to him [III.31].

Section IV: Christ—Crucified and Risen—Challenges Human Power[40]

This section, closely linked with Section I, is primarily an analysis and critique of the uses of power in the church and of church structures in the light of the crucified Christ. Its context is the fact that the two-thirds world sees itself as dominated by the developed world, and under the global influence of superpowers. Only by repentance, the grace of God, and amendment of life can Christians linked with oppressive structures stand in solidarity with Christians in poor lands and experience liberation. Here is Melbourne's theological preamble:

> The proclamation of God's reign is the announcement of a new order which challenges those powers and structures that have become demonic in a world corrupted by sin against God. . . . Jesus of Nazareth rejected coercive power as a way of changing the world. Rather, as signs of God's inbreaking kingdom, he had power to forgive sins, healing power and an authority over demonic, dehumanizing powers. . . . The eye of faith discerns in [Jesus'] cross the embodiment of a God who out-suffers, out-loves and out-lives the worst that powers do. In the decisive events which followed the crucifixion, something radically new happened which seems best described as a new creation. An altogether new quality of power appeared to be let loose among humankind. . . . The most striking picture is that of a sacrificed lamb, slaughtered but yet living, sharing the throne, which symbolized the heart of all power and sovereignty, with the living

God himself. The principle of self-sacrificing love is thus enthroned at the centre of the reality of the universe [IV.3].

The crucified Christ, as the emblem of divine power enthroned at the center of the universe, enables Christians not only to indict themselves for their own unfaithfulness but also to confront the demonic powers at work in public and personal life.

In confronting the powers, churches must avoid imitating the patterns of the powers they seek to confront, or they will become indistinguishable from those worldly powers. "In the light of the reign of God, the fundamental criterion for their use of power must be the good of the poor and their liberation from oppression" [IV.5]. Churches that side with the downtrodden and the oppressed will run the "risk of putting their own institutional life on the line." Challenging the powers in the name of the poor puts churches to the test, makes them agents for transformation, and calls for radical changes in life-style on the part of those who are not poor. "It becomes therefore a missionary obligation to develop a dynamic spirituality including renewed resources for education and a supportive community" [IV.7].

A missionary spirituality based on the power of the crucified and resurrected Christ will be closely linked to Baptism, Eucharist, and the call to discipleship. Some marks of the crucified Christ that characterize the church's style of action will be *suffering, imprisonment, martyrdom,* and *persecution* for the faith. The power of forgiveness replaces the power of vengeance. Loss of status is experienced as spiritual strength. Many Christians lack the experience of the power of the crucified Christ, Melbourne noted, being too easily overcome by grief, pain, or fear:

We are never free from the need for renewal and the need to rediscover the strength that comes from challenging the powers [IV.8-9].

Yet the risen Christ can bring about an inward transformation of suffering so that it takes on a power derived from the power of the cross. Since the practice of nonviolence is "an inalienable part of the Christian obedience," churches must provide support for those who commit themselves to such a path. In other cases, these churches may find themselves called to act in solidarity with those "who become involved

in counter-violence in order to free themselves from the unbearable violence of their oppressors" [IV.11].

Out of this section report, and from the Melbourne Conference Message, there emerges a new picture of an earthly Christ who was laid in a manger, moved toward those on the edges of life, affirmed his lordship by giving it up, and ended up being crucified outside the city gates.[41] Christ incarnate and crucified becomes the model for mission:

> He who is the centre is constantly in movement from the centre to the periphery, towards those who are marginalized, victims of demonic powers, political, economic, social, cultural and even—or especially—religious. If we take this model seriously, we find that we must be with Jesus at the periphery, on the margins of society, for his priorities were clear [IV.20].

The ecclesiological counterpart of the crucified Christ is churches made up of the poor. Indeed, says the report, poor churches should not be viewed paternalistically as *objects* of mission; they have become its *agents* and bearers:

> World mission and evangelism may now be primarily in their hands. Perhaps they alone can waken the world to an awareness of the urgent call of Christ to costly and radical response [IV.21].

It was suggested that the poor and powerless may have the most significant word for the rich and the powerful: that Jesus must be sought on the periphery; that following him involves commitment to the poor; and that only the church of the poor can preach with integrity to the poor of the world [IV.21].

Christ crucified and risen challenges the structures of institutional churches and calls for conversion toward ways in which Christ is expressed in church relationships and in the use of money and power. Melbourne posed searching questions to the churches. Is power used for self-aggrandizement or for the needs of the poor? Is leadership exercised as an expression of selfless love which releases and encourages gifts of the entire community? Does the community perceive leadership as helping to free the poor and the oppressed? Do all persons, regardless of sex, age, handicaps, or status, share in decision making and the exercise of gifts? Are women empowered for ministry and

service? Is knowledge the exclusive monopoly of an elite group [IV.13]? On what basis are accumulated funds invested, and who benefits from church investment policies [IV.14]? Member churches are challenged to review investment policies and to turn their holdings into resources for Christ's mission to the poor and the powerless [IV.26].

MELBOURNE: A PRELIMINARY ASSESSMENT

We can now summarize and restate the main issues and findings of Melbourne.

1. The kingdom as the goal of mission

The kingdom of God, both as a *gift* and as a *task,* stands forth as the most comprehensive biblical expression for the goal of *missio Dei.* In the perspective of the coming kingdom, other terms acquire their respective places and relationships. *Missio Dei* means that the triune God—Father, Son, and Holy Spirit—continues to be the main actor in mission. God does not turn responsibility for mission over to the church; he himself carries it to completion, with or without the church's cooperation. Therefore the life of the church does not express either the source or the fullness of mission. Properly understood, the church is an instrument of the kingdom and an eschatological foretaste of it— in that sense even a "sacrament" of the kingdom, as Melbourne suggested. The kingdom is, in Käsemann's phrase at Melbourne, none other than Jesus Christ, "the royal reign of God in person."[42]

A proper eschatological perspective, such as was considered at Willingen but not adequately developed until Melbourne, is crucial to discerning the church's missionary role. On the one hand, the end of history is anticipated in the death and resurrection of Christ, the new creation is already experienced as a partial reality, and Christ's followers are enabled and encouraged to challenge the demonic powers which have been judged by the cross. On the other hand, the final victory of the kingdom awaits the return of Christ in power and glory. In the "time between," Christ's faithful witnesses can expect to be identified with him in suffering and martyrdom. The ultimate victory of the kingdom is sure, because God is God. Therefore Christians witness in hope, believe and pray, "Come, Lord Jesus. Your kingdom come!"

2. Christology for mission and evangelism

"Melbourne was a Christological conference,"[43] not in the sense of presenting a fully developed Christology, but rather because it highlighted a specific point of the Christological tradition appropriate for sharing good news to the poor. Melbourne said little about the traditional doctrine of the atonement, and not much about the cosmic Christ who unites all things in himself. Melbourne's Christology centered on the "earthly Jesus, the Jew, the Nazarene, who lived as a simple Galilean man, suffered and was executed, dying on the cross."[44] This earthly Christ who came to proclaim good news to the poor (Luke 4) was held up not simply as an object of faith but in a particular way as a model for mission. At Melbourne there occurred a shift from Paul and the apostles as paradigms for mission to Jesus Christ, healer, proclaimer, and caster-out of demons, as the missionary *par excellence:* and a shift away from preaching the message of justification by faith for sinners to enacting the kingdom in history by word and deed.

Jesus, crucified outside the city wall, moves from the center of power to the periphery to be with the poor, the despised, the marginalized, and the oppressed. He calls his people to leave their centers of power and to join him among the poor and the powerless. The consequences of this missionary Christology are to challenge the church to abandon its ethnic and class identifications and to seek the salvation—in a comprehensive spiritual, personal, social, and material sense—of those who have priority in God's promises.

3. The poor as a new missionary yardstick

Melbourne follows the tradition of earlier WCC missionary conferences in redefining the context of mission and, more precisely, relocating its current locus in the world. Previous conferences had defined this locus in such broad categories as "the secular world," "people of other faiths and ideologies," "centers of decision-making responsibility or conflict," or simply "those who do not know or acknowledge Jesus as Lord." Melbourne, following the lead of two Conferences of Latin American Roman Catholic Bishops—at Medellin (1968) and Puebla (1979)—declared that the poor have a prior claim on God's promises and that, as a result, the church has a "preferential option" (cf. I.4) to serve the poor. Commented CWME Director Emilio Castro:

> The relation to the poor inside the church, outside the church, nearby and far away, is the criterion to judge the authenticity and credibility of

the Church's missionary engagement. . . . The missiological principle, the missionary yardstick, is the relation of the Church to the poor.[45]

This would mean (1) a call to the churches to repent, because the credibility of the kingdom is at stake in the attitude of the church to the poor; (2) concern for the poor as a priority in all mission strategies and in missionary vocation; and (3) evangelization of the poor as a call to the poor to become evangelists and to claim the promises of the kingdom.[46]

This new missiological yardstick, if implemented, would impose far-reaching demands and place before churches and mission agencies rigorous new economic and personnel standards.

4. Call for a new missionary life-style

Closely related to the two preceding points is the search for a missionary life-style patterned after Christ's own ministry among the poor and the marginal. It is a life-style based on Christ's *kenosis* as a way of accomplishing his mission:

> Christ refused to impose God's kingdom by taking power and ruling humankind and all creation as the just ruler (cf. temptation story). He manifested God's way of reigning by giving up his being equal to God, becoming a Jew, a Galilean, living among the poor and disenfranchised, dying on the cross in our place. The symbols of God's kingdom are not the sword and crown, but bread and wine—the broken body of our Lord. The call to the disciple is nothing less than to follow that way—in absolute opposition to any reasonable search for accomplishment and success. It is not a call to powerlessness, but to a life that has its source in the power of the Holy Spirit.[47]

Such a life-style possesses a charism which overcomes limits, breaks down walls and barriers, and crosses frontiers to live with people where they are. It makes the witnesses vulnerable and pushes them toward new experiments in living, risk-taking, and pilgrim ways. Because such a life-style is the very antithesis of institutional self-preservation, it may require the continuation of a special kind of missionary vocation within the church. The purpose of a missionary spirituality is to enable the church to be present in the midst of human struggles and to witness to the hope that is in Christ. ''It is in the actual participation with people in the search for solutions to common human problems that we find natural opportunities to name the Name of Jesus Christ, to render witness to his saving and liberating powers."[48]

5. The church as a renewed missionary agent

Beginning at Nairobi, and continuing at Melbourne, the church appears to have been rehabilitated in WCC circles as an instrument for mission. The spoken word—like Baptism and Eucharist—is said to have a sacramental quality; the church itself is called a "sacrament of the kingdom." Melbourne clearly articulated the belief that the Christian community in its various forms is capable of repenting, being renewed, and being equipped for missionary service. In the eschatological perspective of the kingdom, the church attains its rightful place as servant and herald of the kingdom, not its final expression. Liberated from feverish concern for institutional self-preservation, the church is free to give itself up to its proper service of proclaiming Christ and heralding the kingdom by word and deed. Because the mission is Christ's, not its own, the church dares to risk failure, exposes its own weakness and vulnerability, and allows itself to be tested by the Lord's own standards of authenticity and credibility. Its real power lies in its faithfulness to the *kenotic* life-style, and to the cross and the resurrection. In giving up its life for Christ's sake, the church finds it true identity, and becomes a church in mission.

6. Mission practice as an expression of theory

Melbourne posed huge challenges to the churches. It went far toward providing a contemporary reformulation of the theory of mission in a world where most of the people are poor and still waiting for a witness to the gospel that will be really "good news" [I.16]. Could rich churches truly repent and adopt a new missiological yardstick? Could missionary vocation be repatterned after the *kenotic* spirituality of Jesus Christ? Is it too romantic to think of the world's poor as the real evangelists of the future? How and by what means would the engagement take place? Such questions were not answered at Melbourne, which proposed no specific programs or strategies for completing the unfinished task. Melbourne's task was to offer a vision and a theological perspective:

Now that we have a theological perspective—the Gospel announced to the poor, and a vision of God's own missionary style—Jesus emptying himself, going through the cross to the margin of life, we need to engage ourselves in practical discussions with all those who receive today the calling to go to the regions beyond.[49]

The crucial test of the Melbourne vision was whether it could be translated into missionary action by conciliar groups.

MISSION AND EVANGELISM: AN ECUMENICAL AFFIRMATION (1982)

In the interim between its Fifth and Sixth Assemblies at Nairobi (1975) and Vancouver (1983), respectively, the WCC achieved a major breakthrough in the adoption of a document entitled, "Mission and Evangelism—An Ecumenical Affirmation."[50] In 1976, immediately following the Fifth Assembly, the Central Committee of the WCC asked the CWME to prepare a document containing "the basic convictions of the ecumenical movement on the topic of mission and evangelism."[51] Conversations on the subject were held in connection with preparations for Melbourne, and representatives of various confessional groups, including Roman Catholics and Eastern Orthodox, were extensively consulted. In 1982 the document was approved by the Central Committee and sent to the churches for consideration and implementation. While the document has no binding authority for WCC member churches, apart from the intrinsic ability of its content to inspire a response, it may be considered exceptional in view of the widespread favorable acceptance which it has received both within and outside the WCC.[52]

The "ecumenical affirmation" about mission and evangelism is remarkable not because of the novelty of its content—indeed, most of its points had been articulated at CWME meetings from Mexico City (1963) to Melbourne (1980)—but because of the felicity with which it restates and clarifies existing positions. Eschewing polarizing tendencies, the document continues the trend initiated at Nairobi of working toward convergence and consensus. Points of divergence find little expression in the statement. Indeed, the "ecumenical affirmation" in its preface strikes a note of considerable urgency in regard to the church's privilege and obligation to announce the gospel of salvation to every creature. At the same time, the mission task is seen as having its foundation in the revelation of the triune God, with the church receiving its sending mandate to witness to the reign of God in Christ through the Spirit. The post-Melbourne stance is fully set forth in the new document.

The preface declares that "the Church is sent into the world to call people and nations to repentance, to announce forgiveness of sins and a new beginning in relations with God and with neighbours through Jesus Christ."[53] The urgency of the evangelistic calling, set forth in terms of the cultural challenges of all six continents, is given an uncharacteristic emphasis:

> In a world where the number of people who have no opportunity to know the story of Jesus is growing steadily, *how necessary it is to multiply the witnessing vocation of the church!*
>
> In a world where the majority of those who do not know Jesus are the poor of the earth, those to whom he promised the kingdom of God, *how essential it is to share with them the Good News of that kingdom!*
>
> In a world where people are struggling for justice, freedom and liberation, often without the realization of their hopes, *how important it is to announce that God's kingdom is promised to them!*
>
> In a world where the marginalized and the drop-outs of affluent society search desperately for comfort and identity in drugs or esoteric cults, *how imperative it is to announce that he has come so that all may have life and may have it in all its fullness (John 10:10)!*
>
> In a world where so many find little meaning, except in the relative security of their affluence, *how necessary it is to hear once again Jesus' invitation to discipleship, service and risk!*
>
> In a world where so many Christians are nominal in their commitment to Jesus Christ, *how necessary it is to call them again to the fervour of their first love!*
>
> In a world where wars and rumours of war jeopardize the present and future of humankind, where an enormous part of natural resources and people are consumed in the arms race, *how crucial it is to call the peacemakers blessed, convinced that God in Christ has broken all barriers and has reconciled the world to himself (Eph. 2:14; II Cor. 5:19)!*[54]

In this ecumenical affirmation, the churches in all six continents challenge one another to announce that God reigns, to declare that there is hope for a gracious future, and to remind the world that Jesus is coming again and soon!

Two middle sections describe "the call to mission" and "the call to proclamation and witness."[55] The first sets forth the IMC and WCC conviction that there is a close and inextricable relationship "between Christian unity and missionary calling, between ecumenism and evangelization":

> The churches of the WCC are on a pilgrimage towards unity under the missionary vision of John 17:21, "that they may all be one; even as thou, Father, art in me, and I in thee, that they also may be in us, so that the world may believe that thou hast sent me."[56]

The church has as one *constitutive* mark "its being apostolic, its being sent into the world." *Acts* tells the story of the church's expansion, which occurred through faithful witness, persecution, and purposeful ministries. Jesus was the complete revelation of God's love, manifesting both God's *justice* and *forgiveness* in a variety of ways. The church today has the same freedom to develop its mission in response to changing situations and circumstances. Sent into the world by God's love, it seeks to witness to the full realization of God's kingdom in Jesus Christ.

The church's call to proclamation and witness arises from the nature of the church as the body of Christ, sharing in the Lord's twofold ministry of mediation: from God to creation, and from creation to God.

> The Church manifests God's love for the world in Christ—through word and deed, in identification with all humanity, in loving service and joyful proclamation; the Church, in that same identification with all humanity, lifts up to God its pain and suffering, hope and aspiration, joy and thanksgiving in intercessory prayer and eucharistic worship.[57]

Through worship, prayer, intercession, solidarity with the poor, and advocacy of justice even to the point of confrontation with oppressive powers, the churches seek to fulfill their evangelistic vocation. Proclamation of Christ crucified is the starting point; emphasis is laid on Jesus' identification with the poverty of humankind. "To believe in Jesus the King is to accept his undeserved grace and enter with him into the Kingdom, taking sides with the poor struggling to overcome poverty."[58] The church also proclaims Jesus as risen from the dead; through the resurrection, God vindicates Jesus and "opens up a new period of missionary obedience until he comes again."[59]

The "ecumenical affirmation" continues with seven "ecumenical convictions" by which, according to the document, Christians of diverse confessions and traditions "have learned to recognize each other as participants in the one worldwide missionary movement" and "under which they covenant to work for the kingdom of God."[60] These are, in outline: (1) personal conversion; (2) the gospel to all realms of life (wholeness); (3) mission in unity; (4) mission in Christ's way; (5) good news to the poor; (6) mission in and to six continents; and (7) witness among people of living faiths.[61] Only a few summary observations can be made about each.

"The proclamation of the Gospel includes an invitation to recognize and accept in a personal decision the saving lordship of Christ." Each person is entitled to hear the good news. "The calling is to specific changes, to renounce evidences of the domination of sin in our lives and to accept responsibilities in terms of God's love for the neighbour." The call to conversion, as a call to repentance and obedience, should also be addressed to nations, groups, and families. Conversion begins with the "repentance of those who do the calling, who issue the invitation," i.e., the evangelists. Conversion is the daily reenactment of Baptism by dying and rising with Christ.[62]

"The teaching of Jesus on the kingdom of God is a clear reference to God's loving lordship over all human history. The lordship of Christ is to be proclaimed to all realms of life."[63] The good news is a challenge to the structures of society as well as a call to individuals to repent. The church *announces* good news, *denounces* sin and injustice, *consoles* widows and orphans, and *celebrates* life in the midst of death. The realms of science and technology claim special attention today. Christian witness points toward Jesus Christ as "God's wisdom" at the center of all creation, and as the clue to our human stewardship.

Churches are to be a "sign for the world," as Christian mission is "the action of the body of Christ in the history of humankind," into which persons who through conversion and Baptism accept the gospel are incorporated. Sadly, however, "many who are attracted to the vision of the kingdom find it difficult to be attracted to the concrete reality of the Church."[64] Accordingly, churches are in need of a continuing process of renewal so as to become living witnesses to the integrity of the gospel. The weekly celebration of Eucharist is a place for renewal of a congregation's missionary conviction; it provides bread for a missionary people. Christians are called to work for the renewal and transformation of local churches.

Common witness should be the natural result of unity with Christ in his mission. The goal of unity should be not merely a common affirmation of the fundamentals of Christian faith, but also proclamation together of the good news to the world. Since the heart of Christian mission is to multiply local congregations, churches are urged to continue the task of sowing the seed "until there is in every human community a cell of the kingdom, a church confessing Jesus Christ and in his name serving his people. The building up of the church in every place is essential to the Gospel."[65] "Inculturation" occurs when Christians express their faith in the symbols and images of their local cultures. The process of inculturation is stimulated as Christians in a given place participate in the struggle of the less privileged for their liberation. Diversity of cultural expressions is not a serious threat to unity, for "the unity we look for is not uniformity but the multiple expression of a common faith and a common mission."[66] Sharing Christian witness out of different cultural perspectives can be mutually inspiring and corrective.

"Our obedience in mission should be patterned on the ministry and teaching of Jesus."[67] The self-emptying of Christ who lived among the people, shared in their hopes and sufferings, and gave his life on the cross for all humanity, is what is meant by "mission in Christ's way." An imperialistic or crusading spirit was foreign to Jesus. Churches are free to choose the ways they consider best to present the gospel to people in different circumstances, but they should be aware of the distortions caused by methodologies of communication. "Every methodology illustrates or betrays the Gospel we announce."[68] Evangelism happens in interpersonal relations as people share the pains and joys of life. Ordinary people in small caring communities whose life prompts the question "What is the source of the meaning of your life?" are often the primary confessors of the faith.

"The proclamation of the Gospel among the poor is a sign of the messianic kingdom and a priority criterion by which to judge the validity of our missionary engagement today."[69] New awareness exists of the growing gap between wealth and poverty among the nations and *within* each nation. By a "tragic coincidence" most of the world's poor have not heard the gospel or been able to recognize it as "good news."

> This is a double injustice: they are victims of an unjust economic order or an unjust political distribution of power, and at the same time they are deprived of the knowledge of God's special care for them. To announce the Good News to the poor is to begin to render the justice due to them.[70]

This new awareness invites churches to rethink priorities and life-styles, locally and globally. The global nature of poverty and growing interdependence between nations invites—indeed *obliges*—every church and every Christian to find ways to share the good news with the poor today.

In reaching out to the marginalized, the dropouts, and the misfits, churches are learning to overcome the old dichotomies between "evangelism and social action," and between a "spiritual" and a "material" gospel. There should be no evangelism without solidarity, but also no solidarity that does not include sharing the good news of the kingdom.

> There is here a double credibility test: A proclamation that does not hold forth the promises of the justice of the kingdom to the poor of the earth is a caricature of the Gospel; but Christian participation in the struggles for justice which does not point toward the promises of the kingdom also makes a caricature of a Christian understanding of justice.[71]

God's "preferential option for the poor" offers a "valid yardstick" for individual Christians, local congregations, and churches in mission to set new priorities and to develop their lives around gospel values. As they do so, Christians may be gratefully surprised to discover dimensions of the gospel long forgotten or overlooked.

"Everywhere the churches are in missionary situations."[72] Where churches are old and established, life is organized without reference to Christian values; the growth of secularism stands as a challenge to the church. Churches have lost contact with working class people and youth. Movements of migrants and refugees bring "the missionary frontier to the doorstep of every parish." Christian affirmations about worldwide missionary responsibility become more credible if they are authenticated by serious missionary engagement at home. Expressions of solidarity among churches across political frontiers—e.g., in the support of programs to combat racism in Southern Africa—are important symbolic actions and reminders of the church's catholicity. As the local congregation witnesses in its own situation, engages in intercession for churches in other parts of the world, and shares persons and resources, it participates fully in the world mission of the Christian church.

The so-called moratorium on mission means not the end of mission but the freedom to reconsider present engagements to see whether they continue to be appropriate expressions of mission for today. In spite of past ambiguities that have accompanied the carrying of the gospel across national and continental boundaries, that movement needs to continue:

> Each local parish, each Christian, must be challenged to assume responsibility in the total mission of the Church. There will always be need for those who have the calling and the gift to cross frontiers, to share the Gospel of Jesus Christ, and to serve in his name.[73]

The specific calling of individuals or communities which cross cultural and national frontiers in the service of the gospel should not become an "alibi" for the whole church but rather a "symbolic concentration." The traditional exchange of missionary personnel between churches in the northern and southern hemispheres will in future give way to increasing traffic between the poor churches of Asia, Africa, and Latin America. A goal of multilateral sharing should be to loosen "the bond of domination and dependence" that still characterizes relationships between churches in the North and the South.

Christians owe the message of God's salvation "to every person and every people," including those who live by other religious convictions or ideological persuasions. The obligation to witness is without limit, but "true witness follows Jesus Christ in respecting and affirming the freedom of others."[74] The "ecumenical affirmation" recognizes that we have often looked for the worst in others and passed negative judgments on other religions; we need to learn to witness in a humble, repentant, and joyful spirit. Christians, while agreeing that the witness should be given to all, continue to differ on exactly "how this salvation in Christ is available to people of diverse religious persuasions." God as Creator has not left himself without witness, and the Spirit is at work in ways that pass human understanding. In entering into dialog with others, "Christians seek to discern the unsearchable riches of God and the way he deals with humanity."[75] Christians coming from cultures shaped by another faith will find this a special challenge. Christians should join hands with people of other faiths to work for freedom, peace, and mutual respect. They should be in dialog with civil authorities regarding freedom of religion.

Life together with people of other faiths and ideologies is seen as "an encounter of commitments":

> Witness cannot be a one-way process, but of necessity is two-way; in it Christians become aware of some of the deepest convictions of their neighbours. It is also the time in which, within a spirit of openness and trust, Christians are able to bear authentic witness, giving an account of their commitment to Christ, who calls all persons to himself.[76]

To this matter of witness among people of living faiths as an issue challenging the WCC we shall return in a later section.

The WCC "ecumenical affirmation" concludes with a final section entitled "Looking toward the Future." The new frontiers of mission and evangelism are quickly recalled: secularized masses of industrialized societies; emerging new ideologies; movements of workers and political refugees; the people's search for liberation and justice; the uncertain pilgrimage of the younger generation into a future overshadowed by nuclear peril. "The Church is called to be present and to articulate the meaning of God's love for every person and for every situation."[77] Christians are called to bring "their hearts, minds and wills" to the altar of God in faith supported by prayer, contemplation, and adoration. The same Lord who sends his people to cross all frontiers and to enter into unknown territories is the one who assures them, "I am with you to the close of the age."

WCC SIXTH ASSEMBLY AT VANCOUVER (1983): "JESUS CHRIST—THE LIFE OF THE WORLD"

Coming shortly after the CWME Melbourne Conference (1980) and the release of the widely heralded "Mission and Evangelism—An Ecumenical Affirmation" (1982), the Sixth Assembly at Vancouver provided the WCC with an exceptional opportunity to give further exposure to its new consensus on mission and evangelism. The assembly theme, "Jesus Christ—The Life of the World," was admirably suited to this purpose. Yet, apart from brief references in the assembly message and in the report of the first issue group, "Witnessing in a Divided World," the WCC does not appear to have seized on the opportunity of further strengthening its missionary relationships. No major plenary session was devoted to the theme of world mission and evangelism. A group of evangelical observers expressed dismay that the document "Mission and Evangelism: An Ecumenical Affirmation"—one described by evangelicals themselves as "thoroughly evangelical" and widely welcomed in evangelical circles—had not even been mentioned in a plenary address.[78] A Roman Catholic observer at the assembly, referring to the same document, commented that the assembly's treatment of the theme of "witnessing in a divided world" had lagged far behind the "ecumenical affirmation."[79] At the same time, 15 guests from other faiths were cordially received as active participants in the assembly, and 5 of them were invited to address the assembly.[80]

Comments on the "Witness" draft reflected the feeling of some that it was "unscriptural" or "negative" toward the missionary contribution.[81] A few complained of the vagueness of statements on Christology and soteriology; still others missed any mention of the fact that "more than three billion have yet to hear the gospel of Christ."[82]

The evidence cited suggests that the assembly committee had not intended to make of Vancouver a mission event. Hailed as a "worshipping assembly," Vancouver presented the gift of life in Jesus Christ as a challenge to the international Christian community to deal with threats to peace and justice, to renew its ecumenical commitment, and to further the dialog with science and technology, as well as with people of other faiths. In contrast to Nairobi, where the emphasis on evangelization had stood out, the mission theme at Vancouver mission was so tightly woven into the seamless ecumenical garment as to be nearly invisible.

> The Message from the Sixth Assembly included these lines: We renew our commitment to mission and evangelism. By this we mean that deep identification with others in which we can tell the good news that Jesus Christ, God and Saviour, is the Life of the World. We cannot impose faith by our eloquence. We can nourish it with patience and caring so that the Holy Spirit, God the Evangelist, may give us the words to speak. Our proclamation has to be translated into every language and culture.

Whatever our context among people of living faiths and no faith, we remember that God's love is for everyone, without exception. All are invited to the banquet. Jesus Christ, the living bread, calls everyone who is hungry, and his food is unlimited.[83]

The first issue group dealt with "Witnessing in a Divided World."[84] Following a brief introduction, the issue group report deals with five areas of special concern, and concludes with recommendations. The areas of special concern are: (1) culture—the context for our witnessing; (2) worship—the perspective and power with which we worship; (3) witnessing among children; (4) witnessing among the poor; and (5) witnessing among people of living faiths. Apart from the subsections on culture and people of living faiths, few new or substantive concerns are presented. The subsection dealing with witnessing among the poor largely repeats emphases from Melbourne and the "ecumenical affirmation." Our summary will be limited to points related to culture as the context for witnessing, and the approach to people of other faiths.

The report of the discussion on "culture" picks up on an issue dealt with at the Bangkok CWME Conference (1972): how does culture function in the witness to the gospel? Reference is made to the manner in which Western missionaries carrying the gospel to the two-thirds world "by and large denigrated these cultures as pagan and heathen and as inimical to the Gospel."[85]

As they did this, many missionaries did not realize that the Gospel they preached was already influenced by centuries-old interaction with many and different cultures and that they were at this point imposing a culturally bound Christian proclamation on other people. Neither did they realize that they were in fact inhibiting the Gospel from taking root in the cultural soil to which it had come.[86]

Today, however, there are indigenous or local expressions of the Christian faith in many parts of the world, presenting a diversity of forms.

The Gospel message becomes a transforming power within the life of a community when it is expressed in the cultural forms in which the community understands itself.[87]

The subsection report (1) encourages a sharing of the diversity of cultural manifestations of Christian faith, with a particular eye to the unity that binds them together, their Christological centers, and their trinitarian source; (2) warns of the possibility that our witness to the gospel can become captive to presuppositions of a particular culture; (3) calls for a closer investigation into the modern secular global culture being shaped by modernization and technology, and in particular the underlying values associated with it; (4) pleads for care in the preservation of the cultures of minority groups threatened with extinction; and (5) asks for further study of the whole matter of witnessing to the gospel across cultural boundaries, realizing that "listening to and learning from the receptor culture is an essential part of the proclamation of the Christian message."[88]

The subsection on people of other faiths observed:

> Of all the things we do as Christians, witnessing among peoples of living faiths and ideologies causes the most difficulty and confusion. In this task we are hesitant learners and need to acquire sensitivity. . . .[89]

Affirming the uniqueness of Jesus Christ, the group at the same time wished to "recognize God's creative work in the seeking for religious truth among people of other faiths."

> We see, however, the need to *distinguish between witness and dialogue,* while at the same time affirming their inter-relatedness.[90]

The subsection offered the following clarifications:

> 43. Witness may be described as those acts and words by which a Christian or community gives testimony to Christ and invites others to make their response to him. In witness we expect to share the good news of Jesus and be challenged in relation to our understanding of, and our obedience to that good news.
> 44. Dialogue may be described as that encounter where people holding different claims about ultimate reality can meet and explore these claims in a context of mutual respect. From dialogue we expect to learn more about how God is active in our world, and to appreciate for their own sake the insights and experiences people of other faiths have of ultimate reality.
> 45. Dialogue is not a device for nor a denial of Christian witness. It is rather a mutual venture to bear witness to each other and the world, in relation to different perceptions of ultimate reality.

46. While distinctions can be made between dialogue, cooperation and mutual witness, in the real experience of living in a religiously and ideologically pluralistic situation they in practice intermingle and are closely inter-related.[91]

In concluding, the subsection requested deepened theological reflection on the nature of witness and dialog and called for further study of a number of issues, including dialog with people from traditional religions, the question of sharing worship or prayer with people of other faiths, and the influence of new religious movements. It is clear that this issue group with its sharpened distinction between "witness" and "dialog" made an important contribution to the subject.

Among recommendations made by the "witness" section at Vancouver to the member churches were the following:

● to encourage the translation and distribution of "Mission and Evangelism: An Ecumenical Affirmation" as an aid to witness;

● to request churches to study the section on the poor from the Melbourne Conference report;

● to encourage the distribution and study of the WCC Guidelines on Dialogue;

● to share experiences of witness and dialog among people of living faiths, or of no religion;

● to initiate studies on "gospel and culture" in cooperation with regional councils and the WCC.[92]

Other recommendations to the WCC originating from the Sixth Assembly's "Program Guidelines Committee" were the following:

(a) to help member churches in developing an understanding of the relationship between evangelism and culture in respect of both the contextual proclamation of the Gospel in all cultures and the transforming power of the Gospel in any culture;

(b) to seek to develop dialogue with evangelicals not related to the WCC on the meaning and methods of evangelism, particularly with concern for the relation between evangelism and the wholeness of salvation and the criteria for authentic church growth; and

(c) to help to clarify the distinction between evangelism, carried out in the spiritual freedom and power of the gospel, and proselytism in all its forms, particularly in view of activities, some of which evidence an arrogant disregard for people's cultural integrity and which are sometimes—consciously or unconsciously—at the service of foreign political interests.[93]

GUIDELINES ON DIALOG WITH PEOPLE OF LIVING FAITHS AND IDEOLOGIES

The practice of dialog, its theological presuppositions, and its relationships to Christian mission and witness have been a factor in ecumenical discussions on mission since at least the time of Edinburgh 1910.[94] Prior to the Uppsala Assembly (1968) the WCC established a subunit on Dialogue with People of Living Faiths and Ideologies (DFI) as part of its Program Unit on Faith and Witness, but independent of the Commission on World Mission and Evangelism.[95] It is from this time that intensified activities related to dialog take place under the sponsorship of the WCC, and heightened interest is observed at the level of the WCC Central Committee. Because of the close links between dialog and mission at both the theological and practical levels, we shall trace the emergence of an official WCC position on dialog. We have noted that the document "Mission and Evangelism: An Ecumenical Affirmation," in its final "conviction" about "Witness among People of Living Faiths," and the issue group on "Witness in a Divided World" at the Vancouver Assembly each gave special attention to dialog. What, if anything, does the WCC Central Committee's adoption of "Guidelines on Dialogue" (1979) say about the ecumenical style of mission? This question gains additional significance in relation to separate positions on dialog taken by evangelicals and Roman Catholics.

As early as 1971 the WCC Central Committee, meeting in Addis Ababa, received an "interim policy statement" on dialog and adopted preliminary "guidelines." The fact that Christians were living in pluralistic societies was cited as a motivating factor. It was felt that Christians needed special help and encouragement in witnessing to people of other faiths or no faith. Already in the 1971 "interim policy statement," several fundamental assumptions were made explicit, from which the WCC has never departed. These are, on the one hand, commitment to the uniqueness of Jesus Christ, and on the other, respect for the integrity of the dialog partner:

> A Christian's dialogue with another implies neither a denial of the uniqueness of Christ, nor any loss of his own commitment to Christ. . . . Christians enter into all forms of dialogue from the standpoint of their faith in Jesus Christ and their obligation to witness to him. Love requires us to recognize and respect the integrity of our partners who enter into dialogue from the standpoint of their faith and commitment.[96]

Dialog offers Christians the promise of discovering new dimensions of their own faith, and entering into new relationships with people of other faiths. In dialog our Christian faith is tested and strengthened.

Dialogs may be held with various goals: to prepare for common action in society; to promote better mutual understanding; to promote more authentic indigenization of Christian faith in different cultures. Dialog must take place in freedom, allowing each partner to be understood as they understand themselves. No agreement exists, even among Christians, as to the theological implications of dialog. Further study is needed here. So far as the relation between dialog, mission, and witness is concerned, acute differences continue to divide Christians as to whether "the emphasis on dialogue will blunt the cutting edge of mission" or whether the new approach will actually further mission. The interim statement recognized that suspicion existed among dialog partners that "dialog" may simply be "a new name for proselytization." Even so, said the WCC, dialog would lose its meaning unless Christians bore witness to the salvation they receive in Jesus Christ. Such insights and "caveats" were to be found in the interim statement, and they continue to inform the later WCC statement.

In the years which followed, the WCC dialog subunit held a number of bilateral and multilateral meetings with persons of other faiths for further exploration of issues. A consultation held in Chiang Mai, Thailand, in 1977 on the theme "Dialogue in Community"[97] proved to be a turning point in the process. The statement on the community context and the theological rationale for dialog adopted at Chiang Mai was received by the WCC Central Committee at its 1977 meeting with praise for the degree of agreement and mutual understanding achieved.

Revised WCC "Guidelines" for dialog, based on the Chiang Mai statement, were adopted in 1979 and published, together with the previously approved portions, as *Guidelines on Dialogue with People of Living Faiths and Ideologies.*[98]

What had changed between the 1971 and 1979 statements? At Chiang Mai it had become clear that interfaith dialog gained realism and significance when conducted as a dialog between living communities of faith rather than as an exchange of individual scholars or specialists. Christians recognize that they are part of a wider community of humankind under God's creative rule. With their neighbors of other faiths they share many cultural values, while differing in others. Human communities are constantly changing, and both religion and ideology are recognized as potent factors for dividing the human community. As persons committed to peace, liberation, and justice, Christians are called to contribute from their own resources of faith to the development of communities based on reconciliation in a pluralistic world.

Some images which express the experience of churches scattered within the world of human communities are:

● communion in the church as sacrament of the reconciliation and unity of humankind;

● communion with God who in the fullness of the Trinity calls humankind into unity with himself;

● communion in fellowship with all members of the body of Christ through history across distinctions of race, sex, caste, and culture;

● conviction that God in Christ has set the church free for communion with all peoples and everything which is made holy by the work of God.[99]

As a "sacrament of the reconciliation and unity of humankind," Christians are acutely aware of the need to overcome confessional divisions and to work for visible church unity. In a spirit of deep humility, and renouncing all triumphalism, Christians share with fellow human beings in "a compelling pilgrimage."

Christians live out their lives in actual community with people who may be committed to faiths and ideologies other than their own. Dialog reaching across differences of faith, ideology, and culture is a part of Christian service in community. In dialog Christians actively respond to the double love command "to love God and your neighbor as your-self." In dialog Christians speak the truth in love:

> We do not see dialogue and the giving of witness as standing in any contradiction to one another. Indeed, as Christians enter dialogue with their commitment to Jesus Christ, time and again the relationship of dialogue gives opportunity for authentic witness. Thus to member church-es of the WCC we feel able with integrity to commend the way of dialogue as one in which Jesus Christ can be confessed in the world today; at the same time we feel able with integrity to assure our partners in dialogue that we come not as manipulators but as genuine fellow-pilgrims, to speak with them of what we believe God to have done in Jesus Christ who has gone before us, but whom we seek to meet anew in dialogue.[100]

As Christians engage in faithful dialog with people of other faiths and ideologies, they will not avoid asking themselves penetrating questions about the place of these people in the activity of God in history. Ap-proaching theological questions in this spirit, Christians will proceed

> . . . with *repentance*, because they know how easily they misconstrue God's revelation in Jesus Christ, betraying it in their actions and posturing as owners of God's truth rather than, as in fact they are, the undeserving recipients of grace;
> . . . with *humility*, because they so often perceive in people of other faiths and ideologies a spirituality, dedication, compassion and a wisdom which should forbid them making judgments about others as though from a position of superiority;
> . . . with *joy*, because it is not themselves they preach; it is Jesus Christ, perceived by many people of living faiths and ideologies as a prophet, holy one, teacher, example; but confessed by Christians as Lord and Saviour, Himself the faithful witness and the coming one (Rev. 1:5-7);
> . . . with *integrity*, because they do not enter into dialogue with others except in this penitent and humble joyfulness in the Lord Jesus Christ, making clear to others their own experience and witness, even as they seek to hear from others their expressions of deepest conviction and insights. All these would mean an openness and exposure, the capacity to be wounded which we see in the example of our Lord Jesus Christ and which we sum up in the word vulnerability.[101]

In the same spirit Christians will also attempt to address themselves to theological questions posed by other faiths and ideologies. Among these the following are outstanding:

(1) the doctrine of creation, as illuminated by the Trinity and the resurrection and glorification of Christ;

(2) the nature and activity of God, the Spirit, and Christ;

(3) use of the Bible as the basis for Christian reflection on issues arising from dialog;

(4) problems of church unity;

(5) the aim of dialog not as "reduction of living faiths and ideologies to a least common denominator," and not only as a comparison of symbols and concepts, but as "the enabling of a true encounter between those spiritual insights and experiences which are only found at the deepest levels of human life."[102]

Other, even more difficult questions about the activity of God in human history and the scope of divine salvation in relation to people of other faiths and ideologies are also posed, but no answers are offered. A helpful statement on "syncretism" as a possible danger is attached.

The guidelines *proper,* as recommended to the churches for study and action, are preceded by a short preface:

It is Christian faith in the Triune God . . . which calls us Christians to human relationship with our many neighbours. Such relationships include dialogue: witnessing to our deepest convictions and listening to those of our neighbours. It is Christian faith that sets us free to be open to the faiths of others, to risk, to trust and to be vulnerable. In dialogue, conviction and openness are held in balance. . . [dialog] is a way of living out Christian faith in relationship and commitment to those neighbours with whom Christians share town, cities, nations, and the earth as a whole. Dialogue is a style of living in relationship with neighbours. This in no way replaces or limits our Christian obligation to witness, as partners enter into dialogue with their respective commitments.[103]

Here follow 13 specific programmatic recommendations to the churches, printed without explanatory comments:

LEARNING AND UNDERSTANDING IN DIALOGUE

1. Churches should seek ways in which Christian communities can enter into dialogue with their neighbours of other faiths and ideologies.

2. Dialogues should normally be planned together.

3. Partners in dialogue should take stock of the religious, cultural and ideological diversity of their local situations.

4. Partners in dialogue should be free to "define themselves."

5. Dialogue should generate educational efforts in the community.

SHARING AND LIVING TOGETHER IN DIALOGUE

6. Dialogue is most vital when its participants actually share their lives together.

7. Dialogue should be pursued by sharing in common enterprises in community.

8. Partners in dialogue should be aware of their ideological commitments.

9. Partners in dialogue should be aware of cultural loyalties.

10. Dialogue will raise the question of sharing in celebrations, rituals, worship and meditation.

PLANNING FOR DIALOGUE

11. Dialogue should be planned and undertaken ecumenically, whenever possible.

12. Planning for dialogue will necessitate regional and local guidelines.

13. Dialogue can be helped by selective participation in world interreligious meetings and organizations.[104]

Of these guidelines the first, viz., that churches as local communities should seek ways of entering into dialog with their neighbors of different faiths and ideologies, is undoubtedly the most important. For the problem with dialog is not any lack of adequate theory or guidelines but the shortage of actual practice up to this time.

In these WCC Guidelines on Dialogue, along with their theological introduction, we can identify another major ecumenical achievement, paralleling "Mission and Evangelism: An Ecumenical Affirmation" and "Baptism, Eucharist and Ministry" in significance. The WCC wisely decided to detach its subunit on dialogue from the CWME. To have subordinated dialog to planning and theologizing about mission and evangelism would have been injurious to the discussion, despite the close relationship between the two. The WCC Central Committee, to its credit, wisely took a middle road between dialog as a *substitute* for mission and dialog as a *subterfuge* for mission. It maintained the integrity of both dialog in freedom and witness out of commitment.

At Vancouver (1983) the issue group on "Witness in a Divided World," as noted above, insisted on a clearer distinction between "witness" and "dialog." This distinction added nothing new, but merely reiterated the position of the 1979 Guidelines on Dialogue. Similarly, the request from the Vancouver Assembly's Programme Guidelines Committee for help in clarifying the distinction between "evangelism" carried out in the spirit of the gospel and "proselytism" in all its forms had already been adequately addressed in the WCC Guidelines for Dialogue. The request showed that the full implications of the dialog statement had not yet been grasped by the churches.

In the ecumenical movement, dialog was fast becoming more than "a style of living in relationship with neighbours." It was a new style of ecumenical action and an expression of the Christian's approach to a wide range of activities of witness, service and community relationships in a pluralistic world.

5

THE EVANGELICAL MISSIONARY MOVEMENT

For conciliar Protestants after the World Missionary Conference at Edinburgh (1910) and, increasingly after the WCC New Delhi Assembly (1961), for Orthodox as well, the ecumenical missionary tradition as represented by the International Missionary Council and later by the WCC's Commission on World Mission and Evangelism was an important frame of reference for mission planning and cooperation. But there were other organizational frameworks and consultative organs for mission of equal importance to their own constituencies.

For evangelicals, especially those from North America and their two-thirds world counterparts, the Lausanne Committee for World Evangelization (LCWE) represents a comprehensive movement for consultation, coordination, and joint planning of mission efforts. This movement grew rapidly in strength and dynamism after World War II, particularly after the 1960s. It was organized originally in parallel position to, but also partly in conscious opposition to, existing ecumenical organs for missionary cooperation. LCWE represents a conservative evangelical alternative to the conciliar missionary movement in terms of its theology, strategy, and organization. In recent years, however, some contact and dialog has taken place between evangelical representatives and persons from the conciliar and Roman Catholic mission traditions.

EVANGELICAL MISSIONARY THINKING: THE LAUSANNE MOVEMENT

The evangelical stream of missionary thinking as represented by groups related to the work of the Lausanne Committee for World Evangelization (LCWE) is often known as the "Lausanne Movement." It represents a loose coalition of persons, mission agencies, and Christian organizations sharing a common theological position and a common missionary and evangelistic purpose.[1] Following the International Congress on World Evangelization (ICOWE) held at Lausanne, Switzerland, in 1974, these groups have formed a cohesive "movement" under the direction of a governing board, the LCWE, which has met biennially since 1974.

The LCWE and its constituency include some persons and groups who share the traditions of the earlier World Missionary Conference (Edinburgh 1910) or who were involved in the work of the former IMC prior to its integration into the WCC (1961), but later became disenchanted with ecumenical mission. It also includes evangelical groups that have come on the scene more recently and which were never part of the earlier missionary movement.

Traditionally, evangelicals have been characterized by an emphasis on personal Christian experience, a desire to share the faith with others, especially through verbal witness, and a conservative doctrinal position. This position normally includes as essential affirmations: belief in the verbal inspiration and authority of the Scriptures, the Virgin Birth and divinity of Jesus Christ, the substitutionary atonement, and the physical resurrection and bodily return of Jesus Christ in judgment.

The Lausanne Movement has its strongest center in the United States, but it maintains important links with evangelicals in Britain, Scandinavia, Germany, some other European countries, and, through the missionary movement, with persons, churches, and mission organizations in Asia, Africa, and Latin America. Among the more influential members of the coalition are the Interdenominational Foreign Missions Association (IFMA), which is made up of independent faith missions and interdenominational mission societies; the Evangelical Foreign Missions Association (EFMA), the missionary arm of the National Association of Evangelicals in the USA; the Billy Graham Evangelistic

Association; the World Evangelical Fellowship (WEF); World Vision Incorporated and its research arm, MARC (Mission Advanced Research and Communication Center); InterVarsity Christian Fellowship; Campus Crusade International; the evangelical journal *Christianity Today;* and the School of Missions at Fuller Theological Seminary, Pasadena, California.[2] Each of these groups is independently organized. Prior to the 1960s, evangelicals had few formal relationships with one another.

Before 1966 evangelicals worked mainly through separate organizations to carry out their obedience to the Great Commission. Since 1966, however, many have drawn closer together through major public meetings designed to give greater visibility to the evangelical viewpoint and to explore common strategies. A characteristic of these meetings has been the growing desire to make available an evangelical alternative to what is perceived as the liberalism of mainline denominations and the ecumenical movement in general.[3]

At Wheaton, Illinois, the IFMA and the EFMA jointly sponsored a Congress on the Church's Worldwide Mission (April 9-16, 1966) which dealt with a broad agenda of issues and served as a rallying point for worldwide evangelical missionary groups. The purpose of this congress (which brought together 938 delegates from 71 countries) was to enable evangelical leaders to make plain their missionary theology and strategy over against the ecumenical movement, in the belief that the evangelical missionary movement had come of age. The *Wheaton Declaration*[4] unreservedly reaffirmed commitment to "the primacy of preaching the gospel to every creature" and called for the mobilization of the church for the "evangelization of the world in this generation." It declared that "church planting has the priority among all other mission activities"; reflected the maturity of emerging churches in the two-thirds world; and, reminiscent of the IMC Madras Meeting (1938), held that the *local church* was chiefly responsible for the continuing task of mission and evangelism. The declaration admitted the failure of evangelicals to manifest biblical oneness in Christ due to "carnal differences and personal grievances." But the congress could not find an acceptable solution for ongoing church-mission tensions, nor a formula for giving visible expression to the spiritual unity felt by evangelicals. The congress was marked by frequent attacks on the ecumenical movement.[5]

Later the same year (October 24–November 4, 1966) the Berlin World Congress on Evangelism, sponsored by *Christianity Today,* was attended by 1100 conservative evangelical leaders from more than 100 countries.[6] The main aims of this congress were to define biblical evangelism, stress its urgency, and study obstacles to evangelism and ways of overcoming them. Theologically, the Berlin Congress was committed to the final authority of the Bible and rejected all thinking on evangelism not based on Holy Scripture. Obedience to the Great Commission, understood as the practical correlate to biblical authority, required that Christians overcome their lack of zeal and passion for evangelism and engage in evangelizing the earth in the remaining third of the 20th century. Gospel and church were indissolubly related in this task; evangelism was seen as the church's primary task. The congress was particularly sensitive to the relationship between evangelism and social action. Racism within the church, it was said, constituted a denial of the gospel and a deterrent to evangelistic witness. Yet the congress was unable to do more than deplore racism in its final statement. Similarly, it struggled with the issue of evangelical unity but shied away from organizational structures to express it. The main significance of Berlin 1966 was to give larger visibility to the evangelical cause and, like Wheaton, to offer a biblically based alternative to ecumenism.[7]

LAUSANNE 1974: THE INTERNATIONAL CONGRESS ON WORLD EVANGELIZATION

The Lausanne Congress on World Evangelization (July 16-25, 1974) was a stunning advance over earlier evangelical meetings and represented a high-water mark for evangelical identity and solidarity in mission and evangelism. The 2700 participants from 150 nations— 50% of them from the two-thirds world—voiced their praise to God for his salvation and rejoiced in the evangelical fellowship they discovered in common obedience to the Great Commission:

> We are deeply stirred by what God is doing in our day, moved to penitence by our failures and challenged by the unfinished task of evangelization. We believe the Gospel is God's good news for the whole world, and we

are determined by his grace to obey Christ's commission to proclaim it to all mankind and to make disciples of every nation.[8]

Using the newly coined term "evangelization," Lausanne bridged the differences between the more limited emphases at Wheaton 1966 and Berlin 1966 and forged an evangelical united front of persons sharing world mission and evangelism interests. Moreover, the placement of evangelism within the larger and more comprehensive framework of world mission raised important questions about the nature of the gospel proclaimed and the role of the church in its proclamation.

Lausanne achieved a breakthrough in securing the adoption of the *Lausanne Covenant*,[9] a theological consensus on the basis and nature of evangelization. "History may show this Covenant to be the most significant ecumenical confession on evangelism that the church has ever produced."[10]

The Lausanne mandate arising from the 1974 congress was "to hasten the evangelization of all peoples of the world in obedience to the command of Jesus Christ and in anticipation of his return, by multiplying and strengthening the ways in which evangelical believers work together to accomplish this task through churches, missions and other Christian organizations."[11] Among the specific objectives set by LCWE for carrying out the mandate were:

(1) to advance biblical evangelization as reflected in the Lausanne Covenant;
(2) to promote spiritual renewal as a foundation to world evangelization;
(3) to be a motivator and facilitator for world evangelization through networks of relationship;
(4) to measure progress in world evangelization so as to focus prayer and other resources in anticipation of further spiritual breakthroughs.

The overriding goal of the movement—to enable persons to come to know Jesus Christ as Savior and Lord—was to be carried out through specific goals: promoting cooperative evangelistic efforts; promoting studies of biblical theology and strategies of evangelization; stimulating united prayer for world evangelization; encouraging stewardship of resources and sacrificial giving; sharing information about the progress of evangelization; sponsoring meetings at various levels; commissioning persons of vision and experience to share insights and useful models; providing for joint action; encouraging and supporting research and development; and interceding for religious liberty.[12]

How did Lausanne come about? Billy Graham, honorary chairman of the Lausanne Congress, spoke for the planning committee in an address entitled "Why Lausanne?" Graham felt hopeful because the "evangelistic cutting edge of the Church of Jesus Christ worldwide"[13] had come to Lausanne to seek ways of fulfilling Christ's last commission. The congress stood in the great tradition of movements of evangelism from the time of the early apostles until Edinburgh 1910. Their common characteristic, according to Graham, was that they took their stand on the basis of the Scriptures as the word of God, held a definite view of salvation (including the lostness of human beings and their need for redemption), strongly believed in conversion, and were convinced that evangelism was not an option but an imperative.[14]

But after Edinburgh 1910, according to Graham, the world church had "foundered" and lost much of its vision and evangelistic zeal; there were three reasons for this:

(a) loss of the authority of the message of the gospel;

(b) preoccupation with social and political problems;

(c) equal preoccupation with organizational unity.

In the ecumenical movement the spotlight had gradually shifted from evangelism to social and political action; but in the newly constituted evangelical missionary movement it would remain focused on evangelism and missions. "Evangelism," said Graham, "is the one task. . . we are unitedly determined to do."[15]

According to Graham, evangelicals were called to reaffirm their commitment to five biblical concepts essential to evangelism:

(a) the authority of Scripture;

(b) the lostness of human beings apart from Jesus Christ;

(c) that salvation is in Jesus Christ alone;

(d) that witness must be by both word and deed;

(e) the necessity of evangelism.

The congress dealt with "world evangelization," not just evangelism, because the unevangelized world consisted of both "superficially Christian populations" and "unreached" populations.[16] Lausanne must therefore keep its eyes on "the big picture of the whole world for which Christ died," including groups far away and near neighbors. Without using the term "reevangelization," Graham appeared to endorse the concept. "World evangelization means continued and increased send-ings of missionaries and evangelists from every church in every land to the unreached billions."[17]

The goals of Lausanne, as Graham saw them, were:

(a) to frame a biblical declaration on evangelism that would speak with a clear evangelical voice, while at the same time challenging the WCC;

(b) to challenge the church to complete the task of world evange-lization;

(c) to state the relationship between evangelism and social respon-sibility;

(d) to develop a new worldwide *koinonia* or fellowship among evan-gelicals of all persuasions.[18]

For Graham the drama at Lausanne revolved around the vision of Edinburgh 1910, lost by the ecumenical movement but now recovered by the world's evangelicals!

Graham would later say that the Lausanne Congress had "burst upon (the evangelical world) like a bombshell," becoming an "awakening experience" and summoning the evangelical community to "renewed zeal and new commitment."[19]

THE LAUSANNE COVENANT: PLATFORM FOR EVANGELICAL COOPERATION

The solemn act of signing and adopting the 15-point final draft of the *Lausanne Covenant* as presented to delegates at Lausanne was undoubtedly the main achievement of the 1974 Congress. The *Cove-nant* was to become the ongoing basis for evangelical cooperation in world evangelization and a further catalyst to evangelical unity. It takes the form of an affirmation of faith and then invites its signatories to enter into a "solemn covenant with God and with each other to pray, to plan, and to work together for the evangelization of the whole world."[20]

The *Covenant* is a mature, balanced, comprehensive, but concise statement of evangelical mission theology, and constitutes the center-piece and enduring monument of Lausanne. Not all of its statements are of equal import, but some must be singled out as breaking new ground or giving sharper definition to traditional evangelical positions.

THE PURPOSE OF GOD

Paragraph 1, "The Purpose of God," expresses a trinitarian understanding of mission and views the missionary task of the church as a calling of the people of God to be servants and witnesses for the extension of God's kingdom:

> We affirm our belief in the one eternal God, Creator and Lord of the world, Father, Son and Holy Spirit, who governs all things according to the purpose of his will. He has been calling out from the world a people for himself, and sending his people back into the world to be his servants and his witnesses, for the extension of his kingdom, the building up of Christ's body, and the glory of his name [LC 1].[21]

This statement clearly places the *Covenant* within the mainstream of contemporary missiological thinking and offers points of contact with all who adhere to a trinitarian understanding of *missio Dei*. This paragraph, like each subsequent section of the *Covenant,* is grounded in biblical references.

THE AUTHORITY OF THE BIBLE

"The Authority and Power of the Bible," a constant point of reference for evangelicals, stands in second place in the document:

> We affirm the divine inspiration, truthfulness and authority of both Old and New Testament Scriptures in their entirety as the only written Word of God, without error in all that it affirms, and the only infallible rule of faith and practice. We also affirm the power of God's Word to accomplish his purpose of salvation [LC 2].

This statement accurately reflects evangelical priorities: the integrity of mission can only be secured when it is firmly based on biblical authority. The *Covenant* affirms a high doctrine of scriptural authority, but avoids divisive references to modes of inspiration. The reference to the *power* of God's Word is a reminder that the Bible is not merely a *formal* authority but also a *means of grace.*

THE UNIQUENESS OF CHRIST

Another crucial statement, "The Uniqueness and Universality of Christ," deals with soteriology and the knowledge of God. The statement joins together references to the lostness of human beings apart from Jesus Christ, and the conviction that salvation is in Jesus Christ alone, as a basis for reinforcing the necessity of evangelism:

> We affirm that there is only one Savior and only one Gospel, although there is a wide diversity of evangelistic approaches. We recognize that all men have some knowledge of God. . . but we deny that this can save. . . . We also reject as derogatory to Christ and the Gospel every kind of syncretism and dialogue which implies that Christ speaks equally through all religions and ideologies. Jesus Christ, being himself the only God-man, who gave himself as the only ransom for sinners, is the only mediator between God and man. There is no other name by which we must be saved. All men are perishing because of sin, but God loves all men, not wishing that any should perish but that all should repent [LC 3].

The *Covenant* is uncompromisingly Christocentric against all tendencies to view other faiths or religious communities as valid roads to salvation. It asserts a universalism of evangelistic responsibility, but not of salvation:

> To proclaim Jesus as the "Savior of the world" is not to affirm that all men are either automatically or ultimately saved, still less to affirm that all religions offer salvation in Christ [LC3].

In spite of its acknowledgment of a wide diversity of evangelistic approaches, the statement is clearly skeptical about dialog as an approach to evangelism, and negative toward the possibility of discovering Christ more fully through dialog with persons of other faiths. It is, therefore, at odds with some ecumenical and Roman Catholic theologies of dialog and especially with the latter's evaluation of other faiths. LC 4, however, includes a more positive assessment of dialog.

THE NATURE OF EVANGELISM

"The Nature of Evangelism" distinguishes evangelization as such from "Christian presence" and "dialog." It places proclamation and conversion at the center of evangelistic activity:

> To evangelize is to spread the good news that Jesus Christ died for our sins and was raised from the dead according to the Scriptures, and that

as the reigning Lord he now offers the forgiveness of sins and the liberating gift of the Spirit to all who repent and believe. Our Christian presence in the world is indispensable to evangelism and so is that kind of dialogue whose purpose is to listen sensitively in order to understand. But evangelism itself is the proclamation of the historical, biblical Christ as Savior and Lord, with a view to persuading people to come to him personally and so be reconciled to God. . . . The results of evangelism include obedience to Christ, incorporation into his church and responsible service in the world (LC 4).

Further references in this section to the "cost of discipleship," cross-bearing, obedience to Christ, and "responsible service in the world" are indications that conversion is not understood superficially.

In his plenary address at Lausanne, John R. W. Stott agreed with the Uppsala (1968) statement that "a Christian's dialogue with another implies neither a denial of the uniqueness of Christ, nor any loss of his own commitment to Christ." He also called on evangelicals to engage in dialog with others as a token of Christian humility and love; to rid their minds of prejudices and caricatures; to struggle to listen and to see what prevents another person from hearing the gospel and seeing Christ and "to sympathize with him in all his doubts and fears and 'hang-ups.' "[22]

Yet for Stott and evangelicals generally no amount of human sensitivity could be allowed to compromise the presentation of the historic *kerygma*. Dialog and Christian presence were thus viewed as attitudinal prerequisites for evangelism, not as substitutes.

CHRISTIAN SOCIAL RESPONSIBILITY

No section of the *Covenant* was more controversial, and none more indicative of the new direction of evangelicalism, than the one on "Christian Social Responsibility." If the statement on the uniqueness of Christ demonstrated the fundamental theological conservatism of the Lausanne movement, this section witnessed to its growing prophetic consciousness, especially as advocated by the so-called radical evangelicals and many from the two-thirds world. This paragraph introduces the language of *justice* and *reconciliation* in human society and *liberation* from oppression into the heretofore detached and individualistic rhetoric of evangelicalism. It is here that the evangelical movement reaches a new turning point.[23]

We affirm that God is both the Creator and the Judge of all men. We therefore should share his concern for justice and reconciliation throughout human society and for the liberation of men from every kind of oppression. . . . Here too we express penitence both for our neglect and for having sometimes regarded evangelism and social concern as mutually exclusive. Although reconciliation with man is not reconciliation with God, nor is social action evangelism, nor is political liberation salvation, nevertheless we affirm that *evangelism and socio-political involvement are both part of our Christian duty.* For both are necessary expressions of our doctrines of God and man, our love for our neighbor and our obedience to Jesus Christ. The message of salvation implies also a message of judgment upon every form of alienation, oppression and discrimination, and we should not be afraid to denounce evil and injustice wherever they exist. . . . The salvation we claim should be transforming us in the totality of our personal and social responsibilities. Faith without works is dead [LC 5; emphasis added].

Evangelism and sociopolitical involvement were thus seen as coordinate but indispensable expressions of our obedient response to the will of God. They might not be confused, but neither could they be separated. However, their exact relationship in evangelical thinking remained to be specified.

RADICAL DISCIPLESHIP GROUP AT LAUSANNE

An ad hoc group of evangelicals at Lausanne known as the "Radical Discipleship" group sought to move the congress even further in taking a new position on Christian social responsibility. This group called on the congress to "repudiate as demonic the attempt to drive a wedge between evangelism and social action." It spoke of the gospel as "good news of liberation, of restoration, of wholeness, and of salvation that is personal, social, global and cosmic. . . ."

There is no biblical dichotomy between the Word spoken and the Word made visible in the lives of God's people. Men will look as they listen and what they see must be as one with what they hear.[24]

The Radical Discipleship group believed that evangelistic method must center in Jesus Christ, who took our humanity, suffered death, and gave himself in suffering servanthood for others.

He sends his community into the world, as the Father sent him, to identify and to agonize with men, to renounce status and demonic power, and to give himself in selfless service of others for God. Those who proclaim the Cross must be continually marked by the Cross. . . . We need to meet men on their own ground and be particularly attentive to the powerless.[25]

From this it is evident that while many at Lausanne interpreted the section on Christian responsibility primarily as noting an important distinction between proclamation and Christian social involvement, others were prepared to view it as a call for radical changes in existing styles of Christian living and evangelism. In point of fact, the relationship between the *Covenant's* sections on evangelism and on social responsibility continued to be so troubling to many in the evangelical constituency that a major consultation on the subject had to be convened in Grand Rapids in 1982 in order to settle the issue.[26]

CHURCH AND MISSION ISSUES

The next four sections of the *Covenant* (LC 6-9) form a cluster of statements affirming, respectively, church-related missions (but also mission in the world); mission in unity; partnership in mission; and mission from and to all six continents in view of the urgency of the unfinished task. The echo of earlier IMC policy statements is evident in these sections:

Christ sends his redeemed people into the world as the Father sent him. . . . We need to break out of our ecclesiastical ghettos and permeate non-Christian society. . . . World evangelization requires the *whole church to take the whole Gospel to the whole world*. The church is at the very center of God's cosmic purpose and is his appointed means of spreading the Gospel [LC 6; emphasis added].

Visible unity in truth is God's purpose, and evangelism also summons Christians to unity because disunity undermines the gospel of reconciliation.

Organizational unity may take many forms and does not necessarily forward evangelism. Yet we who share the same biblical faith should be closely united in fellowship, work and witness. We confess that our testimony has sometimes been marred by sinful individualism and needless duplication. We pledge ourselves to seek a deeper unity in truth, worship, holiness and mission [LC 7].

The development of regional and functional cooperation for strategic planning and for sharing of resources was seen to be a necessary consequence. The era of Western mission dominance was over:

> We rejoice that a new missionary era has dawned. The dominant role of western missions is fast disappearing. God is raising up from the younger churches a great new resource for world evangelization, and is thus demonstrating that the responsibility to evangelize belongs to the whole body of Christ. All churches should therefore be asking God and themselves what they should be doing both to reach their own area and to send missionaries to other parts of the world. . . . Thus a growing partnership of churches will develop and the universal character of Christ's Church will be more clearly exhibited [LC 8].

CALL FOR MISSIONARY COOPERATION

The scope of the unfinished task and the present receptivity to the gospel call for a concerted effort by churches and parachurch agencies to launch new efforts to achieve world evangelization on a six-continent basis:

> More than 2700 million people, which is more than two-thirds of mankind, have yet to be evangelized. We are ashamed that so many have been neglected; it is a standing rebuke to us and to the whole church. . . . Missionaries should flow ever more freely from and to all six continents in a spirit of humble service. The goal should be, by all available means and at the earliest possible time, that every person will have the opportunity to hear, understand and receive the good news [LC 9].

As an encouragement to the growth of local self-reliance in mission, the *Covenant* gives its qualified endorsement to a partial moratorium on outside resources:

> A reduction of foreign missionaries and money in an evangelized country may sometimes be necessary to facilitate the national church's growth in self-reliance and to release resources for unevangelized areas [LC 9].

The statement reflects a concern to diminish the competing role of Western missions, and above all of parachurch agencies, in the missionary task of local churches.

Other statements deal with "Evangelism and Culture" (LC 10); "Education and Leadership" (LC 11); "Spiritual Conflict" (LC 12), an attack on worldliness and secularism in the church; "Freedom and Persecution" (LC 13); "The Power of the Holy Spirit" (LC 14); and "The Return of Christ" (LC 15). In this faith the delegates at Lausanne entered into "a solemn covenant with God and with each other" to pray, plan, and work together for world evangelization.

LAUSANNE FOLLOW-UP: THEOLOGY, STRATEGY AND CROSS-CULTURAL EVANGELISM

The adoption of the *Lausanne Covenant* was a milestone in the development of the evangelical missionary movement, but not in any sense the end of the road. For, following the 1974 congress, the Lausanne movement applied itself to a series of deferred tasks. Participants at Lausanne had indicated their overwhelming desire to continue the momentum attained through some kind of postcongress body. This was to be achieved with minimal organizational structure by means of a cooperative, mainly volunteer organism utilizing a network of contacts and relationships, and with a small secretariat, all under the guidance of the international Lausanne Committee for World Evangelization (LCWE). At its first meeting LCWE identified four areas of continuing concern and appointed working groups for (1) *theology*, (2) *strategy*, (3) *intercession*, and (4) *communication*. The Theology and Education Group, later renamed the Theology Working Group (TWG), was given the mandate of exploring the implications of the *Lausanne Covenant* and promoting the study of theological issues, including the relation between theology and practice. The Strategy Working Group (SWG), cooperating closely with MARC-World Vision (Mission Advanced Research Center), has concerned itself with resources and methodologies for completing the unfinished task, and since 1979 particularly with the "Unreached Peoples" project.[27]

The Lausanne movement as a whole has been characterized by its intensive engagement in strategy development, research, and evangelistic methodologies based upon biblical foundations but also incorporating management principles and findings from the social sciences.

HOMOGENEOUS UNIT PRINCIPLE

One of the first issues to be examined by the Theology and Education Group was the controversial "homogeneous unit principle" advocated by Donald McGavran and protagonists of the Church Growth Movement. The philosophy of church growth was strongly entrenched at the School of World Missions of Fuller Theological Seminary, and was in many ways the dominant missiological option favored by American evangelicals. According to McGavran, biblically based missions require the discipling of whole peoples. God wills the numerical growth of Christians through "people movements." Factors that assist or hinder church growth can be analyzed through interdisciplinary methods. Churches should normally show a minimal growth of 50% in one decade. Mission agencies should concentrate their resources on rapidly growing churches, avoiding entrapment in other causes.[28]

Serious objections were raised by some evangelicals to McGavran's use of the term "homogeneous unit" and particularly to his assumption that "people like to become Christians without crossing racial, linguistic or class barriers."[29] Could a church organized on the homogeneous unit principle reflect the unity and universality of the church universal as a new reality in Christ? Is numerical growth the priority when considered in relation to the struggle against racism and tribalism? And what about the prophetic task of the church, the call to repentance and reconciliation, and the enunciation of ethical standards? Many evangelicals felt called on the basis of the *Lausanne Covenant* itself to raise such questions.

A consultation called by LCWE's Theology and Education Group at Pasadena, California (May 31–June 2, 1977) to evaluate the "homogeneous unit principle" as applied to evangelistic methodology concluded that a conflict of principle might indeed exist between the methodology of church growth, wrongly applied, and the spirit of the *Lausanne Covenant*. It said:

> No evangelist has the right to conceal either the offence *(skandalon)* of the gospel which is Jesus Christ and his cross, or any ethical implication of the gospel which is relevant to the particular situation in which he is preaching it.[30]

In the consultation process, positive and negative features of the church growth methodology were tested and critically evaluated. A church based on the homogenous unit principle could be legitimate and authentic, it was felt, but never complete in itself.

GOSPEL AND CULTURE CONSULTATION

A follow-up consultation held in Willowbank, Bermuda (January 6-13, 1978), also organized by the Theology and Education Group, dealt with a range of issues connected with "Gospel and Culture." The *Lausanne Covenant* in its paragraph on this subject had made striking statements in support of contextualization and against the wrongful imposition of alien cultures. The goal was "the rise of churches deeply rooted in Christ and closely related to their culture."

> Culture must always be tested and judged by Scripture. . . . The Gospel does not presuppose the superiority of any culture to another. . . . Missions have all too frequently exported with the Gospel an alien culture, and churches have sometimes been in bondage to culture rather than to the Scripture. Christ's evangelists must humbly seek to empty themselves of all but their personal authenticity in order to become the servants of others, and churches must seek to transform and enrich culture, all for the glory of God [LC 10].

The Willowbank Consultation dealt with issues of Christ and culture in much greater detail, considering the role of culture in relation to its biblical meaning, the cultural context of the Scriptures, communicating the gospel through culture, missionary spirituality based on the incarnation, culture in the experience of conversion, and culture in church formation. The subtitle of the consultation, "the contextualization of Word and Church in a missionary situation," accurately reflected the scope of its concerns.

The consultation approved the principle that all churches must "contextualize the gospel in order to share it effectively in their own culture."[31] Here again the Lausanne movement demonstrated its special aptitude for combining the tools of linguistic and cultural analysis with biblical principles in developing a culturally sensitive approach to contextual proclamation and church planting.

SIMPLE LIFE-STYLE CONSULTATION

A third consultation dealing with "An Evangelical Commitment to Simple Life-Style" is of special significance because of the way in which its concerns parallel those of the 1980 Melbourne CWME Conference and the 1979 Puebla Roman Catholic Bishops Conference. The

International Consultation on Simple Life-Style was jointly sponsored by the Lausanne Theology and Education Group and the World Evangelical Fellowship, and held in a London suburb (March 17-21, 1980). It was ostensibly called to deal responsibly with implications of a statement found in the *Covenant:*

> All of us are shocked by the poverty of millions and disturbed by the injustices which cause it. Those of us who live in affluent circumstances accept our duty to develop a simple life-style in order to contribute more generously to both relief and evangelism [LC 9].

The actual content of the London consultation went far beyond simple living, stewardship, or benevolence and touched precisely on God's preferential option for the poor, divine judgment on oppressors, the pattern of Christ's own identification with the poor, the risk of suffering for Christ's sake, and Christian support for changes in the political structures—themes seldom articulated with such passion in evangelical mission circles. Uniting prophetic challenge with evangelistic commitment, the report of the life-style consultation is surely one of the most daring to come from signatories of the *Lausanne Covenant*. Little wonder that the consultation planners found the week "historic and transforming."

Here are some key statements from the text of the consultation, reproduced without comment.[32]

> We are disturbed by the injustice of the world, concerned for its victims, and moved to repentance for our complicity in it. . . .
> *Creation:* We worship God as the Creator of all things. . . . We therefore denounce environmental destruction, wastefulness and hoarding. We deplore the misery of the poor who suffer as a result of these evils.
> *Stewardship:* By unfaithful stewardship, in which we fail to conserve the earth's finite resources, to develop them fully or to distribute them justly, we both disobey God and alienate people from his purpose for them. We are determined, therefore, to honour God as the owner of all things. . . .
> *Poverty and Wealth:* We affirm that involuntary poverty is an offence against the goodness of God. It is related in the Bible to powerlessness, for the poor cannot protect themselves. God's call to rulers is to use their power to defend the poor, not to exploit them. The Church must stand with God and the poor against injustice, suffer with them, and call on

rulers to fulfil their God-appointed role. . . . The kingdom is a free gift offered to all, but it is especially good news for the poor because they benefit most from the changes it brings.

We believe that Jesus still calls some people (perhaps even us) to follow him in a life-style of total, voluntary poverty. He calls all his followers to an inner freedom from the seduction of riches. . . . We resolve to get to know poor and oppressed people, to learn issues of injustice from them, to seek to relieve their suffering, and to include them regularly in our prayers.

The New Community: This principle of generous and sacrificial sharing, expressed in holding ourselves and our goods available for people in need, is an indispensable characteristic of every Spirit-filled church. So those of us who are affluent in any part of the world are determined to do more to relieve the needs of less privileged believers. . . . In the same spirit, we must seek ways to transact the church's corporate business with minimum expenditure on travel, food and accommodation.

Personal Life-Style: Our Christian obedience demands a simple life-style, irrespective of the needs of others. Nevertheless, the fact that 800 million people are destitute and that 10,000 die of starvation every day make any other life-style indefensible. . . . We intend to reexamine our income and expenditure, in order to manage on less and give away more. . . . Those of us who belong to the West need the help of our Third World brothers and sisters in evaluating our standards of spending. . . .

International Development: One quarter of the world's population enjoys unparalleled prosperity, while another quarter endures grinding poverty. This gross disparity is an intolerable injustice; we refuse to acquiesce in it. The call for a New International Economic Order expresses the justified frustration of the Third World.

Justice and Politics: We are also convinced that the present situation of social injustice is so abhorrent to God that a large measure of change is necessary. . . . Poverty and excessive wealth, militarism and the arms industry, and the unjust distribution of capital, land and resources are issues of power and powerlessness. Without a shift of power through structural change, these problems cannot be solved. The Christian church, along with the rest of society, is inevitably involved in politics. . . . Servants of Christ must express his lordship in their political, social and economic commitments and their love for their neighbours by taking part in the political process.

Evangelism: The call to a responsible life-style must not be divorced from the call to responsible witness. For the credibility of our message is seriously diminished whenever we contradict it by our lives. It is impossible with integrity to proclaim Christ's salvation if he has evidently not saved us from greed, or his lordship if we are not good stewards of our possessions, or his love if we close our hearts against the needy. When Christians care for each other and for the deprived, Jesus Christ becomes more visibly attractive.

The Lord's Return: The Lord Jesus is coming back soon to judge, save and to reign. His judgment will fall upon the greedy . . . and upon all oppressors. For on that day, the King will sit upon his throne and separate the saved from the lost. Those who have ministered to him by ministering to one of the least of his needy brothers and sisters will be saved, for the reality of saving faith is exhibited in serving love. . . . All of us need to hear again this solemn warning of Jesus.

The statement closes with a call for humble commitment "to develop a just and simple life-style" and to provide support and encouragement to others in this commitment. In encouraging the publication and study of this paper, the LCWE appends a note that it "does not necessarily endorse every viewpoint expressed in it."

EVANGELISM AND SOCIAL RESPONSIBILITY

Of greater significance for the continuing health and well-being of the Lausanne movement, from an organizational point of view, was the convening of an international consultation in Grand Rapids (June 19-25, 1982) on The Relationship between Evangelism and Social Responsibility.[33] The consultation was jointly sponsored by the Theological Working Group of LCWE and the Theological Commission of the World Evangelical Fellowship.

The urgency of holding this consultation was underscored by remarks attributed to some evangelical delegates at the Pattaya Consultation (1980) that LCWE was insufficiently concerned with social justice, and that the committee had in fact regressed from its earlier firm commitment to "Christian Social Responsibility" as expressed in the 1974 *Lausanne Covenant* (LC 5).[34] At the same time, others on the more conservative end of the evangelical spectrum were suggesting that advocates of a strong position on social responsibility might be deserting the historic gospel of the grace of God.

The Grand Rapids Consultation thus took place at a time of "considerable controversy and confusion among evangelicals."[35] The range of divergent views and disagreements was so marked that fear was even expressed that the consultation might not have a positive outcome. In the face of this explosive potential the LCWE opted to approach the issues by means of serious and unhurried theological reflection, making use of Bible study, prayer, and group discussions.

The *Lausanne Covenant* had affirmed that "in the mission of the church's sacrificial service evangelism is *primary*" (LC 6), but it did not explain the relationship between "the Nature of Evangelism" (LC 4) and "Christian Social Responsibility" (LC 5). The consultation had to frame a biblical response in the face of various alternatives:

● that social responsibility is *a distraction* from, or even a *betrayal* of evangelism;

● that social responsibility *is* evangelism;

● that social responsibility is a *manifestation*—or a *consequence*—or a *partner* to evangelism, etc.;

● that social responsibility and evangelism are *distinct* but *equal* components of the church's ministry.[36]

At stake in these discussions was the unity and continuing effectiveness of the Lausanne movement. In the words of John R. W. Stott, the co-chair:

> For many fear that the more we evangelicals are committed to the one, the less we shall be committed to the other; that if we commit ourselves to both, one is bound to suffer; and in particular that a preoccupation with social responsibility will be sure to blunt our evangelistic zeal.[37]

The above statement succinctly expresses one major difference in style or orientation between the ecumenical or conciliar view of mission and evangelism and that of the Lausanne movement. Would evangelicals be able to live with their profession of *wholeness* as expressed in LC 6 ("world evangelization requires the whole church to take the whole gospel to the whole world") or would they end up by surrendering wholeness for evangelical clarity?

The Grand Rapids Consultation, having affirmed both the "call to world evangelization" and the "call to social responsibility," and having examined their relationship from the standpoint of history and eschatology, was able to settle on a compromise formula reflecting the historic reality of more than one kind of relationship. Said the consultation report:

> What has emerged from our discussion is that there is no one relationship in which they are joined, but that there are at least three equally valid

relationships. First, social activity is a *consequence* of evangelism. That is, evangelism is the means by which God brings people to new birth, and their new life manifests itself in the service of others.

Secondly, social activity can be a *bridge* to evangelism. It can break down prejudice and suspicion, open closed doors, and gain a hearing for the Gospel. Jesus sometimes performed works of mercy before proclaiming the Good News of the Kingdom.

Thirdly, social activity not only follows evangelism as its consequence and aim, and precedes it as its bridge, but also accompanies it as its *partner*. They are like the two blades of a pair of scissors or the two wings of a bird. This partnership is clearly seen in the public ministry of Jesus, who not only preached the Gospel but fed the hungry and healed the sick. In his ministry, *kerygma* (proclamation) and *diakonia* (service) went hand in hand. His words explained his works, and his works dramatized his words.[38]

The first point, social activity as a *consequence* of evangelism and of conversion to Christ, continued the tradition of American evangelicalism advocated by Charles G. Finney in the 19th century. The second point, social activity as a *bridge* to evangelism, had long been recognized in the history of the overseas missionary movement. The third point, social activity as a *partner* to evangelism, had been prominent in the thinking of the WCC Department of Evangelism with its tripartite emphasis on comprehensive evangelism as *kerygma* + *diakonia* + *koinonia*.

The Grand Rapids Report concludes with "Guidelines for Action" which show considerable restraint in comparison to similar guidelines coming from the 1980 International Consultation on Simple Life-Styles. This greater tentativeness is particularly evident in the guideline from Grand Rapids dealing with the church's involvement in sociopolitical action, where various approaches are analyzed but no clear mandate is offered.[39]

Through the Grand Rapids consultation, at any rate, the LCWE had maintained the viability of the Lausanne movement, even if its solution to the problem was more pragmatic than theological. Moreover, the approach taken by LCWE to the solution of a divisive theological issue demonstrated the flexibility of its leadership and the growing plurality of views united under the umbrella of the *Lausanne Covenant*.

STRATEGIES FOR CROSS-CULTURAL EVANGELISM: FINDING AND REACHING UNREACHED PEOPLES

Even as the theological commission appointed by LCWE was carrying out its appointed task, the Lausanne movement's Strategy Working Group, in close collaboration with MARC-World Vision, was actively pursuing novel strategies for cross-cultural evangelism. The theoretical basis for a renewed concentration on cross-cultural evangelism was set forth at the Lausanne Congress in a crucial address by Ralph Winter.[40] Briefly stated, Winter's novel thesis was that the spread of the gospel and the growth of a Christian community in each continent and nation had given rise to a serious misunderstanding, viz., that the traditional missionary task of making disciples from all nations was now essentially completed, and that the work of mission sending could now be easily completed through evangelistic efforts by local churches in each region. This view is mistaken, Winter said, because "most non-Christians in the world today are not culturally near neighbors of any Christians, and . . . it will take a special kind of 'cross-cultural' evangelism to reach them."[41]

Winter described different types of evangelism in terms of linguistic and cultural differences and difficulties involved: $E-0$ stands for the renewal of nominal Christians; $E-1$ is evangelism of near neighbors; $E-2$ is evangelism of culturally or linguistically related groups; $E-3$, the most demanding type, is evangelism of culturally distant groups. Winter sums up the process as follows:

> The master pattern of the expansion of the Christian movement is first for special E-2 and E-3 efforts to cross cultural barriers into new communities and to establish strong, on-going, vigorously evangelizing denominations, and then for that national church to carry the work forward on the really high-powered E-1 level. We are thus forced to believe that until every tribe and tongue has a strong, powerfully evangelizing church in it, and thus an E-1 witness within it, E-2 and E-3 efforts coming from outside are still essential and highly urgent.[42]

Four out of five non-Christians are beyond the reach of any local evangelism, Winter added, and will never have an opportunity to become Christians apart from special cross-cultural evangelism efforts from outside. The vast majority of foreign missionaries are tied down by nurture activities among existing Christian communities. As a consequence, some 827 million Chinese, 664 million Muslims, 502 million Hindus, and 403 million other non-Christians would never have an opportunity of hearing the gospel. Some respondents to Winter at Lausanne disputed his facts, calculations, and anthropological or spiritual assumptions, but he did succeed in lifting up renewed cross-cultural evangelism as a crucial priority in completing the unfinished task.[43]

UNREACHED PEOPLE PROJECT

Following Lausanne, LCWE's Strategy Working Group began the task of identifying, classifying, and reaching an estimated 15,000 to 25,000 "unreached people groups," and this resulted in the production of two manuals on the methodology of reaching "unreached peoples"[44] and a series of annual directories containing data on their identity.[45] A "people group" is a significantly large sociological grouping of individuals who perceive themselves to have a common affinity for one another. An "unreached people" is any group that is less than 20% practicing Christian. When the 20% figure is reached, it is assumed that the local church will be able to complete the evangelistic task. The goal of world evangelization is then in sight when each of the 15,000 to 25,000 unreached and hidden people groups is individually targeted for cross-cultural evangelism. In this view, the world must be evangelized "not one country at a time, not one religion at a time, not one person at a time . . . but one people at a time."[46] The LCWE has analyzed some 2900 unreached people groups in country profiles that are computer-stored for easy availability to any interested group.[47]

Of the world's three billion people who are not Christians, only one billion can be reached by Christians who speak their language and understand their culture (E-1 evangelism). The other two billion are "hidden people," living in places where no Christians can see them. The major tasks facing the church are therefore:

(a) to evangelize the millions of nominal Christians included in the one billion Christians;

(b) to reach the one billion non-Christians with whom we are in immediate contact; and

(c) to discover the more than two billion people who are untouched by any Christian witness and develop strategies for reaching them.[48]

In October 1980 a World Consultation on Frontier Missions was held in Edinburgh with a focus on frontier areas and peoples currently beyond the reach of the gospel. Its slogan was "a church for every people by the year 2000." Both the EFMA and the IFMA have devoted special conferences to problems and progress in reaching the unreached. The U.S. Center for World Mission, established at Pasadena, California, in 1976 under the leadership of Ralph Winter, seeks to enroll and train student candidates for frontier missions and has helped to launch the new *International Journal of Frontier Missions.*[49]

The basic thrust of LCWE's strategy for cross-cultural evangelism appears to be Donald McGavran's assumptions about church growth and "homogeneous units," modified by the addition of Ralph Winter's thesis concerning the evangelization of "unreached peoples," and concretized by MARC's assiduous compilation since 1979 of "hidden people" directories.

CONSULTATION ON WORLD EVANGELIZATION, PATTAYA, THAILAND (1980)

A second major LCWE-sponsored evangelical Consultation on World Evangelization (COWE) met at Pattaya, Thailand (June 16-27, 1980). Its theme, taken from Rom. 10:14-17, was "How Shall They Hear?" Compared to Lausanne 1974, Pattaya was a far smaller "working convention," numbering slightly more than 800 delegates and observers, about 45% of whom came from the two-thirds world, all invited on the basis of their personal support for the *Lausanne Covenant.*

COWE 1980 was in effect two consultations running in parallel: one geared to the development of new strategies for cross-cultural evangelism, and the other to an evaluation of the progress of world evangelization since Lausanne 1974.[50] The "unreached peoples" project was already in operation, and several consultations had already been convened to deal with theological issues. Pattaya's stated purposes were:

(1) to seek fresh vision and power for the task Christ has given to his church until he comes;

(2) to assess the state of world evangelization, its progress and hindrances;

(3) to complete an extended study program on theological and stra-
tegical issues related to world evangelization, already begun in many
regions, and to share its results;

(4) to develop specific evangelistic strategies related to different
unreached peoples; and

(5) to review the mandate of the LCWE and determine the role it
might play in furthering these objectives.[51]

At Pattaya, 17 "miniconsultations" met simultaneously, each under
its own coordinator, for the purpose of studying theological issues and
strategies related to reaching particular groups through cross-cultural
evangelism.

THAILAND STATEMENT

A summary statement was also issued from the consultation. En-
dorsing the *Lausanne Covenant* in its entirety as the continuing basis
for common activity, the Thailand Statement reaffirmed the "mandate
for world evangelization" and the primacy of evangelism over social
action in that mandate:

> We have been freshly burdened for the vast numbers who have never
> heard the good news of Christ and are lost without him. We have been
> made ashamed of our lack of vision and zeal, and of our failure to live
> out the gospel in its fulness, for these things have lessened our obedience
> and compromised our witness.[52]

The mandate was urgent and is still binding on all Christian people,
since two-thirds of the world's four and one-half billion people have
not had a proper opportunity to receive Christ.

> If therefore we do not commit ourselves with urgency to the task of
> evangelization, we are guilty of an inexcusable lack of human compas-
> sion.[53]

The Thailand Statement affirmed the "people group" approach and,
by implication, the priority of cross-cultural evangelism as the task of
the church in all countries. Yet it also drew attention to the importance
of reaching larger numbers of persons who are "already Christians in
name, yet still need to be evangelized because they have not understood
the gospel or responded to it." It recognized the local church as "the

principal agency for evangelism, whose total membership must therefore be mobilized and trained." It called for sensitivity to other people's cultural patterns, and stressed changes in personal missionary attitudes:

• *Love:* we cannot evangelize if we do not love;
• *Humility:* other people's resistance to the gospel has sometimes been our fault;
• *Integrity:* our witness loses credibility when we contradict it by our life or life-style;
• *Power:* we are engaged in a spiritual battle with demonic forces. Strategy and organization are not enough; we need to pray earnestly for the power of the Holy Spirit.[54]

The Thailand Statement also included a section on strengthening evangelical cooperation in global evangelization, and striving for visible expression of oneness in Christ. It reflected keen awareness of continuing obstacles to unity among evangelicals, based on differences in church authority or in evangelistic strategy. "These and other tensions are real and must be frankly faced."[55]

LCWE received from the Thailand Consultation a further mandate to act as "a catalyst for world evangelization," and to stimulate co-operative activity throughout the world on the basis of the *Lausanne Covenant.* The statement closed with 12 pledges recommitting the delegates to Christ and the unfinished task.

MINICONSULTATIONS ON MISSION

Pattaya's enduring accomplishment lay in the holding of 17 parallel miniconsultations concentrating on reaching particular peoples for Christ. These working groups built on a pre-Pattaya study process involving hundreds of local groups which considered issues of evangelistic methodology and strategy. The topics were: (1) nominal Protestants; (2) nominal Orthodox; (3) nominal Roman Catholics; (4) city dwellers, large city; (5) city dwellers, inner city; (6) secularists; (7) traditional religionists, Africa; (8) traditional religionists, Oceania; (9) traditional religionists, Latin America and the Caribbean; (10) Buddhists: (11) mystics and cultists; (12) Hindus; (13) Jews; (14) Marxists; (15) Muslims; (16) Chinese; and (17) refugees.[56]

These consultations concretized the mission task by breaking it down into specific groups needing to be approached contextually and on the basis of methodological considerations. Reevangelizing nominal Christians was a central concern alongside the newer task of identifying unreached peoples. Significantly, the "homogeneous unit principle" could not be strictly applied in dealing with groups presenting as much internal diversity as nominal Protestants, secularists, Marxists, or Buddhists.

The reports are of uneven quality and of unequal value, but they accurately reflect the pragmatic interest of the Lausanne movement in developing concrete strategies and experience-based methodologies for evangelization.

One of the more successful probes coming out of the Pattaya Consultation was the one dealing with the evangelization of large cities. After 1980, strategy consultations and case-study workshops on urban evangelism were held in 38 large cities in Asia, Africa, Latin America, and Europe, and in an additional 18 in North America. Local church leaders received training in multidimensional approaches to ministry in large cities based on cooperation, communication, and joint exploration of resources.[57]

Alongside the evangelization of great *urban* areas in all six continents, LCWE Chairperson Leighton Ford selected three other areas for possible concentration of effort in coming decades: (1) Islam, (2) the secular West; and (3) the poor.[58]

THE LAUSANNE MOVEMENT EVALUATED

In the 20-year period after 1966, evangelicals reconstituted themselves as a distinct alternative to the conciliar ecumenical movement. The Lausanne Movement, as a coalition of individual groups and movements brought together by the Lausanne Congress (1974), reclaimed the historic legacy of Edinburgh 1910 and offered itself as the true inheritor of that older movement. To this challenge the conciliar missionary movement was increasingly sensitive, especially after 1975, and could not avoid responding.

In the *Lausanne Covenant* evangelicals forged a broad-based platform for missionary cooperation. Its distinctive marks were faithfulness to scriptural authority and the offer of salvation exclusively through Jesus Christ. They issued a renewed call to evangelize the two-thirds of the world's four and one-half billion people who have had no proper opportunity to receive Jesus Christ. They resisted various temptations to become preoccupied with sociopolitical issues or organizational unity at the expense of evangelism. In so doing, they accomplished most of the goals set forth by Billy Graham at the outset of the Lausanne Congress.

Evangelicals also contributed significantly to the clarification of theological issues in mission, and to the development of new strategies, methodologies, and analytical approaches to cross-cultural mission. In the 13-year period beginning with 1974, an incredible number (more than 100) of conferences at the national, regional, or world levels were held to deal with some aspect of mission theology, strategy, or cooperation, each appealing in some way to the *Lausanne Covenant.*

Theological reflection and strategy development seemed at times to move in different and almost opposite directions, the first oriented toward biblical revelation and the second more toward measurable results. Soon after Lausanne, this was observable in a confrontation between advocates of church-growth philosophy and other evangelicals who questioned the use of the "homogeneous unit" principle. Could the tools provided by social sciences, computerized data, and business management be so employed as to yield authentic results for the kingdom of God? Evangelicals recognized the tension between the two approaches, and the risks in combining them, but they were not averse to joining prayer to activism, or hitching gospel faithfulness to the newest technology.

Overall, the Lausanne movement appeared to be giving evangelicalism a new spirit—a fresh blend of evangelical tradition with modernity—much as Vatican II had done for Roman Catholics through the process of *aggiornamento.* Evangelicalism was demonstrating that it could adapt to the modern world without surrendering biblical principles or forsaking the missionary mandate. This is seen in the *Lausanne Covenant's* critical reflection on the meaning of culture, its condemnation of imperialist attitudes, and the stress laid on presenting the gospel within the local context.

Evangelicals now moved increasingly toward a church-centered mission stance in which the local church was viewed as the principal agent in evangelism, and elements from older IMC formulas were taken over. Parachurch groups were held accountable for maintaining a spirit of Christian unity, and urged to move toward something like de facto integration with local churches.

In raising the issue of simple life-styles as a missionary concern, and calling for penitence on the part of affluent Christians, evangelicals were leading the way.

Certainly, the theological relationship between evangelism and social responsibility continued to be troubling, but, after the Grand Rapids Consultation (1982), even that vexing issue appeared to be yielding to solution.

EVANGELICALISM'S NEW FACE

Yet, after the Lausanne Congress (1976), but especially after the Pattaya Consultation (1980), not all evangelicals were in agreement that evangelicalism had been given a "new face," and certainly not a unified one. At Lausanne the "radical discipleship" group had given a powerful witness against efforts to "drive a wedge between evangelism and social action," or to create "a dichotomy between the Word spoken and the Word made visible" in people's lives. This group sought a consistent *Christological* understanding of evangelism, based on servanthood and the cross.[59] Its witness was directed against those in the evangelical movement who in their view were not taking the consequences of the gospel seriously enough.

In a 1976 post-Lausanne symposium on "The New Face of Evangelicalism," C. Rene Padilla, a respected Latin American evangelical, enthusiastically observed that Lausanne had updated the evangelical agenda by eliminating North American pragmatism, returning biblical theology to its proper basis, giving a deathblow to superficial church planting, eliminating the dichotomy between evangelism and church renewal, and refusing to separate conversion from a radical change in life-style. In his view, the *Covenant* showed that "biblical evangelism is inseparable from social responsibility and church renewal."[60] Subsequent developments would show that this optimistic estimate was not fully warranted.

At Pattaya 1980 those evangelicals who sought to bring about change and reorientation within the Lausanne movement had even greater cause for disappointment.[61] Deeper underlying tensions were not so much resolved as repressed. The LCWE leadership sought to hold to its firm commitment to give single-minded attention to the completion of the task of world evangelization. This meant that disruptive issues such as social justice, the obligation to the poor and the oppressed, and the call for radical changes in evangelical life-styles—matters strongly advocated at the LCWE Consultation on Simple Life-Style and at the WCC-CWME Melbourne Conference just preceding Pattaya—could not receive more than lip service at Pattaya. Discussion was carefully controlled so as to eliminate deviation from the LCWE-proposed agenda.

At Pattaya "A Statement of Concerns" about the direction of the Lausanne movement, reportedly signed by more than 200 delegates and presented to the LCWE Executive Committee, was never discussed in plenary session. Originating in the concern expressed by some African delegates over the contradiction between evangelical witness and support for apartheid, the statement requested the LCWE leadership to form study groups and to develop guidelines on "how evangelicals who support oppression and discrimination . . . can be reached by the gospel and challenged to repent."[62]

Meeting in the post-Pattaya period, the 1982 Grand Rapids Consultation on the Relationship between Evangelism and Social Responsibility offered yet another opportunity to seek deeper evangelical agreement. It produced a formal compromise statement on the consultation subject, but in reality offered only qualified support for evangelicals seeking a stronger mandate for their participation in movements for justice and liberation.

WHEATON 1983

In 1983, however, the World Evangelical Fellowship convened an international conference on "The Nature and Mission of the Church" at Wheaton, Illinois. Consultation III of this meeting, dealing with "The Church in Response to Human Need," went well beyond the findings of the Grand Rapids Consultation in declaring that noninvolvement in political struggles for justice "lends tacit support to the existing order. There is no escape: either we challenge the evil structures of society or we support them." It affirmed that Christian involvement in the struggle against both personal and societal sin is mandated by the need for "transformation," understood biblically in the light of the good news about Jesus, and best described by the biblical vision of the kingdom of God.[63]

Although the statement by the WEF-sponsored 1983 Wheaton Conference was not binding on LCWE, it could be understood as a critique of the more cautious Grand Rapids statement, as a mild rebuke to LCWE for its hesitancy, and as one more effort by progressive evangelicals to move evangelicalism in the direction of greater commitment to action for justice.

Returning to Pattaya 1980, we may say that *two faces* of evangelicalism met there but failed to resolve their differences. The traditional face, represented by the LCWE leadership, was determined to forward the task of world evangelization seemingly without hindrance or distraction. The other, "radical discipleship" face, joined with many voices from the two-thirds world, continued to ask whether the world *could* or *should* be evangelized on the basis of a gospel interpretation many considered narrow, distorted, or emaciated. Between these two faces undoubtedly lay a variety of other positions.

At Pattaya the evangelical movement was apparently not organizationally secure enough or sufficiently mature to deal with tensions and unresolved differences that threatened to work their way to the surface and to destroy the movement's incipient unity. Differences over the "priority" of evangelism in relation to action for justice and social responsibility in reality concealed deeper differences among evangelicals about the nature of the gospel itself, especially the impact of the gospel upon the world, its claims on the Christian, and the shape of the kingdom.

Pleas for greater unity among evangelicals and for lessening of tension and suspicion between local churches and outside parachurch agencies pointed to unresolved ecclesiological differences which continued to beset the movement. Who was to be the bearer of mission: the local church (as stated by official documents), or free-lance evangelistic agencies sometimes ignoring the existence of these local churches and working in an uneasy and competitive relationship with them?

Underlying this issue was yet another: was the Lausanne movement destined to continue as a movement of interested individuals and groups, or could it grow into a movement of churches?

These same issues erupted time and again in the conciliar missionary movement, but there they proved less disruptive due to that movement's longer experience and greater capacity for tolerating diversity.

As it looked to the future, the Lausanne movement faced a number of possible options. It could adhere closely to the program and goals of the LCWE leadership, rejecting all challenges or distractions from the central task of world evangelization, understood since Pattaya in terms of the strategy of "reaching unreached peoples."

Second, it could modify its position on the goals of the movement, accepting views of the advocates of "radical discipleship" and "simple life-style" as basic to the integrity of the movement, and giving greater prominence to "Christian social responsibility." The ultimate consequences for evangelicalism of moving toward greater wholeness and inclusiveness cannot now be foreseen.

Thirdly, the movement could splinter and break up into rival evangelical segments, each with its own theological character, program, and identity. These movements might remain in dialog with each other—they might indeed all continue to appeal to the same *Lausanne Covenant*—but they would no longer be united as a single evangelical movement for mission.

How evangelicals would respond to these and other challenges would become clearer at the next general consultation of LCWE scheduled to be held in the late 1980s.

6

ROMAN CATHOLIC MISSION THEOLOGY: THE IMPACT OF VATICAN II

Prior to the Second Vatican Council (1962–1965) the doctrinal basis of Roman Catholic missionary activity was never stated in a comprehensive or authoritative manner. Various schools of missiological research existed, and pontifical missionary decrees dealt with specific points of mission practice needing emphasis or clarification, for example, increasing the number of missionaries, fostering indigenous clergy, or making local churches truly indigenous.[1] Not until the Second Vatican Council did the Roman Catholic church begin to issue comprehensive and systematic statements dealing with matters of mission theology and practice.

The purpose of the Second Vatican Council, initiated under the guidance of Pope John XXIII, had been to bring about an internal renewal of the church in faithfulness to the gospel of Jesus Christ and the Scriptures, and promote an updating of the church's approach to the modern world *(aggiornamento)* so as to make the church more effective in its mission. Of crucial importance for reshaping the missionary understanding of the Roman Catholic church was the promulgation by Pope Paul VI of the "Dogmatic Constitution on the Church" *(Lumen Gentium,* 1964) and in close dependence on it the "Decree on the

Church's Missionary Activity" (*Ad Gentes,* 1965).[2] Other important decrees dealt with ecumenism, relations with non-Christian religions, and the task of the church in the modern world. Integrating references to Scripture and tradition, and citations from the church fathers and from earlier pontifical decrees, these documents make explicit the Roman Catholic position on mission and evangelization and provide a rich resource for reflection and planning.

THE CHURCH AS MISSIONARY IN ITS VERY ESSENCE

Lumen Gentium and *Ad Gentes* set forth the nature of the church as the "universal sacrament of salvation" (*LG* 48, *AG* 1) existing for the fulfillment of the mission of the triune God in the world and, by its very nature, missionary. The mystery of salvation is that the Creator did not abandon humankind when it had fallen but chose to raise it up to share in his own divine life. In sending Christ the Redeemer, he purposed to call together in a holy church all who should believe in Christ (*LG* 2). The Son came, sent by the Father who chose and predestined us in him for adoptive sonship. To carry out the Father's will "Christ inaugurated the kingdom of heaven on earth and revealed to us the mystery of the Father. By His obedience He brought about redemption" (*LG* 3). The Holy Spirit was sent to sanctify the church and to guide it into fullness of truth. Following Christ's death and resurrection the church received the mission of proclaiming and establishing the kingdom of Christ and God among all peoples. Through Baptism and the Eucharist, Christ communicates his life to believers and mystically unites them with himself. Jews and Gentiles alike are formed into a new race, a messianic people having Christ as its head and receiving the dignity and freedom of children of God. In their hearts the Holy Spirit dwells, their new law is the commandment to love, and their destiny is the kingdom of God. (*LG* 4-9)

The common priesthood of the baptized and the ministerial priesthood of the ordained both share in the one priesthood of Christ and in his prophetic office (*LG* 10). Besides the Catholic faithful, who are fully incorporated into the church in communion with the pope and bishops, the church knows that "in many ways it is linked with those who, being baptized, are honored by the name of Christian" but do not profess the Catholic faith (*LG* 15). It is even related to those who "through no fault of their own do not know the gospel of Christ or His Church, yet sincerely seek God" (*LG* 16). To procure the glory of God and the salvation of all, the church "continues unceasingly to send heralds of the gospel until such time as the infant churches are fully established and can themselves carry on the work of evangelizing" (*LG* 17). On earth the church journeys like a pilgrim in a foreign land, receiving its perfection and vindication only in time to come (*LG* 48). Conscious of its defects and imperfections, it seeks to remove these so that Christ and God may be more fully praised (*LG* 51). This messianic people is a "sure seed of unity, hope, and salvation for the whole human race" and is sent forth by Christ "as an instrument for the redemption of all" and "as the light of the world and the salt of the earth" (*LG* 9).

The church on earth is by its very nature missionary since according to the plan of the Father it has its origin in the mission of the Son and of the Holy Spirit (*AG* 2). The reason for missionary activity lies in the will of God who wishes all to be saved and to come to the knowledge of the truth. Everyone therefore ought to be converted to Christ, baptized, and incorporated into him and into the church which is his body. "Hence missionary activity today as always retains its power and necessity" (*AG* 7). The period between the first and the second coming of the Lord is the time of missionary activity, when the gospel must be preached to all nations.

> Missionary activity is nothing else, and nothing less, than the manifestation of God's plan, its epiphany and realization in the world and in history; that by which God, through mission, clearly brings to its conclusion the history of salvation [*AG* 9].

The special activities by which preachers of the gospel, sent by the church, go into the whole world to evangelize and implant the church among people who do not yet believe in Christ are called "missions." The principal instrument in this work of implanting is the preaching of the gospel (*AG* 6). There are two billion people—and their number is daily increasing—who have never heard, or barely heard, the gospel message (*AG* 10). Local churches are sent to evangelize all the people in their territory. Laypeople should bear witness to Christ by their life and words. Priests should give themselves generously to the work of evangelization. Bishops, above all, are responsible for promoting mission activity, guiding and coordinating it. Missionaries should be prepared for the task of evangelization through special spiritual and moral formation. The whole church should supply aid to weak or declining dioceses. Young churches should be encouraged to take part in the universal mission as soon as possible. Each diocese should appoint persons to promote the work of missions. The Sacred Congregation for the Propagation of the Faith is the competent body to coordinate missionary work throughout the world (*AG* 29).

In related pronouncements, the Second Vatican Council expressed itself on ecumenical principles ("Decree on Ecumenism," *Unitatis Redintegratio,* 1964), relations with people of other faiths ("Declaration on the Relation of the Church to Non-Christian Religions," *Nostra Aetate,* 1965), and the situation of people in the modern world ("Pastoral Constitution on the Church in the Modern World," *Gaudium et Spes,* 1965).

The Decree on Ecumenism set forth the ecumenical goals of Vatican II:

> The restoration of unity among all Christians is one of the principal concerns of the Second Vatican Council. Christ the Lord founded one Church and one Church only [*UR* 1].

Divisions between Christians contradict the will of Christ, provide a stumbling block to the world, and damage the preaching of the gospel to every creature. The movement for the restoration of Christian unity has as its goal

> one visible Church of God, a Church truly universal and sent forth to the whole world that the world may be converted to the gospel and so be saved, to the glory of God [*UR* 1].

In the relation of the church to non-Christians, the Second Vatican council stated:

> The Catholic Church rejects nothing of what is true and holy in these religions. She has a high regard for the manner of life and conduct, the precepts and doctrines which, although differing in many ways from her own teaching, nevertheless often shed a ray of that truth which enlightens

all men. Yet she proclaims and is in duty bound to proclaim without fail, Christ who is the way, the truth and the life (John 14:6). In him, in whom God reconciled all things to himself (2 Cor. 5:18-19), men find the fulness of their religious life [NA 2].

The church therefore urges its members to enter "with prudence and charity" into dialog and collaboration with people of other faiths and "while witnessing to their own faith and way of life, acknowledge, preserve and encourage the spiritual and moral truths found among non-Christians, also their social life and culture" [NA 2].

Finally, in the lengthy "Pastoral Constitution on the Church in the Modern World," the Second Vatican Council reflected on the "joys and hopes," the "griefs and anxieties" of contemporary culture brought about by increasing power and wealth, ideological polarization, technological change, and the disruption of traditional social structures. It considered in detail threats to human dignity, human cultural development, and peace in the community of nations (GS, passim). These statements amplify the church's position on mission and evangelism.

DEVELOPMENTS AT THE ROMAN SYNOD OF BISHOPS: EVANGELIZATION, JUSTICE, AND LIBERATION

Following the Second Vatican Council, assemblies of the Roman Synod of Bishops were convened at approximately three-year intervals, each synod being a representative and consultative assembly of about 200 bishops selected by national and regional episcopal conferences.

The 1971 Synod took up the topic of "Justice in the World," and produced a notable declaration on the integral relationship between action for justice and evangelization. The bishops were struck by the growth of oppression and serious injustice around the world caused by unjust systems and structures. They shared their awareness of the church's vocation to be present in the heart of the world by proclaiming good news to the poor, freedom for the oppressed, and joy to the afflicted. Through the events of human history God had revealed to them the meaning of his plan of liberation and salvation fulfilled in Christ:

Action on behalf of justice and participation in the transformation of the world fully appear to us as a constitutive dimension of the preaching of the Gospel, or, in other words, of the Church's mission for the redemption of the human race and its liberation from every oppressive situation.[3]

Christian love of the neighbor and justice could not be separated, the bishops said, for love implies a demand for justice, and justice attains inner fullness only in love:

For unless the Christian message of love and justice shows its effectiveness through action in the cause of justice in the world, it will only with difficulty gain credibility with the men of our times.[4]

The church therefore has a proper and specific responsibility to proclaim justice and denounce injustice when the fundamental rights of human beings and their salvation demand it. The bishops also recognize that those who speak to others about justice must first be just themselves. The church is therefore called to examine its modes of acting, its possessions, and its own life-style.[5]

The 1974 Synod of Roman Bishops met on the topic "Evangelization in the Modern World." The Synod confirmed anew that

the mandate to evangelize all people constitutes the essential mission of the Church. . . . The duty to proclaim the Gospel belongs to the whole people of God . . . [and] no real Christian may absent himself from this duty.[6]

In facing the difficulties of evangelization, Christians are called to incessant interior conversion and renewal through prayer, Scripture study, contemplation, and participation in the sacraments. The Synod commended closer collaboration with non-Catholic Christians and the pursuit of the dialog with people of other faiths "to achieve a deeper understanding of the Gospel's newness and of the fullness of revelation, and to be able to show them thereby the salvific truth of God's love that fulfills itself in Christ."[7]

However, the Synod was especially concerned to clarify the relationship between evangelization and "*integral salvation* or the *complete liberation* of peoples":

Let us nurture the hope that the Church, in more faithfully fulfilling the work of evangelization, will announce the total salvation of man or rather his complete liberation, and from now on will start to bring this about.[8]

The meaning of this somewhat ambiguous statement was that the church, as a community engaged in evangelization, must conform to Christ and the norms of the gospel in bringing about the "true and complete liberation" of persons and groups. The church's approach must not be limited to political, social, and economic considerations, but must draw from the Lord himself (Luke 4:18) and from the gospel the incentives for promoting service to the poor and the oppressed and for eliminating the social consequences of sin that are translated into unjust social and political structures. The bishops believed that the church has a duty to be present among the people of our time to bring the presence of Christ, the incarnate word, among them. In so doing the church discovers opportunities to evangelize the world and promote authentic liberation.[9] This request for clarification of the basis and scope of "total salvation" in the church's missionary practice was to have far-reaching consequences.

Thus the 1974 synod, building on the work of the one held in 1971, which called action for justice "a constitutive dimension of the preaching of the Gospel" and of the church's mission, qualified its earlier statement to the extent of distinguishing between political liberation in the secular sense and "total salvation" or "complete liberation" in an evangelical sense. But the synod was unable to complete its work of defining evangelization in a satisfactory manner, and in the end decided to remit to the pastor of the universal church, Pope Paul VI, the task of giving fuller and more mature form to the concerns of the 1974 Synod.

EVANGELII NUNTIANDI:
APOSTOLIC EXHORTATION OF POPE PAUL VI

Paul VI accepted the challenge from the 1974 Bishops Synod with enthusiasm and produced a monumental work in the apostolic exhortation "The Evangelization of the Men of Our Time" (*Evangelii Nuntiandi*, 1975).[10] He considered it a kind of modern *summa* on the problems and requirements of evangelization. Paul VI used the 10th anniversary of the close of the Second Vatican Council to pose the question:

After the Council and thanks to the Council, which was a time given her by God, at this turning point of history, does the Church or does she not find herself better equipped to proclaim the Gospel and to put it into people's hearts with conviction, freedom of spirit and effectiveness [*EN* 4]?

Pope Paul VI's deeper questions were the following: what has happened to the "hidden energy" of the good news? In what ways is it capable of transforming the people of the 20th century? What methods should be followed in order that the power of the gospel might have its effect (*EN* 4)? The pope was deeply convinced that the task of evangelization was not an optional one for the church:

It is the duty incumbent on her by the command of the Lord Jesus, so that people can believe and be saved. This message is indeed necessary. It is unique. It cannot be replaced. It does not permit either indifference, syncretism or accommodation. It is a question of people's salvation. . . . It is truth. It merits having the apostle consecrate to it all his time and all his energies, and to sacrifice for it, if necessary, his own life [*EN* 5].

With the Apostolic Exhortation of Pope Paul VI, evangelization becomes an activity of highest priority on the agenda of the contemporary Catholic church.

In succinct strokes, *Evangelii Nuntiandi* sets out the nature, basis, and scope of evangelization. "Jesus himself, the Good News of God, was the very first and the greatest evangelizer" (*EN* 7). He proclaimed first of all the kingdom of God. As the kernel of good news, Christ proclaims salvation,

this great gift of God which is liberation from everything that oppresses man but which is above all liberation from sin and the Evil One, in the joy of knowing God and being known by him, of seeing him, and of being given over to him [*EN* 9].

The kingdom comes as grace and mercy, but must at the same time be gained through toil and suffering in a life lived according to the gospel and under the cross. Each individual gains the kingdom and salvation through a total interior renewal, a radical conversion, a profound change of mind and heart (*EN* 10).

Evangelization is the proper vocation of the church—of the whole church and of each member. The church begins by being evangelized itself by constant conversion and renewal, in order to evangelize the world with credibility (*EN* 15). There is a profound link between Christ, the church, and evangelization (*EN* 16).

Evangelization can only be grasped in terms of its many-sided wholeness. It is a rich, complex, and dynamic process which must not be oversimplified (*EN* 17). It includes both interior change in persons and transformation of the social and cultural milieux in which they live. This is Paul VI's view:

> For the Church, evangelizing means bringing the Good News into all the strata of humanity, and through its influence transforming humanity from within and making it new: "Now I am making the whole of creation new." But there is no new humanity if there are not first of all new persons renewed by Baptism and by lives lived according to the Gospel. The purpose of evangelization is therefore precisely this interior change, and if it had to be expressed in one sentence the best way of stating it would be to say that the Church evangelizes when she seeks to convert, solely through the divine power of the Message she proclaims, both the personal and collective consciences of people, the activities in which they engage, and the lives and concrete milieux which are theirs [*EN* 18].

This means challenging and overthrowing false value-systems and evangelizing human cultures in a wide and deep sense. The gospel is not identical with culture, but building up the kingdom cannot avoid borrowing elements of human culture. The gospel must permeate all cultures (*EN* 20).

Witness through presence and solidarity is essential, but insufficient. The best silent witness will prove ineffective if it is not explained:

> The Good News proclaimed by the witness of life sooner or later has to be proclaimed by the word of life. There is no true evangelization if the name, the teaching, the life, the promises, the Kingdom and the mystery of Jesus of Nazareth, the Son of God, are not proclaimed [*EN* 22].

Proclamation reaches its full development only when it is listened to, accepted, and assimilated, that is, when it results in adherence to the kingdom. This is revealed concretely by a visible entry into the community of believers (*EN* 23). The ultimate touchstone of evangelization, however, occurs when the one who accepts the Word and gives himself to the kingdom bears witness to it and proclaims it in his turn. Evangelization is thus a complex process made up of varied elements: renewal of humanity, witness, explicit proclamation, inner adherence, entry into the community, acceptance of sacraments, and apostolic initiative. These elements are complementary and mutually enriching (*EN* 24).

To evangelize is to bear witness in a simple and direct way to God revealed by Jesus Christ in the Holy Spirit (*EN* 26). Its foundation, center, and summit will always be the clear proclamation that in Jesus Christ, the Son of God made man, who died and rose from the dead, salvation is offered to all men as a gift of God's grace and mercy. What is the nature of salvation?

> Not an immanent salvation, meeting material or even spiritual needs, restricted to the framework of temporal existence and completely identified with temporal desires, hopes, affairs and struggles, but a salvation which exceeds all these limits in order to reach fulfilment in a communion with the one and only divine Absolute: a transcendent and eschatological salvation, which indeed has its beginning in this life but which is fulfilled in eternity [*EN* 27].

EVANGELIZATION AND LIBERATION

Evangelization thus includes the "proclamation of a hereafter," beyond time and history, beyond the things of this world, and revealed in the future life (*EN* 28). But, at the same time, evangelization takes account of concrete personal and social life here and now; it is, in a word, a message about *liberation* (*EN* 29). In relation to the struggle that condemns millions to remain on the margins of life,

> the Church . . . has the duty to proclaim the liberation of millions of human beings, . . . of assisting the birth of this liberation, of giving witness to it, of ensuring that it is complete [*EN* 30].

Some who wish to commit the church to liberation are tempted to reduce its mission to the dimensions of a simply temporal project, forgetting all spiritual and religious concerns, and using initiatives of a political or societal type. When this occurs, the church loses its fundamental meaning, and its message of liberation is co-opted by ideological systems or political parties. Over against this, Paul VI affirms the "specifically religious finality of evangelization" (*EN* 32), which envisages the whole person "right up to and including his openness to the absolute, even the divine Absolute" (*EN* 33). This transcendent view of the human person cannot be sacrificed to the needs of strategy or short-term efficiency.

In sum, the church links human liberation and salvation in Jesus Christ, but never identifies them. It reaffirms the primacy of its spiritual vocation and refuses to replace the proclamation of the kingdom with the proclamation of human liberation. It knows that God's kingdom is more than human well-being and development. It also knows that temporal and political forms of liberation carry within themselves the germ of their own negation and fail to reach the ideal they propose. Even so, when preaching liberation, the church is not willing to restrict its mission only to the religious field or to dissociate itself from temporal problems. It considers it important to build up structures that are more human, more just, more respectful of the rights of the person and less oppressive and enslaving (*EN* 34-36). The church cannot accept violence and indiscriminate death as the path for liberation, for violence provokes counterviolence and engenders new forms of oppression. "Violence is not in accord with the Gospel" (*EN* 37). The church recognizes that it has strictly evangelical means for participating in human liberation: those which Christ himself announced and demonstrated by his sacrifice on the cross (*EN* 38). Thus Paul VI attempted to define one of the most pressing issues of modern evangelization.

CATHOLIC REGIONAL DEVELOPMENTS IN MISSION: LATIN AMERICA—MEDELLIN TO PUEBLA

Among the various regional developments that occurred in the Roman Catholic church as a result of the Second Vatican Council, the response of the Latin American bishops was of decisive importance for the theme of evangelization. The Second and Third General Conferences of Latin American bishops at Medellin, Colombia (CELAM II, August–September 1968) and Puebla, Mexico (CELAM III, January 1979) carried Roman Catholic thinking on missionary theology and practice forward to a new stage and contributed to a reshaping of the

Roman Catholic response, not only in Latin America but throughout the world.

CELAM II, meeting at Medellin in the presence of Pope Paul VI, attempted to "search for a new and more dynamic presence of the Church in the present transformation of Latin America, in the light of the Second Vatican Council."[11] Latin America stood at a "decisive crossroads" in history, marked by such tragic signs as underdevelopment, hunger and misery, illness, illiteracy, marginality, inequality and social tension, and outbreaks of violence. Discerning the signs of the times, the bishops sought to develop an "integral vision" of the people of Latin America seeking their own liberation and growth in humanity through incorporation and participation in the liberation process.[12]

> We are on the threshold of a new epoch in the history of our continent. It appears to be a time full of zeal for full emancipation, of liberation from every form of servitude, of personal maturity and of collective integration.[13]

The three broad areas under study were human efforts towards justice and peace, the need for adaptation in evangelization and faith, and the reform of the church and its structures.

Medellin was a turning point in the identity and mission of the church in Latin America. It is particularly remembered for its clear articulation of the people's cry for justice and liberation; its espousal of the cause of the poor; and its recognition of base Christian communities as primary centers for Christian community and evangelization.[14]

The church has a message for all who hunger and thirst for justice, declared the Catholic bishops at Medellin. It is that the God who created humans in his image and likeness sent his Son to liberate them from slavery to sin, including hunger, misery, oppression, and injustice caused by human selfishness. To bring about justice, it is not enough to change political structures. People need to be authentically converted to the "kingdom of justice, love and peace; . . . there will be no new continent without new men, who know how to be truly free and responsible according to the light of the Gospel."[15]

God's salvation is an action of "integral human development and liberation," which incorporates people into Christ through faith and Baptism, and through the Spirit transforms them into new creatures.

Love is the dynamism that motivates Christians to realize justice in the world. Temporal progress is not equated with the kingdom of God, but it contributes to the better ordering of society. Accordingly, the church rejects any dualism that separates temporal tasks from inner sanctification. To enable victims of injustice to participate in the process of determining their own destiny, the church's pastoral action includes *concientizacion* and education aimed at changing structures and observing justice.[16]

The church could not be indifferent in the face of social injustice which keeps the majority of the people of Latin America in poverty and wretchedness:

> A deafening cry pours from the throats of millions of men, asking their pastors for a liberation that reaches them from nowhere else.[17]

The church's luxurious buildings, vehicles, and attire, together with secrecy about finances, all contribute to the notion that the church is rich and make the poor feel that the bishops do not care about them.

> Because of the foregoing we wish the Latin American Church to be the evangelizer of the poor and one with them, a humble servant of all our people.[18]

Christ not only loved the poor but, being rich, he *became* poor, lived in poverty, and founded his church as a sign of that poverty. In this context a "poor church" denounces the unjust lack of this world's goods, preaches, and lives in spiritual poverty "as an attitude of spiritual childhood and openness to the Lord," and tries to translate that spirit of poverty into authentic attitudes and actions pointing to Christ:

> The poverty of the Church and of its members in Latin America ought to be a sign and a commitment—a sign of the inestimable value of the poor in the eyes of God, an obligation of solidarity with those who suffer.[19]

The Lord's command to evangelize the poor calls for a redistribution of apostolic resources and personnel that gives *preference* to the poorest and most needy sectors of society. Solidarity with the poor means that the church makes their problems its own and enters into their struggle against injustice. In these convictions from Medellin lay the seed of the powerful idea which would have its later impact on Puebla 1979 and Melbourne 1980.

Medellin also considered the renewal of pastoral structures in the light of the Second Vatican Council. Its encouragement of the formation of "base Christian communities" must be understood in the context of promoting justice in society and expressing solidarity with the poor. Christians should normally find their spiritual communion in local communities that correspond to the reality of the homogeneous group and are small enough to allow personal participation. The church's pastoral efforts should be directed toward transforming these communities into the "family of God," each with its own fellowship of faith and cultic life.

> This community becomes then the initial cell of the ecclesiastical structures and the focus of evangelization, and it currently serves as the most important source of human advancement and development.[20]

Here the saints are to exercise their ministry and to become a sign of the presence of God in the world. Thus Medellin placed its seal of approval on what was to become the most creative structural innovation of the period after the Second Vatican Council.

THE EVANGELIZATION OF LATIN AMERICA: PUEBLA 1979

The Third General Conference of Latin American bishops met in Puebla, Mexico (January 27—February 13, 1979), on the topic "Evangelization in Latin America's Present and Future." Following the example of his predecessor, Paul VI, who went to Medellin, Pope John Paul II traveled to Puebla to inaugurate the momentous gathering. "The future is in God's hands," he told the bishops, then adding, "but somehow God is also placing the future of a new evangelization impetus in your hands."[21] He later wrote that Puebla had been "a great step forward for the Church's essential mission, i.e. evangelization."[22] The personal appearance of John Paul II gave added publicity to the cause of evangelization and demonstrated its high priority for the church.

Recognizing that the Medellin conclusions were the "point of departure" for Puebla, the new pope skillfully drew upon Paul VI's apostolic exhortation *Evangelii Nuntiandi* as the basis for his own opening address on evangelization.[23] As his own personal touch, John Paul II added a burning desire to promote human dignity and protect human rights. He coupled this with the strongest warning that the church must be concerned with the *whole* human being and not reduce liberation in Christ to a political program. In its own final documents the Puebla conference reaffirmed the church's preferential option for the poor and the role of base Christian communities as agents of evangelization. The pope expressed the hope that other local churches would take note and follow the example of Latin America.

The bishops should know, said John Paul II, that their chief duty is to be "teachers of the truth that comes from God." It is this truth that sets people free, and it is what they are looking for when the church announces the good news. The truth about *Jesus* is at the core of evangelization and forms its real content. A solid Christology sheds light on all other doctrinal themes and pastoral questions. Christ's message and mission

> has to do with complete and integral salvation through a love that brings transformation, peace, pardon and reconciliation. . . . Any form of silence, disregard, mutilation, or inadequate emphasis on the whole of the mystery of Jesus Christ that diverges from the Church's faith cannot be the valid content of evangelization.[24]

The truth about the *church* is that "evangelizing is the essential mission, the specific vocation, the innermost identity of the church, which has been evangelized in turn."[25] Evangelization is a profoundly ecclesial action, and therefore a correct vision of the church is indispensable for a correct view of evangelization. The truth about *human beings* is that they are the image of God and cannot be reduced to mere fragments of nature. The truth is that "the human being is single, unique, and unrepeatable, someone thought of and chosen from eternity, someone called and identified by name."[26] This truth is the basis of the church's social teaching and of its proclamation of authentic liberation.

The pope spoke at length about the relationship between the church's work of evangelization and its promotion of human dignity:

> If the Church gets involved in defending or promoting human dignity, it does so in accordance with its mission. For even though that mission

is religious in character, and not social or political, it cannot help but consider human persons in terms of their whole being.[27]

The church has learned that works on behalf of justice and human dignity are an indispensable part of its evangelizing mission—so said the 1971 Roman Bishops Synod. The church did not need to have recourse to ideological systems in order to love, defend, and collaborate in the liberation of human beings.

At the center of its own message, said John Paul II, the church finds inspiration for acting in favor of brotherhood, justice, and peace and against all forms of domination and slavery. The church wishes to maintain its distance from competing social and economic systems "in order to opt solely for the human being." The church is concerned about the whole person, and it has the duty of proclaiming liberation in the deeper, fuller sense made known by Jesus:

> It is liberation made up of reconciliation and forgiveness. It is liberation rooted in the fact of being the children of God. . . . If we are to safeguard the originality of Christian liberation and the energies that it is capable of releasing, we must at all costs avoid reductionism and ambiguity.[28]

In proclaiming authentic liberation in Christ, the bishops are responsible for teaching the church's social doctrine to the faithful and forming their social conscience at all levels.

The above reflections on "authentic liberation," developed by John Paul II for CELAM III on the basis of *Evangelii Nuntiandi,* were fully incorporated into the schema of the Puebla final document.

The official conclusions of Puebla 1979 contain five parts: (1) a pastoral overview of Latin America; (2) God's saving plan for Latin America; (3) evangelization in Latin America as communion and participation; (4) a missionary church serving evangelization in Latin America; and (5) a closing section on pastoral options. Only a few points may be noted.

With regard to base Christian communities, Puebla was pleased to report that small communities were creating more personal interrelations, and fostering acceptance of God's word, reexamination of the people's life, and reflection on reality in the light of the gospel:

> They accentuate committed involvement in the family, one's work, the neighborhood, and the local community. We are happy to single out the

multiplication of small communities as an important ecclesial event that is peculiarly ours, and as the "hope of the church."[29]

More attention needed to be paid, however, to training leadership for base Christian communities.

Puebla reaffirmed the Medellin position on the preferential option for the poor:

> We are going to take up once again the position of the Second General Conference . . . in Medellin, which adopted a clear and prophetic option expressing preference for, and solidarity with, the poor. . . . We affirm the need for conversion on the part of the whole Church to a preferential option for the poor, an option aimed at their integral liberation.[30]

The object was to proclaim Christ the Savior to the poor, to enlighten them about their dignity, and help them in efforts to liberate themselves. This option was demanded by the scandalous reality of economic imbalances in Latin America. The gospel demand for poverty, understood as solidarity with the poor, required that the church reexamine its structures and undergo a conversion both in its thinking and its life-styles. With its *preferential,* yet not exclusive, love for the poor, the bishops conference at Puebla attempted to keep alive the summons given at Medellin.

> In conclusion, the bishops at Puebla declared: We opt for a Church that is a sacrament of communion, . . . a servant Church that prolongs down through the ages Christ, the Servant of Yahweh, . . . a missionary Church that joyously proclaims to people today that they are children of God in Christ. . . . Being a missionary and an apostle is the very condition of the Christian.[31]

In these words the Catholic bishops at Puebla identified the church's very existence with the fulfillment of the mission of God.

ASIAN MISSIONARY CONGRESS: MANILA 1979

The first Catholic International Mission Congress to be held in Asia took place in Manila (December 2-7, 1979), under the joint sponsorship of the Sacred Congregation for the Evangelization of Peoples, the Asian Bishops Conference and the Pontifical Mission Aid Societies of the Philippines. Its topic was "Toward a New Age in Mission: Good News of God's Kingdom to the Peoples of Asia."[32] Its historic significance was recognized by the pope's envoy, Cardinal Rossi, who declared it "an important step in the history of civilization." Said Rossi:

Just as in the case of Latin America, so also Asia is emerging in the Catholic Church as an active missionary force.[33]

Exceedingly well prepared, the Manila congress built on the texts of *Ad Gentes* and *Evangelii Nuntiandi* but also on the work of conferences and workshops of Asian bishops and other church leaders over a 15-year period. Its starting point was "the Asian context" and the present-day situation of Asia seen in the light of the gospel. Its special emphasis was on the building up of the *local church* as the focus of the task of evangelization.

Reflection on the *Asian* task was accomplished in working groups concentrating on the "three dialogs"—with local culture, with Asian religious traditions, and with the life of the people, especially the poor. The practice of dialog, Puebla's "preferential option for the poor," and the concept of "grassroots ecclesial communities" were all familiar to the delegates of the Manila Congress.

The "message"[34] and consensus papers of the Asian Missionary Congress, published in the three-volume report, would become important sources for Catholic missiological thinking.

The delegates to the Manila congress were consciously situating the work of evangelization "within the context of this vast and varied, this restless and swiftly changing world of nearly two and one-half billion people, nearly two-thirds of all mankind." They could discern a common search for *light* in the midst of confusion, *life* in the midst of suffering, and *love* in an age of violence and oppression. The ancient religions which shaped the histories of Asian peoples and the fabric of its cultures "have reawakened in a remarkable manner" in the last decades (§§4-6). Asian Christians and the churches in Asia are part of a common search:

In this Congress we have realized anew how great a challenge this moment of history places before the Gospel and the Church. We have heard the imperatives it addresses to all of us who, in all unworthiness, have yet been chosen to tell the story of Jesus, to speak His message before our brothers and sisters, and as His people to carry His Spirit and live His life in our own . . . [§7].

Throughout Asia a profound religious sense remains, but materialism, secularism, and ideologies have made deep inroads. Asians have met Christ and the gospel in diverse ways and been deeply attracted to them, yet the *church* has been a stumbling block to belief:

> With sorrow we confess that many have not been equally drawn to the Church because so often they did not see in us, in our institutions and in our lives the image and the realization of the Good News we proclaim. Have we not too frequently made His message mere words and doctrines, His deeds mere precepts and practices, His life merely a complex of rites and institutions [§8]?

Asian Christians remain convinced that "what our peoples are seeking they will find in Jesus and His Gospel."

> And yet somehow we have not been able to find ways to release this power of the Gospel, so that it can truly reach and move the minds and hearts of multitudes of Asian peoples. We have not spoken His Word and lived out His deeds in such a way that these are heard and seen as bearing the promises and hopes of the future of mankind [§9].

Thus Asian communities of faith are "challenged to an ever renewed conversion to God's Word . . . and to a constant reevangelization of themselves." They are summoned to a deeper life of faith and the experience of the power of the Spirit.

> They must respond creatively to the imperatives of a deeper and more extensive inculturation of the Christian life, so that our Asian peoples may find the Christian existence and message truly transparent to Jesus and His Gospel . . . [§10].

Signs of renewal are also seen, and these signs give hope that God through the Spirit is readying the Asian churches *"for a true renewal of mission in Asia and throughout the world."* Among these signs are a hunger for prayer and contemplation among the young, a longing to hear and reflect on the Word in community, increased participation in the Eucharist, a desire for greater simplicity of life-styles, and a growing sense of solidarity with the poor. The rapid multiplication of "grassroots ecclesial communities" and new mission ventures by Asian churches are further signs [§12].

NEW AGE IN MISSION

What is the newness of this "new age of Mission"? Asian churches could discover it in their growing maturity as sending churches, each related to its own local culture:

"Mission" is no longer, and can no longer be, a one-way movement from the "older churches" to the "younger churches," from the churches of the old Christendom to the churches in the colonial lands. Now—as Vatican II already affirmed with clarity and force—every local church *is* and cannot be but missionary. Every local church is "sent" by Christ and the Father to bring the Gospel to its surrounding milieux, and to bear it also into all the world. For every local church this is a *primary task*. Hence we are moving beyond both the vocabulary and the idea of "sending churches" and "receiving churches," for as living communities of the one Church of Jesus Christ, every local church must be a sending church, and every local church (because it is not on earth ever a total realization of the Church) must also be a receiving church. Every local church is responsible for its mission, and co-responsible for the mission of all its sister-churches. Every local church, according to its possibilities, must share whatever its gifts are, for the needs of other churches, for mission throughout mankind, for the life of the world [§14].

Also new is the church's fresh appropriation of local cultures:

We believe that the Spirit of the Lord calls each people and each culture to its own fresh and creative response to the Gospel. Each local church has its own vocation in the one history of salvation, in the one Church of Christ. In each local church each people's history, each people's culture, meanings and values, each people's traditions are taken up, not diminished or destroyed, but celebrated and renewed, purified if need be, and fulfilled . . . in the life of the Spirit [§15].

Local Christian communities become manifestations of the joy, freedom and purity which the grace of Christ brings to flowering in the heart of every people. The Holy Spirit "quickens God's people to new life, to new initiatives" [§§16-17].

Much remains to be done in many areas, but the crux of the Asian church's renewal for evangelization is described thus:

> It suffices for the present to indicate here the continued building up of the local church as the focus of the task of evangelization today, with dialogue as its essential mode, through a more resolute, more creative, and yet truly discerning and responsible inculturation; through interreligious dialogue undertaken in all seriousness; through solidarity and sharing with the poor and the advocacy of human rights; through the creation of "grassroots ecclesial communities" with structures of genuine co-responsibility and ministries of charism and service; through the fostering of evangelizing education in schools and by non-formal education modes, and through an adequate media-ministry [§19].

Through the Asian Mission Congress, the churches gained a new awareness of what mission today and in the future demands of Christians in Asia:

> We have reached a decisive turning point in the mission history of the Third World. There is no return to the past, neither to the past mission theories, nor to past mission methods, nor to the past mission goals [§22].

Despite the numerical weakness of Christians in Asia, delegates were challenged not to lose heart but to trust wholly in the power of the Spirit.

As a symbolic token of the missionary seriousness of the Asian churches, the congress was concluded with the conferring of the mission mandate and cross—a kind of commissioning rite—on 70 Filipino men and women who would bear the Word of the Lord as missionaries to all corners of the earth. Absent Chinese brethren were remembered in prayer. The desperate plight of Indo-Chinese refugees was brought to the attention of various governments. Consensus papers from congress workshops were commended to local churches for study and implementation.

Through regional conferences and consultations involving representatives of diverse local churches, the Roman Catholic church was finding yet another way of developing its mission theology and practice.

The universal magisterium of the Vatican combined with decrees of Roman Bishops Synods and recommendations from national or regional conferences of bishops or specialists would prove very useful in allowing the church to gain wisdom, maintain communication, and express authority at various levels— global, regional, national, and local.

MISSION AGENDA FOR THE FUTURE: THE 1981 SEDOS RESEARCH SEMINAR

Another valuable perspective on Roman Catholic missions is that provided by the church's own mission agencies or sending "institutes." The SEDOS Research Seminar on the Future of Mission held in Rome (March 8-19, 1981) was attended by representatives of 45 mission Catholic communities from six continents, all committed to the mission *ad gentes*.[35] The seminar focused on the new roles of mission institutes in relation to the changed world situation but also in recognition of the fact that *local churches* rather than mission institutes were now the principal factor in determining the expression of mission within the universality of the church. It produced an "agenda for future planning, study and research in mission"[36] which is expected to set trends for coming decades. Basing its work on the foundation of the church's established teaching, especially as set forth in *Evangelii Nuntiandi,* the seminar was concerned not so much with the *why* of mission as with the *how.*

The SEDOS Seminar found four main activities in the church's missionary action, all interrelated, which stood out as basic but which also required further exploration in detail: proclamation, dialog, inculturation and liberation.

PROCLAMATION

"The authentic proclamation of the Gospel is a witness by Word, by the silent witness of action, or by the even more silent presence of Gospel life lived faithfully among others. At the same time, it is a listening to life, discovering the presence of God's Word and Spirit among a people, a presence which has preceded the missionary." There are two different but complementary models:

(1) the *centripetal* model of leading people into the church and extending the church's visible communion; and

(2) the *centrifugal* model of allowing the power of the gospel to move out and to encounter humanity in its struggles, thereby furthering the values of the kingdom.

The seminar believed that the second model was "achieving more prominence today and may be directing us to what will become the priority in much future missionary proclamation."[37]

DIALOG

"If proclamation is concerned chiefly with presenting Christ, dialogue seeks also to find Him already present in a given situation. Dialogue involves the humble discernment of the Word of God in other persons, in the institutionalized forms of other faiths, in various ideologies and in secular realities."

It is not a "diminished form of mission" or an expedient to be used when direct proclamation is impossible. "It is missionary action and is implied in all genuinely missionary activity. The immediate goal of dialogue is the deeper *recognition* of Christ in the other through honest and respectful conversion, which involves risks on both sides."

Dialog is then a "genuine form of Christian witness" which transforms persons and through them societies and cultures. For Christians, dialog with persons of other faith or no faith becomes a "self-evangelization."[38]

INCULTURATION

Inculturation has its source in the Incarnation, the mystery of the Word made flesh in Jesus Christ. "Inculturation, therefore, becomes another way of describing Christian mission. If proclamation sees mission in the perspective of the *Word* to be proclaimed, inculturation sees mission in the perspective of the *flesh*, or concrete embodiment, which the Word assumes in a particular individual, community, institution or culture."

What is inculturated is the gospel or, more accurately, *faith* in the gospel. Inculturation is essential to all authentic missionary action. It cannot be artificially induced but needs to flow spontaneously from the faith of people expressed within symbols of their own culture. It will mean for the church a new discovery of the gospel and an enrichment of the life of the church.[39]

LIBERATION

Liberation is a dynamic woven into all the challenges faced in mission today. "The message which Jesus preached was Good News to the poor, freedom for captives. Jesus' own direction of His message of liberation in a special way to the poor is the basis for liberation theology." "The Gospel as liberation of the poor emphasizes the prophetic aspect of evangelization. It calls for an *analysis* of the anti-Kingdom values in a situation and a *witness* to the Kingdom values. . . ."

The poor should not be understood as objects of evangelization but as its *agents,* since the gospel is meant for them in a special way. The "poor" are those who are systematically deprived of the means for the fullness of life.

"Commitment to the saving message of Jesus Christ entails commitment to the liberation of the oppressed. This commitment means engagement in the struggle for justice and an end to oppressive structures." Liberation is closely linked to proclamation, dialog, and inculturation. The church is in need of a "new missionary spirituality" that responds to the poor.[40]

CENTRAL ROLE OF THE LOCAL CHURCH

The local church, and not primarily the mission institutes, is the bearer and recipient of the activities of proclamation, dialog, inculturation, and liberation.

> The Church is a communion directed towards mission, a mission whose goal is communion in Christ, among all people. It is a people gathered to be sent, and sent to be gathered. . . . The Church is called and sent to be the sign and the instrument of communion and solidarity among all people, a foretaste of the coming Kingdom. It fosters and deepens communion together with its constitutive dimensions of justice and peace, wherever they occur already, and seeks to create them where they are not. A "worthy" participation in the Eucharist, source and summit of the Church, presupposes a lived communion among people.

For its missionary action the church needs not only a conversion of hearts but of *structures* which recognizes spiritual gifts (charisms), fosters new ministries, and stimulates *co-responsibility* at the grass-roots level. Communion requires *interdependence,* not dependence. Catholic communion is meant to be a pluriform "unity in diversity," achieved from below, and not created by Vatican *fiat.* Local churches have an equal share in the mission of the church; they have a right and duty to initiate new missions without gaining the sanction of the *Propaganda Fide.* "Structures geared to excessive centralism do not help such missionary initiatives to flower in local churches."

The old distinction between mission-sending and mission-receiving churches is becoming blurred by the increase in vocations in the "young churches" and their decrease in the "older churches." All churches are mission-sending as well as mission-receiving; their mutual mission to one another is a reinforcement of the communion of local churches. Among the greatest needs are the sharing of funds, personnel, and information. According to the principle of subsidiarity, whatever can be decided or executed at the grass-roots level is not to be decided or executed at a higher level.[41]

The mission institutes provide a continuing vehicle for persons in local churches to respond to the missionary call. Such institutes are in the process of clarifying their roles, improving programs of formation, and establishing closer links of communications both between themselves and between the institutes and local churches.[42] While their roles will be dramatically changed, they will be nonetheless significant for the future.

REFLECTIONS ON DIALOG AND MISSION: THE VATICAN'S SECRETARIAT FOR NON-CHRISTIANS

In 1984, on the 20th anniversary of the creation by Pope Paul VI of the Secretariat for Non-Christians as a Vatican office "to search for methods and ways of opening up a suitable dialogue with non-Christians," that secretariat issued its own statement on the relationship between dialog and mission.[43] The purpose was to reflect on the church's experiences with dialog over 20 years, as well as to offer a partial solution to "difficulties which can arise from the duties of evangelization and dialogue which are found together in the mission of the church."[44] The statement appeals to "The Declaration of the

Relation of the Church to Non-Christian Religions" (*Nostra Aetate*, 1965) as well as to other documents from Vatican II and later, in an effort to dispel confusion and ambiguity within and outside the church about the precise relationship between mission and dialog.

Mission, says the document, is the special activity by which the church makes itself fully present among peoples in which it has not yet taken root. It is a complex reality which includes (1) "the simple presence and living witness of the Christian life"; (2) the service of humanity, with activity for social development and in the struggle against poverty; (3) liturgical life, prayer, and contemplation; (4) "dialogue in which Christians meet the followers of other religious traditions in order to walk together towards truth and to work together in projects of common concern"; and (5) announcement and catechesis in which the good news of the gospel is proclaimed. Each local church is responsible for the totality of mission, and every Christian is involved in some degree. Jesus' own ministry contains *all* the elements of mission, and so also does the New Testament provide a composite picture. Mission revolves about the *human* in full respect for human freedom. Mission work should refrain from all coercive action, and demonstrate love and respect for all that is good in the religious commitment of the neighbor.[45]

Dialog is the name given to the new attitude fostered by the Second Vatican Council toward non-Christian religions. It is rooted in the social experience of human community, but "the church feels itself called to dialogue principally because of its faith":

In God, the Father, we contemplate a pervasive love unlimited by space and time. The universe and history are filled with His gifts. Every reality and every event are surrounded by his love. In spite of the sometimes violent manifestations of evil, in the vicissitudes in the life of each individual and every people there is present the power of grace which elevates and redeems. The church has the duty of discovering and bringing to light and fullness all the richness which the Father has hidden in creation and history, not only to celebrate the glory of God in its liturgy but also to promote among all mankind the movement of the gifts of the Father.[46]

Christ is the Word who enlightens every person, "the redeemer present with grace in every human encounter." Every person without exception has been redeemed by Christ, and Christ is united with each person without exception, even when that person is unaware of it. The Spirit "acts in the depths of people's consciences and accompanies them on the secret path of hearts towards the truth." The church is called, along with the rest of humanity, to advance along the path toward the reign of God in which all humankind will live in perfect communion as brothers and sisters.

Christ is the guarantee for the church and the world that the "last days" have begun, and the "final age of history is already fixed." It is this vision of the final consummation which induced the Fathers of the Second Vatican Council to affirm that there are "elements which are true and good," "precious things both religious and human," "seeds of contemplation," "elements of truth and grace," "rays of the truth which illumines all mankind" to be found in the great religious traditions of humanity. These "merit the attention and esteem of Christians" and constitute an invitation to dialog, both in the things which unite and in those which divide. Quoting *Ad Gentes:*

> Just as Christ penetrated to the hearts of men and by a truly human dialogue led them to the divine light, so too his disciples, profoundly pervaded by the Spirit of Christ, should know and converse with those among whom they live, that through sincere and patient dialogue these men might learn of the riches which a generous God has distributed among the nations. They must at the same time endeavor to illuminate these riches with the light of the Gospel, set them free, and bring them once more under the dominion of God the Saviour [*AG* 11].

Dialog is before all else "a manner of acting, an attitude and a spirit which guides one's conduct." It implies concern, respect, and hospitality toward the other. It leaves room for the other person's identity, his modes of expression, and his values. Dialog is thus the norm and necessary manner for every form of Christian mission. All Christians are called to "live dialog" in their daily lives.[47]

What, then, is the relationship between dialog and mission? According to the 1984 statement by the Secretariat, "missionary proclamation has conversion as its goal," and "all persons are constantly called to this conversion." Here conversion is understood as the "humble and penitent return to the heart of God" of persons who under the action of the Spirit open their hearts to the Lord so that they may adhere to him. Each conversion is a work of grace in which the principal agent is not any human being, but the Holy Spirit. "The Christian is but a simple instrument and co-worker of God." Each partner may feel a valid desire to share faith with the other. In the process of conversion, which must be entirely free and voluntary, no one must be constrained to act against conscience, nor impeded from acting according to conscience. The statement implies that conversion may follow witness, but that it need not.

Quite independently of the missionary proclamation that leads to conversion, the statement continues, the church is encouraged to practice dialog to recognize "seeds of goodness and truth" wherever they exist, to build up genuine peace in the world, to promote social transformation, to overcome racial, social, and religious differences, and to bring about mutual enrichment.

> God never ceases to reconcile persons to Himself by the work of His Spirit. The church relies on the promise made by Christ that the Spirit will guide it in history towards the fullness of truth (John 16:13). For this reason it goes out to meet individuals, peoples and their cultures, aware that in every human community are found the seeds of goodness and truth, and conscious that God has a loving plan for every nation (Acts 17:26-27). The church therefore wants to work together with all in order to fulfill this plan and by so doing recognize the value of the infinite and varied wisdom of God and contribute to the evangelization of cultures.[48]

In the same way the church seeks dialog with all who acknowledge God, preserve in their traditions elements of religion and humanity, or respect high-minded human values, regardless of the source. Even enemies of the gospel and persecutors of the church are not excluded. Dialog thus becomes a source of hope and a factor in the transformation of human community. Because God's "mysterious and silent Spirit" directs the carrying out of God's design in history and "opens the path of dialogue," one may be confident that God's children dispersed by sin will one day be reunited.[49]

In so saying, the secretariat appears to make a clear distinction between the motives, methods, and expectations that belong to "mission and conversion," on the one hand, and those that pertain to "dialogue for the building of God's reign," on the other. Proclamation, as we have seen, may lead to personal conversion and thus it contributes to the extension of Christian community. Dialog, however, recognizes goodness and truth wherever these are found and helps to transform human community into the reign of God by overcoming racial, social, religious, and other differences, thus fulfilling God's eschatological plan.

Dialog is the "norm and necessary manner for every form of Christian mission," we are told, yet the goals of dialog appear to be markedly different from those of mission. Despite the effort of the Secretariat for Non-Christians to clarify the relationship between dialog and mission, the ambiguity remains.

JOINT DOCUMENTS: ECUMENICAL STATEMENTS ABOUT MISSION

The Roman Catholic position on mission is further revealed in the publication of documents or statements resulting from bilateral conversations between Catholics and other groups. Two of these are briefly examined here: first, the study document entitled *Common Witness,* issued by the Joint Working Group of the Roman Catholic church and the World Council of Churches in 1980;[50] and, second, "The Evangelical—Roman Catholic Dialogue on Mission, 1977–1984: A Report,"[51] issued by participants in this dialog in 1986. The first document is a progress report on experiences of common witness involving Catholics and others in the recent past, with an invitation to continue and to intensity such efforts in the future. The second is an exploratory report which, while falling far short of consensus, indicates a sufficient degree of agreement to make conversations between Catholics and Evangelicals promising and worthwhile.

Common Witness takes for granted that unity in witness and witness in unity are both a theological necessity and an established fact in many places in the world. The impulse to common witness comes from Jesus Christ. The document notes that the World Council of Churches in its Fifth General Assembly at Nairobi (1975), the Lausanne Committee for World Evangelization in its *Lausanne Covenant* (1974), and both Pope Paul VI in *Evangelii Nuntiandi* (1975) and Pope John Paul II in *Redemptor Hominis* (1979) all have appealed for greater common witness to Christ in the work of evangelization (CW 11-12).[52] Common ground for Christian witness is given in the gospel message and in Baptism; its source is the triune God and the commission given to the entire church by its Lord. Witness is nurtured by the deepening of spiritual life, and becomes a channel of divine love to all people. When incarnated into life, and seen by others as a conviction worth dying for, proclamation becomes credible. Since words alone cannot give sufficient expression to the love of God in Christ, witness demands comprehensive expression by every Christian and by the church in every part of life. Witness helps to extend the fellowship of the Spirit, and creates new Christian community. Through common witness the church is called to bring the message of love and reconciliation to even the most difficult situations, giving an account of "the hope that is in us," proclaiming the cross and resurrection of Jesus Christ, and becoming the mouth and voice of the poor and the oppressed in the presence of the "powers that be" (CW 15-38).[53]

Common Witness becomes concrete in dealing with occasions and possibilities for joint witness, and also recognizing problems and tensions. The principle of the Lund Faith and Order Meeting (1952) is invoked in inviting churches "to do all things together except where fidelity of conscience would forbid." We are not yet putting this principle into practice, the report says (CW 40). Joint evangelization efforts through preaching, retreats, Bible study, and action groups express a common commitment to the gospel. Coordinated pastoral and missionary actions prepare the way for Christian unity (CW 44). Faithful witness given by one church in a particular place can be part of the rich and diverse witness of the whole church, leading to greater solidarity and mutual intercession (CW 46). Divided witness, however, can become a "counter witness." When churches are still divided and not yet one in their understanding of the gospel, witness to Christ may be distorted by unworthy motives, attitudes, behavior, and methods. "Proselytism" replaces selfless love by group egotism, and substitutes one's own methods and programs for the Spirit's activity (CW 47-53). Accordingly, common witness calls for common efforts to reach unity in the understanding of the gospel. Common witness is needed at all levels of church life—local, regional, national, and global. Ecumenical groups and religious communities can play a key role by discovering and putting into practice new ways of expressing Christian life and common witness that transcend conventional barriers (CW 54-62).[54]

Common Witness closes with an appeal "to join forces to proclaim the Gospel of the kingdom to all peoples." Such common witness is not "an abstract theological concept" or simply "friendly ecumenical relations." It is a task of great urgency when measured against the growing threats to human civilization: drug traffic, armaments, the power of the mass media. "Witness that dares to be common is a powerful sign of unity coming directly and visibly from Christ and a glimpse of his kingdom" (CW 63-64). The report cites growing evidence of common witness being practiced: in diaconic service, witness to non-Christians, promotion of human rights, common Bible translations, theological dialogs, joint arrangements for religious education in schools and teacher training.[55]

Common Witness is offered as a study document to elicit reaction and criticism, and to promote discussion on the nature, urgency, and forms of common witness. The document has generally received a favorable reception in Roman Catholic and conciliar circles, but needs to become better known and more widely used if it is to have its intended impact.

"The Evangelical—Roman Catholic Dialogue on Mission, 1977–1984: A Report,"[56] (ERCDOM) is the result of a series of three meetings which took place between Roman Catholics and selected evangelical participants over a period of seven years. The Roman Catholic participants were named by the Vatican Secretariat for Promoting Christian Unity while the evangelicals, some of whom were related to the Lausanne movement, in the present case represented not churches or movements but only themselves. The very fact that such a series of meetings could be held and its results published is in itself an indication of a surprising rapprochement between these groups, and a testimony to their sincere mutual desire for dialog.

The dialog on mission between evangelicals and Roman Catholics was possible, according to the report, for two reasons. First, both groups have recently been concentrating their attention on evangelism. Second, the *Lausanne Covenant* (1974) and the apostolic exhortation *Evangelii Nuntiandi* (1975) reveal a degree of convergence and lay the groundwork for a serious dialog on the nature of evangelism.

The report is extensive in content and detailed in its treatment of key issues. The outline follows: (1) revelation and authority; (2) the nature of mission; (3) the gospel of salvation; (4) our response in the

Holy Spirit to the gospel; (5) the church and the gospel; (6) the gospel and culture; (7) the possibilities of common witness. The report is not an "agreed statement" but rather a faithful record of the ideas shared.

The participants in ERCDOM offer this report to other evangelicals and Roman Catholics "as a sign of their conviction that fidelity to Jesus Christ requires that we take his will for his followers with a new seriousness." Their hope is that the dialog will be continued and developed.

CATHOLIC MISSION THEOLOGY: EVALUATION AND CRITIQUE

Since the Second Vatican Council the Roman Catholic church has defined and clarified its mission theology and principles. The documents reviewed above, originating from various sources such as council decrees, pontifical pronouncements, Roman Bishops Synods, regional bishops conferences, and mission agency seminars, provide us with a synoptic picture of Catholic missionary thinking. Difficulties arise because statements coming from widely varying sources—including several Vatican Secretariats—are not well integrated, and may sometimes give the impression of being in conflict with one another. Moreover, this picture does not begin to take into account the views of individual Catholic mission theologians, some of whose writings appear at times to deviate widely from the church's official magisterium. A further problem arises when it comes to establishing the precise authority of statements which do not bear the Vatican *imprimatur.* Who speaks for the church, other than the pope? Given these limitations, it is possible to make some critical observations about Catholic missionary thinking since Vatican II.

1. The church is understood as missionary in its entirety, and the task of evangelizing all peoples constitutes the church's essential vocation (*EN* 14, 59; *AG* 1, 35). *Evangelii Nuntiandi,* building on the missionary awareness of the Second Vatican Council, and on the specific mandate of the 1974 Roman Bishops Synod, is an extended meditation on the church's missionary obligation. There is little doubt that *Evangelii Nuntiandi* and the council documents provide the strongest support and motivation for missionary activity, not simply for the evangelization of non-Christians but for the reevangelization of nominal Christians as well.

Catholic ecclesiology with reference to mission is well developed, and there is a forward movement from *Ad Gentes* (1965) to *Evangelii Nuntiandi* (1975) and later statements. The entire church is missionary by nature, and this is true universally as well as in terms of each local church. The local church has the privilege and obligation of being involved in mission where it is, as well as of participating in the wider mission of the universal church. The distinction between "sending" and "receiving" churches has become obsolete. It is also true that the church is missionary at every level—global, regional, national, and local—and in all its parts—bishops, clergy, religious, laity, and special institutes. The former hierarchical view of apostolic authority is now balanced by the sense that mission is the task of all the faithful. Special rights formerly reserved exclusively for the Congregation for the Propagation of the Faith (*AG* 29) in providing central coordination and direction for mission work are not even mentioned in *Evangelii Nuntiandi,* which is far more concerned with encouraging lay participation in mission and developing resources at the local level. Regional mission conferences now strongly affirm the importance of developing mission theology in the context of local cultures and in response to local needs. The matter of co-responsibility between local churches and the Vatican for the mission of the universal church is not forgotten, but it receives a new expression as a result of the increasing dynamism of regional movements and the demand for increased local autonomy.

2. With regard to the relation between evangelization and advocacy of justice along with the promotion of human rights, the documents demonstrate unambiguously that liberation from everything that oppresses human beings—but above all liberation from sin and from the "evil one"—belongs to the kernel and center of the good news of salvation which Christ proclaims (*EN* 9). The 1971 Roman Bishops Synod on "Justice in the World" firmly established that "action on behalf of justice and participation in the transformation of the world" are a "constitutive dimension of the preaching of the Gospel, or, in other words, of the Church's mission for the redemption of the human race and its liberation from every oppressive situation." To that extent, any separation between *salvation* in Christ and *liberation* from every form of oppression would appear to be ruled out.

The real problem has to do with the scope of liberation and its theological interpretation. We have seen that evangelicals associated with the LCWE had difficulty in stating the precise relationship between evangelism and social responsibility. A special consultation (Grand Rapids, 1982) was required to deal with the problem. Similarly, for Roman Catholics, particularly after the Roman Bishops Synod of 1971, the question is not *whether* justice and liberation are integral components of mission and evangelism (they are), but exactly how liberation is to be understood theologically.

Pope Paul VI in *Evangelii Nuntiandi* (*EN* 30-35, 1975) and Pope John Paul II speaking at Puebla (1979) went to considerable lengths to underscore the spiritual character of liberation, and to distinguish it from any kind of political, economic, or ideological project. The official position is that liberation envisages the *total* human being, and that it is rooted in the gospel and in the fact of our being children of God. Liberation cannot be reduced to the dimensions of a simply *temporal* project; the *eschatological* dimension of the kingdom of God must not be forgotten. Thus human liberation and salvation in Jesus Christ are closely linked, but never identified (*EN* 35), for the church knows that not every notion of liberation is consistent with an evangelical vision of human nature and of the promise of the kingdom.

How far then may local churches go in supporting movements of human liberation? Can these be understood in a wholly religious sense independent of ideological interpretation or of political involvement? What are the criteria for the valid participation by local churches and individual Christians in movements of liberation? Are they different for Catholic laity than for clergy? And what about basic ecclesial communities involved in movements for human liberation—is their activity validated by the gospel, and if so up to what point? The precise relation between the proclamation of salvation in Jesus Christ and support for liberation from every form of oppression—including concrete forms of oppression traceable to particular historical structures—needs further clarification if the link between mission and liberation is to be more than a rhetorical one.

3. The Catholic position on dialog, together with various Catholic interpretations of the theological significance of other religions, is troubling in view of the multiplicity of such statements and continuing ambiguity about their precise meaning. This is particularly true when

Catholic statements on dialog are compared with the very precise WCC statement and "Guidelines on Dialogue." The WCC statement, while strongly advocating the practice of dialog, consistently avoids taking any theological position on other religions, and holds that there is no incompatibility between commitment to mission and the practice of dialog. Some Catholic statements, by contrast, appear to speak of mission as a form of dialog, while others seem to draw a sharp distinction between the two.

In general, Catholic statements about "seeds of truth" and "spiritual and moral truths" to be found in other religions (cf. *AG* 2) are considerably more optimistic and positive on the subject than similar statements by most other Christians on this subject. At the same time, it is noteworthy that statements of judgment or condemnation of other faiths are virtually absent. While council statements do not explicitly state that *all will be saved* apart from the knowledge of the gospel and of faith in Jesus Christ, they move strongly in the direction of soteriological universalism. It is at least a serious question, and one calling for further dialog between Catholics and non-Catholics, whether this extraordinarily high Catholic estimation of non-Christian beliefs, practices, and peoples does not in some way undercut the 1974 Bishops' declaration that "the task of evangelizing all people constitutes the essential mission of the church" (*EN* 14).

Statements coming from Catholic mission seminars and from regional church conferences tend to be clear and unambiguous about the *practice* of dialog. The SEDOS seminar declared that dialog was not a diminished form of mission but was itself "missionary action" and implicit in all genuinely missionary activity. The Asian bishops strongly endorsed dialog in its threefold form as a necessity for local churches engaged in mission: dialog for inculturation; interreligious dialog; and dialog with people, especially the poor. No debate exists about dialog as an essential *attitude* which expresses the Christian's approach to people of other religions and cultures (*NA* 1, *EN* 18-20, 63). Indeed, substantial agreement can be found between Catholic, conciliar, and evangelical Christians about the necessity of practicing dialog as an attitude and spirit guiding Christian behavior in all areas. The Secretariat for Non-Christians is precisely right in declaring that "dialogue is thus the norm and necessary manner of every form of Christian mission."

Difficulties arise only when the theological and philosophical presuppositions for dialog in Catholicism are spelled out more clearly, along with stated Catholic expectations for entering into conversation with peoples of other faiths. As the 1984 statement of the Vatican Secretariat for Non-Christians reminds us, Catholicism has traditionally held that the power of divine grace is found in the life of every people and of each individual through creation. In some way Christ is the Logos which enlightens all persons, whether they have heard and received the gospel or not. The Spirit not merely accompanies but even anticipates the church's ministry of Word and sacraments. When these theological assumptions—shared by non-Catholics in varying degrees—are linked to the view that "rays of truth illumine all mankind" (*NA* 2) and reinforced by the conviction that the church should reject "nothing of what is true and holy in these religions," there is strong basis for the assumption that the Catholic church's normal relationship to non-Christian peoples need not be one which seeks to evangelize and convert them, but may well be carried out at the level of dialog for the purpose of mutual sharing and enrichment. The 1984 statement of the Secretariat for Non-Christians on "The Attitude of the Church towards the Followers of Other Religions" implies an alternative soteriological possibility according to which the church no longer has a necessary mandate to "make disciples of all nations" but may instead invite people of other faiths to become, as it were, "honorary participants" in the reign of God through a process of dialogical sharing leading to global reconciliation and transformation. It would be difficult to find a clear biblical basis for such an expectation.

The Second Vatican Council did not state, as some individual Catholic theologians have stated, that other religions are "means of salvation" per se. It did, however, clarify that sincere non-Christians can be saved by the grace made available through Christ apart from explicit faith in the gospel. Most Protestants, whether conciliar or evangelical, would feel that there is a basic contradiction between the evangelical mandate to preach the gospel and make disciples of all nations, on the one hand, and the expectation, on the other hand, that the world is being steadily reconciled and transformed, and the kingdom inaugurated, apart from proclamation of Jesus Christ as Lord and acceptance of that faith. The persistence over the years of this soteriological vision within Catholicism, and the cruciality of the issue for missionary motivation, suggests that Christians everywhere concerned about the future of the mission enterprise, in West and East and in the two-thirds world, should urgently engage one another in dialog on this subject.

7

TOWARD A NEW ERA OF MISSION: QUESTIONS AND DIRECTIONS OF THE FUTURE

Our survey of current trends in mission theology—conciliar, evangelical, and Roman Catholic—has shown both change and continuity, convergence and divergence, between the traditions. Each group as it develops and refines its own mission theology will benefit from the insights of other traditions. The common commitment which all traditions share to doing mission in unity requires that all communities engage in dialog with a view to strengthening their common witness and removing obstacles to cooperation in the unfinished task. This dialog of Christian traditions about mission, an example of which was the 1977–1984 Evangelical—Roman Catholic Dialogue on Mission, is only beginning and needs to go much further.

As Christian communities share their deepest convictions about mission with one another, they will grow in trust and understanding and discover new ways of manifesting their essential oneness in faith, not only through prayer, study, and eucharistic worship, but eventually also through acts of common witness before the world.

What are the crucial issues of mission theology that need further dialog and understanding as we look forward to doing mission in the new era? Are there clues available for future directions? In this concluding chapter we shall attempt to summarize and restate some of the unresolved issues touched on in previous chapters. In a brief "thesis" following each set of questions, we shall set forth a direction for further exploration or outline a necessary task. Here are *15* issues demanding missiological reflection in the new missionary era.

WHO IS JESUS CHRIST?

The question of Jesus Christ is foundational for all mission theologies, for it determines what kind of gospel will be preached, and how mission is understood. Our picture of Jesus Christ, and our understanding of the gospel of salvation and liberation, determines our mission practice and our witness to the kingdom.

All traditions agree on common Christological marks based on Scripture and creeds, but there are wide variations in emphasis. Lausanne spoke of only one Savior, who gave himself as a ransom for sinners and is the only mediator between God and human beings. At Melbourne, Jesus became the kenotic crucified one who calls his followers to join him alongside the poor at the peripheries and challenges human power structures. In *Evangelii Nuntiandi* we encountered the liberating Christ who offers "integral salvation" for the whole person. Each statement about Jesus Christ embodies some important element of the gospel, but many statements are one-sided or unbalanced and fail to do justice to the wholeness of Christian witness. A biblically balanced and complete witness to the whole Christ is a mission priority.

THESIS: Mission theology should seek to develop a more adequate, balanced, and unified picture of Jesus Christ which is historically normative (i.e., in conformity with Scripture and creeds) but also relevant missiologically and applicable in cross-cultural situations. Such a unified picture would involve the integration of divine and human attributes, showing Christ as both transcendent and preexistent Lord and also as incarnate and suffering human being. It would maintain a constant and complete interchange of characteristics between the earthly Jesus and the exalted Lord, i.e., the crucified and the risen Lord.

WHAT KIND OF CHURCH IS THE BEARER OF GOSPEL WITNESS?

Mission theologies now agree that mission is the essential task of the whole church, and that every local congregation must become a primary instrument in evangelization. The church as people of God witnesses to the kingdom and is itself a foretaste and sign pointing to the future perfection of the kingdom.

But what kind of church can become the instrument of *missio Dei?* Is it a church equipped with the "three-self" marks? A church composed of homogeneous units, or a diverse and multicultural church? A church marked by rapid growth in numbers? A church with its own deep sense of cultural identity? A suffering and cross-bearing church? A poor church, or a church organized at the grass roots? A church which equips all baptized believers for participation in mission? Mission theologies have identified these and other elements essential to a missionary church, while missionary structure studies have pointed to the danger of rigidly holding on to outmoded or inflexible structures not adapted functionally to mission. Mission theology can be of further service in developing the functional profile of a missionary congregation.

THESIS: The church which has mission as its essential calling is to be understood as "God's people" (1 Peter 2:8-9) (rather than as an institution) which in its earthly pilgrimage may through the Spirit avail itself of a variety of structures, expressions, and relationships to carry out its mission and ministry in the world. Adaptability for mission should be one test for church structures at all levels. Apart from the mandate to preach the gospel to the whole creation and administer the sacraments, all structures may be regarded as provisional and subject to change or renewal in the light of the church's calling.

WHAT IS THE GOAL OF THE MISSION OF GOD?

All traditions agree that the kingdom of God is in some sense the final goal, but they differ on what that may mean and how it affects the ongoing task and priorities of the church during the interim period. Does the goal of mission remain making converts and planting churches wherever they do not exist, or does the expectation of the kingdom shift the church's priorities to activities which somehow anticipate a "new heaven and a new earth"? If church reproduction is no longer the final goal, can it be properly described as a still valid intermediate goal? Are church structures and activities provisional, and will they disappear in the *eschaton* in order that Christ's kingdom may become all in all?

How is the task of the church changed by the expectation of the coming kingdom? What is the relation between the existence of a messianic people on earth of God and the ultimate promise of God's kingdom? Will the whole earth be incorporated into the plan of God's kingdom and, if so, by what means? What is our hope for the future in Christ, and what does the Lord's coming again mean for our present (denominational) churches? Mission theology in an age of religious pluralism and proximity to the coming kingdom demands that we make our vision of the future clearer so as to prepare for Christ's return in the way the Lord wishes.

THESIS: The church in the interim between Christ's resurrection and his return must remain committed to the dual task of proclaiming faith, receiving converts, forming Christian communities, and administering the sacraments, while at the same time witnessing to the kingdom and preparing for the return of Christ in the most comprehensive sense (including prayer for the kingdom and denunciation of the demonic forces which oppose the kingdom). The final result belongs to divine providence. The church is thus called to be a faithful steward of its given missionary task, even when it lacks clear answers or a clear vision of the events of the end-time. Therefore, witness to the kingdom cannot be abandoned for church planting, or vice versa.

WHAT KIND OF UNITY IN CHRIST IS NECESSARY FOR MISSION?

All traditions affirm an essential relationship between mission and unity, while differing on exactly how much unity is needed for fellowship in Christ, and how that unity is to be expressed. What kind of unity is required by our confession of oneness in Christ and in what does it consist? Is creedal unity or unity based on faith and order agreements essential? Is organic union among divided churches required for cooperation in mission, or may groups divided in structure share the proclamation of the gospel and the sacraments? What about mutual recognition of members and ministries—can it facilitate co-operation in mission?

Is it agreed that the New Delhi (1961) Faith and Order formula for unity ("all in each place," etc.) represents a valid proposal for local unity? Does "conciliar fellowship" at the local level express the goal of unity among divided churches? Would agreement on "Baptism, Eucharist and Ministry" (Lima, 1982) establish the possibility for common witness? Mission theology in collaboration with ecumenical studies can assist the churches in their mission effort by clarifying the basis and conditions for cooperation in mission.

THESIS: As all churches are under obligation to continue the pursuit of Christian unity and to find ways of manifesting unity in Jesus Christ before the world, they should seek opportunities for common study, fellowship in the gospel as conscience allows, and partnership in Christian witness before the world. Unity is a gift from God, and its ultimate expression is eschatological, but Christians are responsible to bring their missionary service into conformity with the will of Christ who prayed that "they may all be one" (John 17:21).

WHAT STRUCTURES OF MUTUALITY AND PARTNERSHIP ARE NEEDED?

What structures are needed to express the spiritual reality that participation in mission is the common privilege of churches in all lands and in all six continents in the new era? Are there still limits to cooperation between Christians of differing denominational or theological positions? Can Christians of different national or denominational backgrounds engage in common witness to the gospel, joint catechesis, or cooperative mass media outreach? What about preparation for ministry and service to society?

Are traditional bilateral structures of partnership still adequate, or do they tend to perpetuate older differences between "donors" and "receivers"? What new structural models are available to bring together Christians of different theological, church, national, or cultural backgrounds in a "six-continent" missionary witness? Are international and interdenominational witness and service teams a possibility? Can churches in different continents share resources and planning in a common effort? Mission theology must prepare the way for creative new expressions of missionary partnership which underscore the supranationality of the gospel and the universality of Christ's lordship.

THESIS: As current structures tend to maintain the dominance of wealthy Western partners, do not express the international and interracial character of mission, and are therefore inadequate for expressing oneness in Christ, high priority should be given to designing structures for sharing mission resources and engaging in joint planning on a regional, national, or local basis. This is especially necessary in the case of Western sending agencies and growing churches of the two-thirds world.

WHAT IS THE RELATIONSHIP BETWEEN EVANGELISM AND SOCIOPOLITICAL RESPONSIBILITY?

In the preceding pages, the relation between evangelism and sociopolitical responsibility has been identified as a key issue. Conciliar Christians say that God's justice manifests itself both in the justification of sinners and in social and political justice for the oppressed, and that God's power changes both persons and structures. Evangelicals say that evangelism and social action are both part of our Christian duty, but that evangelism is primary. Catholics hold that action on behalf of justice and participation in the transformation of society are a "constitutive dimension" of preaching the gospel, but nevertheless evangelization should not be reduced to a political program.

Are evangelism and divine justice merely related externally, as coordinate elements, or are they part of the same offer of the gospel? Is one formula more faithful to the Scriptures than another, or can all interpretations serve the mission of God? Which forms of sociopolitical responsibility are appropriate in Christian mission, and which not? Who decides on these matters?

THESIS: As there is now very nearly complete consensus on the basic proposition that evangelism and sociopolitical responsibility are inseparable in mission, the issue should be regarded as no longer divisive, but Christians holding different convictions should engage in further study and dialog to promote fuller understanding and more effective witness to the gospel.

IS THE CHURCH'S PREFERENTIAL OPTION FOR THE POOR BINDING?

Is the church's "preferential option for the poor" a faddish idiosyncrasy or a binding yardstick for the future? Who are the poor, and what is their priority in the mission of God? Are solidarity with the poor, the practice of "spiritual poverty," the call to authentic life-styles, and the renunciation of power and influence obligatory for all churches, including those in affluent nations? What is the meaning of the preferential option for middle-class churches in Western society? What would it mean for churches already ministering in the context of poverty?

Is the call to identify with the poor and to become "churches of the poor" to be taken literally or only symbolically? What are its implications for the redistribution of church wealth? For the life-styles of religious professionals and laity? For church structures? Churches and mission agencies in all six continents, but especially in the West, have so far paid little more than "lip service" to the challenge of the poor.

THESIS: All churches and mission organizations need to take this option with the utmost seriousness, consider its implications, and seek to recruit persons who possess the charism of being able to work with and alongside the poor.

WHAT FURTHER WORK NEEDS TO BE DONE ON GOSPEL AND CULTURE?

What further missiological work is needed on the relation between gospel and culture? The importance of cultural identity and the need to contextualize the gospel and faith within each local cultural setting are by now almost universally accepted, but significant differences remain. Is there a mandate to maintain cultures intact, or does the gospel transform and modify all cultures through its permeation? Is it true that God wants people to become Christians in their own homogeneous groups? What is the relation between the church's prophetic ministry and its approach to local culture? Can culture become an obstacle in expressing the wider unity of Christians? In the case of tribalism, caste, and apartheid, is it the Christian's obligation to affirm Christ regardless of cultural consequences? When it comes to religious language, concepts, or ritual rooted in the local culture, are there limits to "borrowing" from indigenous religions? Mission theology needs to continue the task of developing criteria and guidelines for the inculturation of the gospel in various cultural contexts.

THESIS: While the matter of cultural adaptation or inculturation is now happily a virtual nonissue, further research is necessary to clarify how the understanding of the gospel is affected by receptor cultures, not merely in the linguistic transmission of the gospel message but in the actual understanding of the gospel and its appropriation within a given culture. We need to study more about how the gospel is understood in diverse cultural contexts, thereby increasing our understanding of the richness of God's revelation.

WHAT ABOUT DIALOG BETWEEN CHRISTIAN FAITH AND OTHER FAITHS?

What is the theological value of other religions, and their relation to God's revelation in Jesus Christ? How does religious pluralism affect the call to evangelize all peoples? And how should dialog between Christians and people of other faiths and ideologies be understood: as a requirement for effective Christian witness, or as a substitute for such witness?

We have noted apparent differences between the goals and expectations of Roman Catholic and conciliar approaches to dialog. These in turn are rooted in different theological perspectives about other faiths. The consequences of these differences for mission practice are likely to be far-reaching if taken to their logical conclusions, and to give rise to fragmentation and disunity.

Can dialog be understood as an exercise by Christians who wish to affirm ethical and spiritual truths found in other religions while at the same time remaining faithful to their own sincere convictions about Christ? Can the conviction that there is "no other name" be combined with an attitude of mutual trust and respect toward other religionists? Mission theology must seek to clarify the goals of Christians in dialog and the theological understanding that underlies those goals, while also giving guidance to persons preparing for such encounters.

THESIS: Dialog as an attitude, spirit, and style of approach to persons of other faiths is to be unconditionally affirmed as valid, but the goal of dialog and its underlying theological presuppositions, particularly with regard to the salvific power or value of other faiths, must be closely examined and clarified on the basis of Scripture and tradition. This will require an ecumenical "dialog about dialog."

WHAT EQUIPPING IS NEEDED FOR MISSION AND EVANGELISM?

What equipping of the saints is needed for participation in mission and evangelism? It is a truism to state that mission is the task of every baptized believer, and of every congregation. But how does this equipping take place, and why does so much church activity fail to equip Christians for mission and evangelism? Is a more realistic combination of theory and practice needed, along with nurture and support? What is lacking in the ordinary catechetical preparation and worship experience of Christians that fails to motivate them to mission?

Where professional missionaries are concerned, are there new approaches to training and formation? How can parish pastors be equipped to lead in programs of education for mission and evangelism? Such questions are not theoretical but touch on the effectiveness of the local church in its missionary awareness and outreach.

THESIS: The equipping of missionaries and of all baptized Christians for participation in mission must become much more practice-based to be effective, and such elements as cross-bearing, discipleship training, changes in life-style, and actual practice in sharing one's faith must be central to all such equipping.

WHAT STRATEGIES ARE NEEDED FOR THE UNFINISHED TASK?

What strategies are needed for reaching the unreached? Is it still feasible to speak of evangelizing the world in our generation? What are reasonable goals for global mission today? These are important questions in the new missionary era.

Does effective mission practice depend on using such methodologies as church growth analysis, or identifying and targeting unreached peoples? How can such strategies be useful, and what are their limits? Is strategy development, in relation to mission theology and motivation, an essential component of mission practice? We have noted that the evangelical mission movement, in comparison to conciliar and Roman Catholic missions, places heavy emphasis on strategy development, evangelistic methodologies, and the employment of research tools derived from the social sciences. Mission theology must seek to render a judgment on the value and importance of these contributions.

THESIS: Research on mission strategies and methodologies should be carried out and the results utilized when clearly beneficial to mission, but such considerations must never be allowed to override or obscure clear theological principles and goals. Further missiological study will disclose whether claims made for the homogenous unit principle or for strategies for reaching the "hidden billions" are genuine revelations of God's Spirit.

WHAT MOTIVATION IS NEEDED FOR MISSION AND EVANGELISM?

What motivation can impel Christians to cross boundaries to share the gospel with others? Expressing a compelling missionary motivation in the new missionary era is a serious problem for all Christian communities. What has happened to the "hidden energy" of the good news in our time? asked Pope Paul VI. What statement of the gospel will motivate Christians to spontaneous and joyful witness? All traditions suffer from a steady erosion of evangelistic commitment due to the inroads of secularism.

Evangelicals continue to appeal to the Great Commission but also to the lostness of three billion human beings without Christ. Catholics speak of the essential missionary nature of the church and of its apostolic tradition and obligation. Conciliar Christians say "there is no participation in Christ without participation in his mission" but interpret the motive in different ways. Many modern Christians feel guilt or embarrassment about sharing the gospel with others, especially in the West. Mission theology should make an ecumenical study of the question of a valid and compelling biblical motivation for doing mission in our day.

THESIS: Studies should be made, on an ecumenical basis, of missionary motivation in the new age of missions, clearly separating the motive for mission today from Western colonialism, cultural imperialism, and other false motives, but expressing the continuing validity of the Great Commission.

WHAT IS THE AUTHORITY OF THE BIBLE FOR MISSION?

How does biblical authority become normative in the practice of mission and evangelism? Underlying many of the preceding questions is a prior question about the use of the Bible as a basis and frame of reference, and its authority in shaping mission theology and practice.

All groups affirm the authority of the Holy Scriptures, but they use them in significantly different ways. No single question about mission and evangelism can be approached without an adequate biblical hermeneutic. With the collapse of the old missionary order and the repudiation of mission practices stemming from humanitarianism and Western paternalism, answers influenced by assumptions of an earlier period have become untrustworthy. Pragmatism or traditionalism in mission policy can represent a betrayal of the norm of *sola scriptura,* even when covered by a cloak of piety. The entire basis, methdology, and goal of mission today must be rigorously thought through in faithfulness to the Scriptures, but also in the light of the new situation. Mission theology has the duty to insure that mission practice is developed in conformity with the Word of God.

THESIS: In the reflection on the basis, goal, and means of carrying out the mission of God, the Scriptures are to be regarded primarily as foundational, i.e., as the source and norm for understanding the salvation history which testifies to God's saving action for the world in Christ, but the Scriptures also must be seen as providing valuable illustrations and paradigms for mission today (for example, ministry to the whole person, protest against injustice, God's love for the lost and the poor, etc.).

WHAT IS MISSION TODAY?

What is "mission" and what is "evangelism"? How do both terms relate to "evangelization"? What about the "mission of God" *(missio Dei)?* Discourse about mission is hampered by a growing lack of preciseness about what any given speaker means when speaking of mission. Clearer definitions of the scope, content, and goal of each of these terms, biblically grounded and related to the meaning of *missio Dei,* are needed to guide the church's activity.

In the context of mission from and to six continents, earlier distinctions between "mission" (overseas) and "evangelism" (at home) have become irrelevant. The church in each place is called both to share the good news in its neighborhood and to participate in God's mission to the ends of the earth. Every place has become a mission field, and each church is now a sending body.

The Roman Catholic church first used the term "missions" (pl.) to designate authorized acts of sending under the *propaganda fide* to implant the church where it did not exist. Catholics during the Second Vatican Council began speaking of the church as missionary in its very being. In 1975, Pope Paul VI spoke of "evangelization" as a comprehensive activity directed toward atheists, nonbelievers and nonpracticing Christians alike, and including witness by word and by life, entry into a visible community of Christians, and bearing witness—in that sequence. Conciliar Christians, under the continuing influence of John R. Mott and Edinburgh 1910, still speak of the classic missionary aim of furthering "the proclamation to the whole world of the gospel of Jesus Christ to the end that all men may believe in him and be saved." For them, the precise meaning of mission may vary according to the context and occasion. The WCC-CWME combines the activities of mission and evangelism in a single unit as inseparable.

Evangelicals since Lausanne have used "evangelization" to refer to both cross-cultural missions (*E-2* and *E-3*) but also to the evangelizing of nominal Christians (*E-0*) and non-Christians living close to a Christian community (*E-1*). The purpose of evangelization is to "give individuals and groups a valid opportunity to accept Jesus Christ as Lord and Savior, and serve him in the fellowship of the church."

Mission theology should assist in the task of producing an agreed terminology to guide the efforts of various groups in their mission outreach.

THESIS: "Mission" should normally be used in the sense of the total activity of the church in preaching, teaching, healing, nurturing Christian communities, and witnessing to the kingdom, including advocacy of justice and service to humanity, while "evangelization" will be reserved for the specific task of awakening or reawakening faith in Jesus Christ where it no longer exists or has already ceased to exist. Evangelization is a decisive part of Christian mission, but is not identical with it.

WHO IS A MISSIONARY?

Who is a missionary today? Who goes or is sent? The question looks deceptively simple but actually calls for a thorough revision and updating of our concept of *who* and *what* a missionary is in the new missionary era. Our new theological understanding speaks of the church as missionary in its very purpose and being, and of every Christian as being called to participation in God's mission by Baptism. Yet no church or mission body has gone so far as to abolish the category or function of professional and set-apart missionaries, understood either on a career or short-term basis. Our actual practice is suspended somewhere between the older concept of missionary professionalism and careerism, on the one hand, and the theological ideal of the lay priesthood, according to which every baptized believer is a minister with Christ and a witness to the kingdom, on the other.

Given the bewildering reality of change which makes the missionary terminology of the older missionary era obsolete—mission activities by churches in the two-thirds world, missionaries from the two-thirds world serving in the West, travel by Christian laypersons for business or pleasure, refugee migration movements, recognition of the West as a "mission field," new religious movements eroding Christian faith, inevitable encounters with persons of other faith, dialog in the local community as a lay activity—the functional relationship between the missionary witness of every Christian and the work of the missionary professional needs to be spelled out.

Every local pastor becomes in some sense a motivator and equipper for the mission of the local church in its outreach at home and its participation in the global mission of the church. The task of specially trained and equipped cross-cultural missionaries now becomes evangelization in the "regions beyond" and the crossing of frontiers (however defined) to reach those who would not otherwise receive the witness of the gospel. The effective coworking of all missionary agents in their mutual roles is critical for the success of God's mission.

THESIS: Mission theology should assist with the task of creating a fresh vocabulary for missionary function in the new missionary era, taking into account that mission is the task of the church in all six continents, and with attention to the distinctions but also the interrelationships between cross-cultural missionaries, lay Christians, pastors, and other church workers.

NOTES

CHAPTER 1. Introduction: From an Old to a New Missionary Era

1. Cf. Kenneth Scott Latourette, *Christianity in a Revolutionary Age: A History of Christianity in the Nineteenth and Twentieth Centuries,* vol. 3, *The Nineteenth Century Outside Europe* (New York and Evanston: Harper and Row, 1961), pp. 484ff.; and vol. 5, *The Twentieth Century Outside Europe* (New York and Evanston: Harper and Row, 1962), pp. 501ff.
2. C. Howard Hopkins, *John R. Mott, 1865–1955: A Biography* (Geneva: World Council of Churches, and Grand Rapids: Eerdmans, 1979), pp. 24-27; Dana L. Robert, "The Origin of the Student Volunteer Watchword: 'The Evangelization of the World in this Generation,' " *International Bulletin of Missionary Research,* 10/4 (October 1986): 146-149.
3. Hopkins, *John R. Mott,* pp. 60ff.
4. R. Rouse and S. C. Neill, eds., *A History of the Ecumenical Movement, 1517–1948,* 2nd ed. (Philadelphia: Westminster, 1967), pp. 355-362; J. A. Scherer, "Ecumenical Mandates for Mission," in Norman A. Horner, ed., *Protestant Crosscurrents in Mission: The Ecumenical-Conservative Encounter* (Nashville and New York: Abingdon, 1968), pp. 21-25.
5. Rouse and Neill, *A History,* pp. 405ff., and Scherer, "Ecumenical Mandates," pp. 25-26.
6. Rouse and Neill, *A History,* pp. 366ff., and Scherer, "Ecumenical Mandates," p. 23.
7. Rouse and Neill, *A History,* p. 367.
8. Ibid., pp. 368-370.
9. Pope Paul VI, Apostolic Exhortation *Evangelii Nuntiandi,* "On Evangelization in the Modern World" (Rome: Congregation for the Evangelization of Peoples, n.d.), §4.
10. Hendrik Kraemer, "The Missionary Implications of the End of Western Colonialism and the Collapse of Western Christendom," *History's Lesson for Tomorrow's Mission: Milestones in the History of Missionary Thinking* (Geneva: World's Student Christian Federation, n.d.), pp. 195-206.
11. Cf. J. A. Scherer, *Missionary, Go Home! A Reappraisal of the Christian World Mission* (Englewood Cliffs, N.J.: Prentice-Hall, 1964).
12. David B. Barrett, ed., *World Christian Encyclopedia: A Comparative Survey of Churches and Religions in the Modern World.* A.D. *1900–2000* (Nairobi, Oxford, New York: Oxford University Press, 1982), p. 7.

13. Dean R. Hoge and David A. Roozen, eds., *Understanding Church Growth and Decline, 1950–1978* (New York/Philadelphia: Pilgrim, 1979), p. 17.
14. "Membership Changes in the Lutheran Church in America," Resource Sheet Distributed by the Office for Evangelical Outreach, Division for Parish Services, Lutheran Church in America, 2900 Queen Lane, Philadelphia, PA 19129 (1986).
15. Ibid.; cf. also Statistical Summaries, *LCA Yearbook* (Philadelphia: Board of Publication of the Lutheran Church in America, various years).
16. Lutheran World Information 32/85 (Geneva: Lutheran World Federation), p. 19.
17. Merton P. Strommen, *Our Compelling Need: Evangelization of the Baptized, ALMS Theological Lectures for Laity and Clergy 1982*, p. 5.
18. W. A. Visser 't Hooft, "The General Ecumenical Development Since 1948," *The Ecumenical Advance: A History of the Ecumenical Movement*, vol. 2, 1948–1968, ed. Harold E. Fey (London: SPCK, 1970), p. 4.
19. *World Christian Encyclopedia*, Global Table 2, p. 4.
20. Cf. Walbert Bühlmann, *The Coming of the Third Church: An Analysis of the Present and Future of the Church* (Maryknoll, N.Y.: Orbis, 1977); David B. Barrett, "A.D. 2000: 350 Million Christians in Africa," *IRM* 59/233 (January 1970): 39-54.
21. Lesslie Newbigin, "Mission to Six Continents," in *The Ecumenical Advance*, 2:175.
22. Lesslie Newbigin, *The Other Side of 1984: Questions for the Churches*, Risk Book Series 18 (Geneva: World Council of Churches, 1983); idem, *Foolishness to the Greeks: The Gospel and Western Culture* (Grand Rapids: Eerdmans, 1986).
23. Johannes Verkuyl, "Mission in the 1980's," *Occasional Bulletin of Missionary Research*, 3/3 (July 1979): 94.
24. Charles W. Forman, "A History of Foreign Mission Theory in America," *American Missions in Bicentennial Perpsective*, ed. R. P. Beaver (South Pasadena, Calif.: William Carey Library, 1977), pp. 109-110.
25. *The Missionary Obligation of the Church: Willingen, Germany, July 5-17, 1952* (London: Edinburgh House, 1952).
26. "The Lausanne Covenant," *Let the Earth Hear His Voice: International Congress on World Evangelization, Lausanne, Switzerland; Official Reference Volume*, ed. J. D. Douglas (Minneapolis: World Wide Publications, 1975), pp. 3-9.
27. Pope Paul VI, Apostolic Exhortation, *Evangelii Nuntiandi*, "On Evangelization in the Modern World" (Rome: Congregation for the Evangelization of Peoples, n.d.).
28. "Mission and Evangelism: An Ecumenical Affirmation," *IRM* 71/284 (1982): 427-451.
29. Samuel Wilson, "Current Trends in North American Protestant Ministries Overseas," *IBMR* 5/2 (1981): 74ff.
30. *Mission Handbook 1985–86* (Washington: U.S. Catholic Mission Association, 1986), p. 42.
31. David E. Barrett, "Annual Statistical Table on Global Mission: 1986," *IBMR* 10/1 (1986): 23.
32. Ibid., p. 22.
33. "Mission and Evangelism: An Ecumenical Affirmation," preface.
34. *Budapest 1984; "In Christ—Hope for the World": Official Proceedings of the Seventh Assembly of the Lutheran World Federation, Budapest, Hungary, July 22—August 5, 1984*, ed. Carl H. Mau Jr.; LWF Report No. 19/20 (Geneva: Lutheran World Federation, 1984), pp. 192-197.

35. Information from a press release, "The Fourth Chinese National Christian Conference," August 16-23, 1986, Beijing, China.

CHAPTER 2. Lutheran Mission in Historical Perspective

1. *The Book of Concord: The Confessions of the Evangelical Lutheran Church*, trans. and ed. Theodore G. Tappert (Philadelphia: Fortress, 1959), p. 25.

2. Gustav Warneck, *Outline of a History of Protestant Missions from the Reformation to the Present Time: A Contribution to Modern Church History* (New York/Chicago/Toronto: Fleming H. Revell, 1902), p. 10.

3. Werner Elert, "Missions," in *The Structure of Lutheranism* (St. Louis: Concordia, 1962), 1:385-402.

4. Walter Holsten, "Reformation and Mission," *Archiv für Reformationsgeschichte*, 44/1 (1953):1-31.

5. *Geschichte der lutherischen Mission nach den Vorträgen des Prof. D. Plitt*, ed. Otto Hardeland (Leipzig: A. Deichertsche Verlagsbuchhandlung, 1894–1895), vol. 1.

6. Cf. Johannes Aagaard, "Missionary Theology," in *The Lutheran Church Past and Present*, ed. Vilmos Vajta (Minneapolis: Augsburg, 1977), pp. 206-210. For a Lutheran interpretation of *missio Dei* see Georg F. Vicedom, *The Mission of God: An Introduction to a Theology of Mission* (St. Louis: Concordia, 1965).

7. Large Catechism (Third Part: The Lord's Prayer), *The Book of Concord*, pp. 426-427, §51.

8. Ibid., p. 427, §52.

9. Ibid., §53.

10. Ibid., §54.

11. Ibid., p. 428, §62.

12. Ibid., p. 429, §65.

13. Ibid., §68.

14. Paul Drews, "Die Anschauungen reformatorischer Theologen über die Heidenmission," *Zeitschrift für praktische Theologie* 19 (1897): 1-26. Cf. also Volker Stolle, *Kirche aus allen Völkern: Luther-Texte zur Mission* (Erlangen: Verlag der evangelischen lutherischen Mission, 1983), for examples.

15. Cf. especially H.-W. Gensichen, "Were the Reformers Indifferent to Missions?" *History's Lessons for Tomorrow's Mission* (Geneva: WSCF, 1960), pp. 119-127; H. Dörries, "Luther und die Heidenpredigt," *Mission und Theologie* (Göttingen: H. Reise, 1953), pp. 61-77; W. Maurer, "Reformation und Mission," *Lutherisches Missionsjahrbuch*, 1963, pp. 20-41.

16. WA 12, 267, 3-7; 318, 25-319, 6. Cited by Stolle, *Kirche*, p. 15.

17. WA 11, 411, 31-413, 6. Cited by Stolle, *Kirche*, pp. 16-17.

18. Ibid.

19. *The Book of Concord*, pp. 416-417, §§42, 51-53.

20. Adolf Schlatter, "Luther und die Mission," *Evangelisches Missionsmagazin* 61/7 (1917): 281-288.

21. Heinrich Frick, *Die evangelische Mission: Ursprung, Geschichte, Ziel* (Bonn and Leipzig: Kurt Schröder Verlag, 1922); Paul Althaus, "Um die Reinheit der Mission," *Evangelische Missions-Zeitschrift* 10 (1953): 97-104; Martin Kähler, *Angewandte Dogmen: Dogmatische Zeitfragen* (Leipzig, 1908), 2:340ff.

22. Karl Holl, "Luther und die Mission," *Gesammelte Aufsätze zur Kirchengeschichte*, vol. 3: *Der Westen* (Tübingen: J.C.B. Mohr—Paul Siebeck, 1928), pp. 234-243.

23. WA 47, 463, 7-468, 3. Cited in Stolle, *Kirche*, pp. 28-34.
24. "On War against the Turks," WA 30, 2, 79-148; "Army Sermon against the Turks," WA 30, 2, 160-197.
25. Rudolph Mau, "Luthers Stellung zu den Türken," *Leben und Werk Martin Luthers von 1526 bis 1546*, vol. 1 (Berlin: Evangelisches Verlagsanstalt, 1983), pp. 647-662.
26. Johann Gerhard, *Loci Theologici* (Berlin, 1866), vol. 2, tome 5, pp. 422-434.
27. Ibid., vol. II, tome 6, pp. 52-53, 146-156.
28. Cited in W. Grössel, *Die Mission und die evangelische Kirche im 17. Jahrhundert* (Gotha, 1897), pp. 85-89.
29. W. Grössel, *Justinianus von Weltz* (Leipzig, 1891); J. A. Scherer, *Justinian Welz: Essays by an Early Prophet of Mission* (Grand Rapids: W. B. Eerdmans, 1969); F. Laubach, "Justinian von Welz," *Evangelische Missions-Zeitschrift* 21/4 (1964): 158-165.
30. Philip Jakob Spener, *Pia Desideria*, trans. Theodore G. Tappert (Philadelphia: Fortress, 1964), pp. 87-122.
31. Cf. *Pietists: Selected Writings*, ed. Peter C. Erb (New York, Ramsey, and Toronto: Paulist, 1983).
32. Cf. Gary R. Sattler, *God's Glory, Neighbor's Good: A Brief Introduction to the Life and Writings of August Hermann Francke* (Chicago: Covenant, 1982).
33. Cf. J. A. Scherer, *Mission and Unity in Lutheranism: A Study in Confession and Ecumenicity* (Philadelphia: Fortress, 1969), pp. 25-29.
34. Cf. Vergilius Ferm, *The Crisis in American Lutheran Theology* (New York and London: Century, 1927).
35. J. A. Scherer, *Mission and Unity in Lutheranism*, pp. 41-42.
36. Ibid.
37. Lutheran World Federation Constitution, Article 3, 2, a.
38. The story is told by Frederick K. Wentz, *Lutherans in Concert* (Minneapolis: Augsburg, 1968), and in J. A. Scherer, *Mission and Unity in Lutheranism*.
39. J. A. Scherer, . . . *That the Gospel May Be Sincerely Preached throughout the World* (Geneva: LWF Report 11/12, 1982), pp. 188-189.
40. *In Christ—A New Community: The Proceedings of the Sixth Assembly of the Lutheran World Federation, Dar es Salaam, Tanzania. June 13-25. 1977*, ed. Arne Sovik (Geneva: LWF, 1977).
41. "Southern Africa: Confessional Integrity," *In Christ—A New Community*, pp. 179-180, §§55-56 (emphasis added); "Appeal to Lutheran Christians in Southern Africa concerning the Unity and the Witness of Lutheran Churches and Their Members in Southern Africa," ibid., p. 215. The statement identified the three alien principles undermining faith and unity in Christ as *(a)* loyalty to an ethnic group as a basis for church separation; *(b)* belief that unity of the church is only spiritual and need not be manifested; and *(c)* belief that structures of society are shaped by natural laws only and are not answerable to the criterion of God's love as revealed in the biblical message.
42. "Socio-Political Functions and Responsibilities of Lutheran Churches," in *In Christ—A New Community*, p. 176, §§24-26.
43. Cf. *Lutheran Contributions to the Missio Dei* (Geneva: LWF Department of Church Cooperation, 1984), and Volker Stolle, *Kirche aus allen Völkern: Luther-Texte zur Mission* (Erlangen, 1983).

44. "Report of Section II: World Missions," in *The Proceedings of the Second Assembly of the Lutheran World Federation, Hannover. Germany, July 25—August 3, 1952*, ed. Carl E. Lundquist (Geneva: LWF, 1952), p. 137.
45. Statement of a consulation, Justification and Justice: A Meeting of Lutheran Theologians of the Americas, Mexico City, December 7-14, 1985; *Word and World* 8 (Winter 1987): 79.

CHAPTER 3. Ecumenical Missionary Thinking in Its Recent Development

1. *Renewal and Advance: Christian Witness in a Revolutionary World*, ed. C. W. Ranson (London: Edinburgh House, 1948), p. 173.
2. Ibid., pp. 206-207.
3. Ibid., p. 174.
4. Ibid., p. 175.
5. Ibid., p. 181.
6. *The Missionary Obligation of the Church: Willingen, Germany, July 5-17, 1952* (London: Edinburgh House, 1952), p. iii.
7. Ibid., p. 1.
8. Ibid., p. v.
9. Ibid., p. 6.
10. Ibid., p. 8.
11. Ibid., pp. 14-15.
12. Ibid., pp. 19-21.
13. Rodger C. Bassham helpfully traces the complex ideas, interests, and personalities competing for expression at Willingen; see "Seeking a Deeper Theological Basis for Mission," *IRM* 67 (1978): 329-337.
14. J. C. Hoekendijk, "The Church in Missionary Thinking," *IRM* 41 (1952): 332-334.
15. J. C. Hoekendijk, "The Call to Evangelism," *IRM* 39 (1950): 170-171.
16. Rodger C. Bassham, "Seeking a Deeper Theological Basis for Mission," cites the relationship between the church and its mission, the relation between the church and the kingdom of God, and eschatology as being areas of disagreement.
17. Wilhelm Andersen, *Towards a Theology of Mission: A Study of the Encounter between the Missionary Enterprise and the Church and Its Theology* (IMC Research Pamphlet No. 2; London: SCM, 1955), p. 10.
18. *The Missionary Obligation of the Church*, pp. 1-5.
19. Ibid., pp. 2-4.
20. Ibid., p. 5.
21. *The Ghana Assembly of the International Missionary Council, 28th December, 1957, to 8th January, 1958: Selected Papers, with an Essay on the Role of the IMC*, ed. Ronald K. Orchard (London: Edinburgh House, 1958), p. 10.
22. Ibid.
23. Ibid., p. 172.
24. J. A. Mackay, "The Christian Mission at This Hour," ibid., p. 120; W. Freytag, "Changes in the Pattern of Western Missions," ibid., p. 141.
25. *The Ghana Assembly of the International Missionary Council*, p. 19.
26. Cf. Ernest A. Payne and David G. Moses, *Why Integration? An Explanation of the Proposal Before the World Council of Churches and the International Missionary Council* (London: Edinburgh House, 1957).
27. *The Ghana Assembly of the International Missionary Council*, pp. 156-160.

28. Ibid., Cf. also Karsten Nissen, "Mission and Unity: A Look at the Integration of the International Missionary Council and the World Council of Churches," *IRM* 63 (1974): 539-550. Nissen cites the views of Max Warren, Stephen Neill, and others in opposition to the integration proposal, and concludes that integration has not in fact promoted unity in mission work. He also notes the opposition of the Norwegian Missionary Council.
29. *The Ghana Assembly of the International Missionary Council*, pp. 167-168.
30. Erik W. Nielsen, "The Role of the I.M.C.: Some Reflections on the Nature and Task of the I.M.C. in the Present Situation," ibid., pp. 223-224.
31. Walter Freytag, "Changes in the Pattern of Western Missions," *The Ghana Assembly of the International Missionary Council*, pp. 139-143.
32. Ibid., 143-144.
33. Ibid., pp. 145-146.
34. Lesslie Newbigin, *One Body, One Gospel, One World: The Christian Mission Today* (London and New York: IMC, 1958). Though drafted by Newbigin, the essay is extensively based on earlier IMC conference statements.
35. Ibid., p. 12.
36. Ibid., pp. 14-15.
37. Ibid., p. 17.
38. Ibid., pp. 24ff.
39. Ibid., p. 31.
40. Ibid., p. 36.
41. Ibid., p. 29.
42. Ibid.
43. Ibid., p. 43.
44. *The New Delhi Report: The Third Assembly of the World Council of Churches, 1961*, ed. W. A. Visser 't Hooft (New York: Association Press, 1962), pp. 55-60.
45. Ibid., p. 5.
46. Ibid., p. 4. Some 20 years later, Newbigin acknowledged that not all the hopes of 1961 for the missionary transformation in the life of the WCC and its member churches had been realized, but he still affirmed that the decision was right and that "it created the context in which a true rebirth of the missionary concern of the churches can take place." Cf. Lesslie Newbigin, "Integration: Some Personal Reflections, 1981," *IRM* 70 (1981): 250.
47. *The New Delhi Report*, p. 429.
48. Ibid., pp. 421, 429.
49. *Breaking Barriers, Nairobi 1975: The Official Report of the Fifth Assembly of the World Council of Churches, Nairobi, 23 November—10 December 1975*, ed. David M. Paton (London: SPCK; Grand Rapids: Wm. B. Eerdmans, 1976), p. 390.
50. *Bangkok Assembly 1973: Minutes and Reports of the Assembly of the Commission on World Mission and Evangelism of the World Council of Churches, Dec. 31, 1972 and Jan. 9-12, 1973* (Geneva: WCC, n.d.), pp. 116-117.
51. *The New Delhi Report*, pp. 77-90.
52. Ibid., p. 190.
53. *Witness in Six Continents: Records of the Meeting of the Commission on World Mission and Evangelism of the World Council of Churches Held in Mexico City, Dec. 8-19, 1963*, ed. Ronald K. Orchard (London: Edinburgh House, 1964).
54. Ibid., p. 175.
55. Ibid., pp. 153-154.

56. Ibid., pp. 154-155.
57. *The Church for Others and the Church for the World, a Quest for Structures for Missionary Congregations: Final Report of the Western European Working Group and the North American Working Group of the Department of Studies in Evangelism* (Geneva: WCC, 1968); *Planning for Mission: Working Papers on the Quest for Missionary Communities,* ed. Thomas Wieser (New York: U.S. Conference for the World Council of Churches; London: Epworth, 1966).
58. Report of Section II, "Renewal in Mission," *The Uppsala Report 1968: Official Report of the Fourth Assembly of the World Council of Churches, Uppsala, July 4-20, 1968,* ed. Norman Goodall (Geneva: WCC, 1968), pp. 21-38.
59. *The New Delhi Report,* p. 189.
60. Ibid., p. 190.
61. *The Church for Others,* p. 3.
62. *Planning for Mission,* p. 6. J. G. Davies, chairman of the Western European Working Group, located the theological problem in these areas: (1) the relation of God to church and world; (2) the relationship between church and world; (3) the distinction between church and world; (4) whether Christ should be seen primarily as Savior or as Lord; (5) the relationship of worship and mission (ibid., pp. 8-11).
63. Ibid., p. 11.
64. "The Quest for Structures of Missionary Congregations," ibid., pp. 220-228.
65. Ibid., p. 227. Cf. Hans Joachim Margull, "We Stand in Our Own Way," *Ecumenical Review* 17 (1965): 331. Margull makes the following points on the basis of reformation doctrine: (1) The structure of the church is *always open to change.* (2) The form of the church is to be placed entirely at the service of the gospel. (3) The structure of the church is "provisional." No structure is fixed forever, eternal, or sacred.
66. Cf. J. C. Hoekendijk, "Notes on the Meaning of Mission(ary)," *Planning for Mission,* pp. 37-48, and *Mission in God's Mission,* Report of the Western European Working Group, Driebergen, 1965, ibid., pp. 48-53. Thus Hoekendijk achieved the theological breakthrough he had been denied at Willingen where his proposal ran into resistance from traditional defenders of mission.
67. *The Church for Others,* p. 14.
68. *Planning for Mission,* pp. 51, 54.
69. Ibid., pp. 37, 39.
70. Ibid., p. 41.
71. Ibid., p. 43.
72. Ibid., p. 52.
73. Ibid., p. 53.
74. *The Church for Others,* pp. 16-17. The same point is affirmed in the North American report (*The Church for Others,* p. 69).
75. Ibid., p. 18.
76. Ibid., p. 20.
77. Ibid., pp. 77-78.
78. Ibid., p. 78.
79. Herbert T. Neve, *Sources for Change: Searching for Flexible Church Structures. A Contribution to the Ecumenical Discussion on the Structures of the Missionary Congregation by the Commission on Stewardship and Evangelism of the Lutheran World Federation* (Geneva: World Council of Churches, 1958).

80. Ibid., pp. 7, 13. The commission was particularly critical of the tenor of the Western European report, and somewhat more accepting of the North American report.
81. Ibid., pp. 16-17, 18-44 (the quote is from p. 38).
82. Werner Krusche, "Parish Structure: A Hindrance to Mission? A Survey and Evaluation of the Ecumenical Discussion on the Structures of the Missionary Congregation," ibid., pp. 51-100.
83. Ibid., p. 81.
84. Ibid., p. 82.
85. Ibid., p. 83.
86. Ibid., pp. 83-84.
87. Ibid., p. 84.
88. Ibid.
89. Ibid., p. 85.
90. Ibid., p. 86.
91. Ibid., p. 87.
92. Ibid., p. 88.
93. Ibid., p. 89.
94. Ibid., pp. 90-91
95. Ibid., p. 92.
96. Philip Potter, "Evangelism and the World Council of Churches," *Ecumenical Review* 20 (1968): 171.
97. Ibid., p. 173. Potter did not comment on the study's controversial theological basis, except to say that "humanisation" had been lifted up as the missionary goal in *The Church for Others,* citing the statement that "the dominant concern of the missionary congregation must therefore be to point to the humanity in Christ as the goal of mission" (*The Church for Others,* p. 78; cf. Potter, p. 176).
98. *A Theological Reflection on the Work of Evangelism* [Special Issue of the WCC Division of Studies Bulletin, vol. 5, Nos. 1 and 2, November 1959, p. 14]; cited by Potter, p. 175.
99. Report of the Advisory Commission on "Christ—The Hope of the World" (1954), pp. 16-17; cited by Potter, p. 176.
100. Norman Goodall, editorial, *The Uppsala Report* 1968, p. xvii.
101. "The Church for the World," Report of the North American Working Group, *The Church for Others,* p. 78.
102. "Renewal in Mission," p. 28. In an introductory statement, Canon John V. Taylor pleaded that "humanity" be understood not as an abstract term but in the sense of "the new man," Jesus of Nazareth, and the new being in Christ which human beings put on by adoption as children of God with faith and conversion (*The Uppsala Report 1968,* pp. 22-25).
103. A Norwegian delegate, Dr. Per Lønning, particularly objected to statements from *The Church for Others* and to the phrase, "moving with history towards the coming of the new humanity," which appeared in the final version of the Section II Report (*The Uppsala Report 1968,* pp. 25, 32).
104. *The Uppsala Report 1968,* p. 28.
105. Ibid.
106. W. A. Visser 't Hooft, "The Mandate of the Ecumenical Movement," ibid., p. 138.
107. Ibid., p. 320. Similarly, John V. Taylor, speaking to the Section II plenary, said that "the apparent opposition between the gospel of personal conversion and the

gospel of social responsibility" was the main underlying theological issue, and that delegates must "face the issue and think it through to a synthesis, not a compromise" (ibid., p. 24).

108. "Renewal in Mission," Part II, "Opportunities for Mission," and Part III, "Freedom for Mission." Both the chairman of Section II, Metropolitan Lakdasa de Mel, and the Vice-Chairman, Dr. Arne Sovik, expressed the view that these parts of the report would have the greatest lasting significance.

109. *The Uppsala Report 1968*, pp. 30-32.

110. Ibid., p. 32.

111. Sovik referred to "inclusive" but "purposefully ambiguous phraseology" and "well-worn theological platitudes" (ibid., p. 36).

112. John R. W. Stott, a leading Anglican evangelical, active in the Lausanne movement, criticized the draft for its lack of reference to the millions who are perishing without Christ (*The Uppsala Report 1968*, p. 26). In America, Dr. Donald McGavran, the father of the "church growth" school, asked, "Will Uppsala betray the two billion?" (*Church Growth Bulletin*, vol. 4, no. 5, May 1968).

113. *From Mexico City to Bangkok: Report of the Commission on World Mission and Evangelism of the WCC 1963–1972* (Geneva: WCC, 1972), p. 43. The CWME aim was "to further the proclamation to the whole world of the Gospel of Jesus Christ to the end that all men may believe in him and be saved."

114. Ibid., pp. 43-44. These were published as *Salvation Today and Contemporary Experience: A Collection of Texts for Critical Study and Reflection* (Geneva: WCC, n.d.).

115. *From Mexico City to Bangkok*. pp. 43-44, and Thomas Wieser, "Report on the Salvation Study," *IRM* 63 (1973): 170-179. Some evangelicals were scandalized at the inclusion of Maoist salvation parables.

116. *Bangkok Assembly 1973*, p. 1.

117. Ibid., pp. 88-89.

118. Ibid., p. 91.

119. Ibid., pp. 32-33.

120. Ibid., p. 73.

121. Ibid., p. 103.

122. Jacques Rossel said: "We know very little about the proper use of power by the churches and by groups of Christians and still less of the use by churches and groups of political power" ("The implications of the Conference on Salvation Today for CWME," ibid., p. 66).

123. *Bangkok Assembly 1973*, p. 107.

124. Emilio Castro, "Bangkok, The New Opportunity," *IRM* 62 (1973): 140.

125. Ibid., pp. 142-143.

CHAPTER 4. "Confessing Christ Today": Consolidation and Reconciliation in Ecumenical Mission

1. Cf. David M. Paton's comment in *Breaking Barriers: Nairobi 1975* (London: SPCK, and Grand Rapids: Eerdmans, 1976), p. 35. Other aspects of consolidation and reconciliation were the prominence of Orthodox viewpoints in Section I and the receptivity to the contributions of evangelicals.

2. Cf. "The Report of the Moderator of the Central Committee" on "The Concept of Evangelism in the Modern World," *Breaking Barriers: Nairobi 1975*, pp. 231-236.

3. *Breaking Barriers: Nairobi 1975*, pp. 17-19. The full text of Bishop Mortimer Arias' address, "That The World May Believe," is found in *IRM* 65 (1976): 13-26, and is followed by the responses (pp. 26-43).
4. Report of Section I, "Confessing Christ Today," *Breaking Barriers: Nairobi 1975*, pp. 41-57.
5. Cf. *The Struggle Continues: Official Report of the Third Assembly of the All Africa Conference of Churches, Lusaka, Zambia, 12-24 May, 1974* (Nairobi: AACC, 1975), pp. 31-35. Among the recommendations of the AACC were the following: "that the church should regard evangelization as the total witness in word and deed to the whole life of persons and communities, leading to liberation and fulness of life"; "that the African Church be stimulated to think of itself as a missionary sending church, crossing the borders of countries and/or cultures, both within Africa and beyond the shores of this continent"; "that the African Church accept the challenge and responsibility of evangelizing in frontier situations in this continent"; and "that it be the African Church that determines what external help it needs."
6. Ion Bria, "Confessing Christ Today: An Orthodox Consultation," *IRM* 64 (1975): 67-94. The Orthodox contribution to Section I at Nairobi was reflected in the emphasis on confessing Christ as an activity of the believing community, the central place given to Baptism, conversion, and Eucharist, and the trinitarian references.
7. *Let the Earth Hear His Voice: International Congress on World Evangelization, Lausanne, Switzerland, Official Reference Volume*, ed. J. D. Douglas (Minneapolis: World Wide Publications, 1975).
8. Declaration from the Roman Synod of 1974, cited in *Mission Trends No. 2: Evangelization*, ed. G. H. Anderson and T. F. Stransky, CSP (New York: Paulist, and Grand Rapids: Eerdmans, 1975), pp. 259-264.
9. Philip A. Potter, "Evangelization in the Modern World," *Mission Trends No. 2*, pp. 162-175. Potter reiterated the view that "evangelization is the ecumenical theme par excellence" and called it "the test of our ecumenical vocation."
10. "The Report of the Moderator of the Central Committee," *Breaking Barriers: Nairobi 1975*, pp. 231-232.
11. Ibid., p. 232. However, Thomas also recognized continuing divergences in understanding over the relation between the personal, social, and cosmic dimensions of salvation in Jesus Christ; the nature of the Christian action in history, which expresses the eschatological hope; the future that faith expects and works for in history; and the locus and identity of the church as the bearer of salvation.
12. Ibid., p. 234.
13. Ibid. The Orthodox concern was to emphasize the eschatological nature of human beings as extending beyond their present existence on earth and finally embracing the *eschaton*.
14. Ibid.
15. Mortimer Arias, "That the World May Believe."
16. Ibid., p. 13.
17. Ibid., p. 15.
18. Ibid., pp. 15-16.
19. Ibid., p. 18. Such holistic evangelism, he added, is also contextual, incarnational, costly, vulnerable, and local.
20. John Stott, "Response to Bishop Mortimer Arias," *IRM* 65 (1976): 30.
21. Ibid., pp. 30-33. Cf. also *Breaking Barriers: Nairobi 1975*, pp. 18-19.

22. Stephen Neill, *Salvation Tomorrow: The Originality of Jesus Christ and the World's Religions* (Guildford and London: Lutterworth Press; Nashville: Abingdon, 1976), p. x.
23. *Breaking Barriers: Nairobi 1975*, p. 23.
24. Ibid.
25. Ibid., pp. 52-54.
26. *Your Kingdom Come: Mission Perspectives. Report on the World Conference on Mission and Evangelism, Melbourne, Australia, 12 to 25 May, 1980* (Geneva: WCC, 1980). All references cited are from this official English edition.
27. Cf. Johannes Verkuyl, "The Kingdom of God as the Goal of Missio Dei," *IRM* 68 (1979): 168-175, extracted from *Contemporary Missiology: An Introduction*, trans. and ed. Dale Cooper (Grand Rapids: Eerdmans, 1978), pp. 197-204.
28. The section reports are included in *Your Kingdom Come*, pp. 171-223. In addition, an abridged version of the reports was published in *IRM* 69 (1980-1981): 388-435.
29. The six preparatory issues of *IRM* are: "Edinburgh to Melbourne" 67/267 [1978]; "Australia," "Your Kingdom Come," and "The Kingdom of God and Human Struggles" (68/269, 270, 272 [1979]); and "The Kingdom of God and Power" and "The Church Witnesses to the Kingdom" (69/273, 274 [1980]. The two follow-up issues are "Melbourne Conference Notes" and "Melbourne Reports and Reflections" (69/275-277 [1980-1981]). Cf. also the 12 issues of the occasional preparatory papers which preceded Melbourne (all available from WCC-CWME).
30. The plenary presentations are included in *Your Kingdom Come*, pp. 1-71.
31. Philip Potter, "From Edinburgh to Melbourne," in *Your Kingdom Come*, p. 6.
32. Ibid., p. 8.
33. Soritua Nababan, "Your Kingdom Come," in *Your Kingdom Come*, p. 1.
34. Krister Stendahl, "Your Kingdom Come: Notes for Bible Study," in *Your Kingdom Come*, p. 72.
35. "The Eschatological Royal Reign of God," in *Your Kingdom Come*, p. 61.
36. For the report of Section I, see *Your Kingdom Come*, pp. 171-178.
37. The Norwegian and West German preparatory studies sharply disputed any tendency to identify the poor in the New Testament solely with the materially poor.
38. For the report of Section II, see *Your Kingdom Come*, pp. 179-192.
39. For the report of Section III, see ibid., pp. 193-207.
40. For the report of Section IV, see ibid., pp. 208-223.
41. "Message to the Churches," in *Your Kingdom Come*, p. 235.
42. Ernst Käsemann, "The Eschatological Royal Reign of God," in *Your Kingdom Come*, p. 62.
43. Jacques Matthey, "Melbourne: Mission in the Eighties," in *Your Kingdom Come*, p. xi.
44. Ibid.
45. Emilio Castro, "Reflection after Melbourne," in *Your Kingdom Come*, p. 228.
46. Ibid., p. 229.
47. Matthey, ibid., pp. xvii-xviii.
48. Ibid., pp. xvi-xvii.
49. Castro, "Reflection after Melbourne," ibid., p. 231.
50. "Mission and Evangelism: An Ecumenical Affirmation," *IRM* 71 (1982): 427-451 (other printed versions also exist).
51. Ibid., pp. 421-422.

52. For some Roman Catholic, Orthodox, and Protestant responses to the "Ecumenical Affirmation," cf. ibid., pp. 452-457.
53. Ibid., p. 427.
54. Ibid., pp. 427-428.
55. Ibid., pp. 428-430, 430-432.
56. Ibid., p. 428.
57. Ibid., p. 430.
58. Ibid., p. 431.
59. Ibid., p. 432.
60. Ibid.
61. Ibid., pp. 432-446.
62. Ibid., pp. 432-434.
63. Ibid., p. 434.
64. Ibid., p. 436.
65. Ibid., p. 438.
66. Ibid.
67. Ibid., p. 439.
68. Ibid.
69. Ibid., pp. 440-441.
70. Ibid., p. 440.
71. Ibid., p. 441.
72. Ibid., p. 443.
73. Ibid., p. 445.
74. Ibid., p. 446.
75. Ibid.
76. Ibid., p. 447.
77. Ibid.
78. *IRM* 72 (1983): 598.
79. Ibid., p. 547 (citing Fr. Thomas Stransky).
80. *Gathered for Life: Official Report of Sixth Assembly of the World Council of Churches, Vancouver, Canada, 24 July-10 August, 1983*, ed. David Gill (Geneva: WCC; Grand Rapids: Eerdmans, 1983), p. 8.
81. *Gathered for Life*, p. 31.
82. *IRM* 72 (1983): 598.
83. *Gathered for Life*, p. 3.
84. Ibid., pp. 31-42.
85. *Gathered for Life*, p. 33.
86. Ibid.
87. Ibid.
88. Ibid., pp. 33-34.
89. Ibid., p. 40.
90. Ibid. (emphasis added).
91. Ibid., pp. 40-41; paragraph numbers refer to paragraphs in the section report.
92. Ibid., pp. 41-42.
93. Ibid., p. 254.
94. Cf. Diana L. Eck, *Ecumenical Review* 37 (1985): 412ff.; Carl F. Hallencreutz, *Living Faiths and the Ecumenical Movement*, ed. S. J. Samartha (Geneva: WCC, 1971), pp. 57-71.

95. "The WCC and Dialogue with People of Living Faiths and Ideologies," in *Living Faiths and the Ecumenical Movement,* ed. S. J. Samartha, pp. 47-54 (= *Ecumenical Review* 24 [1971]).

96. *Living Faiths and the Ecumenical Movement,* pp. 48-49.

97. *Dialogue in Community: Statements and Reports of a Theological Consultation, Chiang Mai, Thailand, 18-27 April 1977* (Geneva: WCC, 1977).

98. *Guidelines on Dialogue with People of Living Faiths and Ideologies* (Geneva: WCC, 1979).

99. Ibid., Part I, pp. 7-8.

100. Ibid., Part II, p. 11.

101. Ibid., p. 12 (emphasis added).

102. Ibid., pp. 12-13.

103. Ibid., Part III, p. 16.

104. Ibid., pp. 17-22. The explanatory notes appended to each guideline should be read for fuller understanding.

CHAPTER 5. The Evangelical Missionary Movement

1. Cf. Edward Dayton, "Ten Historic Years," in *The Future of World Evangelization: The Lausanne Movement.* ed. E. R. Dayton and S. Wilson (Monrovia, Calif.: MARC, 1984), pp. 47-57. Unlike the WCC (which is constituted by member churches) and the WCC's Commission on World Mission and Evangelism (which works through representative member councils), the evangelical missionary movement as represented by the Lausanne Committee for World Evangelization is not officially constituted as a council of member churches or missionary organizations. The basis of participation is personal and validated by signing the *Lausanne Covenant,* the theological foundation of the movement.

2. Rodger C. Bassham, *Mission Theology: 1948–1975; Years of Worldwide Creative Tension, Ecumenical, Evangelical and Roman Catholic* (Pasadena, Calif.: William Carey Library, 1979) provides a useful profile of these groups (pp. 173-198). The EFMA and the IFMA along with other unaffiliated evangelical groups are responsible for more than 90% of the total of 45,000 full- and short-term Protestant missionaries sent out from the United States. Mission agencies related to the National Council of Churches now account for less than 9% of the total. Cf. Samuel Wilson, "Current Trends in North American Protestant Ministries Overseas," *IBMR* 5 (1981): 75.

3. Cf. Rodger C. Bassham, *Mission Theology: 1948–1975,* p. 54.

4. The full text of the Wheaton Declaration is to be found in the Proceedings of the Congress, *The Church's Worldwide Mission: An Analysis of the Current State of Evangelical Missions and a Strategy for Future Activity,* ed. Harold Lindsell (Waco, Texas: Word, 1966), pp. 217-237; quotations are from pp. 235, 237, 228, and 231.

5. This summary of the Wheaton Congress is based on Bassham, *Mission Theology,* pp. 210-220. Most frequent charges against the ecumenical movement were theological liberalism, loss of evangelical conviction, universalism in theology, substitution of social action for evangelism, and the search for unity at the expense of biblical truth (ibid., pp. 211-213).

6. For the report of the Berlin Congress see *One Race, One Gospel, One Task: World Congress on Evangelism, Berlin, 1966,* ed. Carl F. Henry and W. Stanley Mooneyham, 2 vols. (Minneapolis: World Wide Publications, 1967).

7. This summary of the Berlin Congress is based on Bassham, *Mission Theology,* pp. 220-230.
8. Introduction to the Lausanne Covenant, *Let the Earth Hear His Voice,* p. 3.
9. The *Covenant,* which underwent three draft revisions, was produced by a drafting committee under the leadership of John R. W. Stott. It was reportedly signed by 2200 persons at Lausanne, and became the basis for participation in the Pattaya Consultation (COWE, 1980). The full text of the *Covenant* is to be found in *Let the Earth Hear His Voice,* pp. 1-9. Citations are from the major sections or paragraphs into which the *Lausanne Covenant* (LC) is divided.
10. An unnamed Asian theologian cited in *The Lausanne Covenant: An Exposition and Commentary by John Stott* (Minneapolis: World Wide Publications, 1975), p. 1. Stott's commentary was reissued as Lausanne Occasional Paper (LOP) No. 3 (Wheaton, Ill.: Lausanne Committee for World Evangelization, 1978).
11. *The Future of World Evangelization: The Lausanne Movement,* p. 34.
12. Ibid., pp. 35-36.
13. Billy Graham, "Why Lausanne?" in *Let the Earth Hear His Voice,* p. 22.
14. Ibid., p. 25.
15. Ibid., pp. 26-28.
16. Ibid., pp. 28-30.
17. Ibid., pp. 32-33.
18. Ibid., p. 34. It is evident that Graham's goals for the congress were all in some sense fulfilled.
19. *The Future of World Evangelization,* pp. 7-8.
20. Conclusion of the Lausanne Covenant, *Let the Earth Hear His Voice,* p. 9.
21. This and subsequent quotations from the *Lausanne Covenant* are from *Let the Earth Hear His Voice,* pp. 1-9; abbreviations refer to paragraphs from the LC.
22. John R. W. Stott, "The Biblical Basis of Evangelism," in *Let the Earth Hear His Voice,* p. 72. Cf. "Renewal in Mission," in *The Uppsala Report, 1968,* p. 29.
23. For an extended discussion on the change and how it was brought about, cf. C. R. Padilla, "How Evangelicals Endorsed Social Responsibility 1966–83," *Transformation,* vol. 2, no. 3, pp. 27-33.
24. "Theology and Implications of Radical Discipleship," *Let the Earth Hear His Voice,* p. 1294.
25. Ibid.
26. *The Future of World Evangelization,* pp. 69-70, 73-77. Cf. *Grand Rapids Report: Evangelism and Social Responsibility: An Evangelical Commitment,* LOP No. 21 (LCWE and WEF, 1982).
27. *The Future of World Evangelization,* pp. 37-39, 48-52.
28. Cf. Donald A. McGavran, *Understanding Church Growth* (Grand Rapids: Eerdmans, 1970).
29. Cf. *The Pasadena Consultation—Homogeneous Unit Principle,* LOP No. 1 (Wheaton, Ill.: LCWE, 1978), p. 3.
30. Ibid., p. 7.
31. *The Willowbank Report: Report of a Consultation on Gospel and Culture Held at Willowbank, Somerset Bridge, Bermuda, from 6-13th January 1978,* LOP No. 2 (Wheaton, Ill.: LCWE, 1978), p. 33.
32. *An Evangelical Commitment to Simple Life-Style: Exposition and Commentary by Alan Nichols,* LOP No. 20 (Wheaton, Ill., LCWE, 1980), pp. 7-31.
33. *Grand Rapids Report: Evangelism and Social Responsibility,* ed. John R. W. Stott, LOP No. 21 (LCWE and WEF, 1982).

34. "A Statement of Concerns on the Future of the Lausanne Committee for World Evangelization," presented to LCWE Executive Committee at Pattaya, June 1980, with 200 signatures; printed in Andrew Kirk, *The Good News of the Kingdom Coming* (Downers Grove: InterVarsity Press, 1985), pp. 148-151

35. Cf. John Reid, in *The Future of World Evangelization,* p. 74, and John Stott, *Grand Rapids Report*, p. 69.

36. John Reid, *The Future of World Evangelization,* pp. 75-76.

37. John Stott, Introduction to *Grand Rapids Report: Evangelism and Social Responsibility,* LOP No. 21, p. 9.

38. Ibid., pp. 21-23.

39. Ibid., pp. 47-48.

40. Ralph D. Winter, "The Highest Priority: Cross-Cultural Evangelism," in *Let the Earth Hear His Voice,* pp. 213-225, 226-241.

41. Ibid., p. 213.

42. Ibid., p. 216.

43. See the responses to Winter's presentation by Philip Hogen, Jacob Loewen, and others in *Let the Earth Hear His Voice,* pp. 242-258.

44. Edward R. Dayton, *That Everyone May Hear: Reaching the Unreached,* special edition for the Pattaya, Thailand Consultation on World Evangelization (Monrovia, Calif.: MARC, 1979), is an introduction to the methodology for identifying and reaching unevangelized peoples. Edward R. Dayton and David A. Fraser, *Planning Strategies for World Evangelization* (Grand Rapids: Eerdmans, 1980) is a much more detailed approach to the same subject.

45. The series entitled *Unreached Peoples* (annual directories available from 1979 onward) is published by the David C. Cook Publishing Co., Elgin Ill.

46. Cf. *That Everyone May Hear,* pp. 21-29.

47. The new profiles are published annually in the series *Unreached Peoples.*

48. Cf. *That Everyone May Hear,* p. 19.

49. W. Webster, in *The Future of World Evangelization,* pp. 134-135.

50. Edward R. Dayton, in *The Future of World Evangelization,* p. 52.

51. Program and Information Booklet, Consultation on World Evangelizaton, Pattaya, Thailand, June 16-27, 1980, p. 5.

52. "The Thailand Statement," in *The Future of World Evangelization,* p. 148.

53. Ibid., p. 150.

54. Ibid., pp. 152-153.

55. Ibid., pp. 153-154. As part of COWE, a Commission on Cooperation in World Evangelism appointed by LCWE met at Pattaya and later published guidelines for cooperation as LOP No. 24 *(Cooperating in World Evangelization: A Handbook on Church/Para-Church Relationships).*

56. Cf. *Future of World Evangelization,* pp. 211-212. Reports of miniconsultations were published as LOP nos. 5-24.

57. Ray Bakke, in *The Future of World Evangelization,* pp. 121-128.

58. Leighton Ford, in *The Future of World Evangelization,* pp. 266-268.

59. "Theology and Implications of Radical Discipleship," *Let the Earth Hear His Voice,* p. 1294.

60. *The New Face of Evangelicalism: An International Symposium on the Lausanne Covenant,* ed. C. Rene Padilla (Downers Grove: InterVarsity Press, 1976), p. 11.

61. Cf. Andrew Kirk, *The Good News of the Kingdom Coming* (Downers Grove: InterVarsity Press, 1985), pp. 14-16.

62. "A Statement of Concerns on the Future of the LCWE," printed as an appendix in ibid., pp. 148-150.
63. "The Church in Reponse to Human Need," Report of Consultation III, Conference on the Nature and Mission of the Church, sponsored by the World Evangelical Fellowship, Wheaton, Illinois, 20 June to 1 July 1983.

CHAPTER 6: Roman Catholic Mission Theology: The Impact of Vatican II

1. *Catholic Missions: Four Great Missionary Encyclicals,* ed. Thomas J. M. Burke (New York: Fordham University Press, 1957), contains important mission decrees from the pre-Second Vatican Council period.
2. *Documents of Vatican II,* ed. Austin P. Flannery (Grand Rapids: Eerdmans, 1975), pp. 350-426 *(Lumen Gentium = LG)* and 813-856 *(Ad Gentes = AG).*
3. Declaration from the Roman Bishops Synod of 1971, cited in *Mission Trends No. 2* (New York: Paulist, and Grand Rapids: Eerdmans, 1975), p. 255.
4. Ibid., p. 256.
5. Ibid., pp. 257-258.
6. Declaration from the Roman Bishops Synod of 1974, cited in *Mission Trends No. 2,* p. 259.
7. Ibid., p. 262.
8. Ibid., p. 263.
9. Ibid., pp. 263-264.
10. Pope Paul VI, *The Evangelization of the Men of Our Time (Evangelii Nuntiandi = EN),* with an introduction by Agnelo Cardinal Rossi (Rome: Sacred Congregation for the Evangelization of Peoples, 1975); also published by United States Catholic Conference, Washington, D.C. under the title *On Evangelization in the Modern World* (1976). Sections quoted from *EN* are taken from the Rome edition.
11. *The Church in the Present-Day Transformation of Latin America in the Light of the Council: Second General Conference of Latin American Bishops, Medellin, August 26–September 6, 1968,* vol. 2: *Conclusions* (Washington: National Conference of Catholic Bishops, 1979), p. 29.
12. Ibid., pp. 19-20.
13. Ibid., p. 27.
14. Ibid., Chapters 1, 14, and 15.
15. Ibid., p. 33.
16. Ibid., p. 40.
17. Ibid., p. 172.
18. Ibid., p. 175.
19. Ibid.
20. Ibid., p. 185.
21. Pope John Paul II, "Opening Address at the Puebla Conference," *Puebla and Beyond: Documentary and Commentary,* ed John Eagleson and Philip Scharper, trans. John Drury (Maryknoll, N.Y.: Orbis, 1979), p. 71.
22. Pope John Paul II, "Letter to the Latin American Bishops," March 23, 1979, *Puebla and Beyond,* p. 111.
23. Pope John Paul II, "Opening Address at the Puebla Conference," ibid., p. 57. John Paul II referred to *Evangelii Nuntiandi* as Paul VI's "spiritual testament," "into which he poured his whole pastoral soul as his life drew to a close" (p. 58).
24. Ibid., p. 60.

25. Ibid., p. 62.
26. Ibid., pp. 63-64.
27. Ibid., p. 66.
28. Ibid., p. 68.
29. "Evangelization in Latin America's Present and Future: Final Document of the Third General Conference of the Latin American Episcopate," §629, *Puebla and Beyond*, p. 211.
30. Ibid., §1134, p. 264.
31. Ibid., §§1302-1304, p. 284.
32. *Toward a New Age in Mission: The Good News of God's Kingdom to the Peoples of Asia. International Congress on Mission (IMC), Manila, 2-7 December 1979,* three books (Manila: Theological Conference Office, International Mission Congress. IMC/TCO, 1981).
33. Ibid., Book 1, p. 1.
34. Ibid., Book 1, pp. 21-29. Paragraphs refer to the text of the Official Message of the Manila Congress.
35. *Mission in Dialogue: SEDOS Research Seminar on the Future of Mission, March 8-19, 1981, Rome. Italy,* ed. Mary Motte, F.M.M. and Joseph Lang, M.M. (Maryknoll: Orbis, 1982), pp. xi-xii, 1-4.
36. Ibid., pp. 633-649.
37. Ibid., pp. 634-635.
38. Ibid., p. 636.
39. Ibid., p. 638.
40. Ibid., pp. 640-641.
41. Ibid., pp. 642-644.
42. Ibid., pp. 645-649.
43. "The Attitude of the Church toward the Followers of Other Religions: Reflections and Orientations on Dialogue and Mission," Secretariat for Non-Christians, Vatican City 56 (1984), XIX, 2. Reprinted in *IBMR* 9/4 (1985): 187-191.
44. Ibid., p. 188.
45. Ibid., pp. 188-189.
46. Ibid., p. 190.
47. Ibid.
48. Ibid., p. 191.
49. Ibid.
50. *Common Witness:* A Study Document of the Joint Working Group of the Roman Catholic Church and the World Council of Churches. Published jointly by the Secretariat for Christian Unity, Roman Catholic Church, and the Commission for World Mission and Evangelism, World Council of Churches (Geneva: WCC, 1980). An earlier and more limited version of this same document was issued by the Joint Working Committee of the Roman Catholic Church and the World Council of Churches in 1971 as "Common Witness and Proselytism: A Study Document," and may be found in *Mission Trends No. 2: Evangelization,* pp. 176-187.
51. "Evangelicals and Roman Catholics Dialogue on Mission, 1977–1984: A Report" (ERCDOM), reprinted in *IBMR* 10/1 (1986): 2-21; available in book form as *The Evangelical Roman Dialogue on Mission, 1977–1984,* ed. John R. Stott and Basil Meeking (Grand Rapids: Eerdmans, 1986).

52. *Common Witness*, p. 10; paragraph numbers refer to the text of *Common Witness*.
53. Ibid., pp. 12-20.
54. Ibid., pp. 20-27.
55. Ibid., Appendix, pp. 29-54.
56. "Evangelicals and Roman Catholics Dialogue on Mission, 1977-1984: A Report."

BIBLIOGRAPHY

A. ECUMENICAL AND CONCILIAR SOURCES

International Missionary Council (IMC)

Ranson, C. W., ed. *Renewal and Advance: Christian Witness in a Revolutionary World. The Whitby Meeting of the IMC, July 1947.* London: Edinburgh House, 1948.

The Missionary Obligation of the Church: Willingen, Germany, July 5-17, 1952. London: Edinburgh House, 1952.

Goodall, Norman, ed. *Missions under the Cross: Addresses delivered at the Enlarged Meeting of the Committee of the International Missionary Council at Willingen, in Germany, 1952; with Statements Issued by the Meeting.* London: Edinburgh House, 1953.

Newbigin, Lesslie. *One Body, One Gospel, One World: The Christian Mission Today.* London and New York: International Missionary Council, 1958.

Orchard, Ronald K., ed. *The Ghana Assembly of the International Missionary Council, 28th December 1957 to 8th January 1958: Selected Papers, with an Essay on the Role of the IMC.* London: Edinburgh House, 1958.

Payne, Ernest A., and Moses, David G. *Why Integration? An Explanation of the Proposal before the World Council of Churches and the International Missionary Council.* London: Edinburgh House, 1958.

World Council of Churches (WCC)

Visser 't Hooft, W. A., ed. *The New Delhi Report: The Third Assembly of the World Council of Churches, 1961.* New York: Association Press, 1962.

Wieser, Thomas, ed. *Planning for Mission: Working Papers on the New Quest for Missionary Communities.* New York: The U.S. Conference for the World Council of Churches. London: Epworth, 1966.

The Church for Others and the Church for the World: A Quest for Structures for Missionary Congregations. Final Report of the Western European Working Group and North American Working Group of the Department of Studies on Evangelism. Geneva: World Council of Churches, 1968.

Goodall, Norman, ed. *The Uppsala Report 1968: Official Report of the Fourth Assembly of the World Council of Churches, Uppsala, July 4-20. 1968.* Geneva: World Council of Churches, 1968.

Neve, Herbert T., ed. *Sources for Change: Searching for Flexible Church Structures. A Contribution to the Ecumenical Discussion on the Structures of the Missionary Congregation by the Commission on Stewardship and Evangelism of the Lutheran World Federation.* Geneva: World Council of Churches, 1968.

Paton, David M., ed. *Breaking Barriers, Nairobi 1975. The Official Report of the Fourth Assembly of the World Council of Churches, Nairobi, 23 November—10 December 1975.* London: SPCK; and Grand Rapids: Eerdmans, 1976.

Gill, David, ed. *Gathered for Life: Official Report, VI Assembly, World Council of Churches, Vancouver, Canada, 24 July–10 August 1983.* Geneva: World Council of Churches. Grand Rapids: Eerdmans, 1983.

WCC Commission on World Mission and Evangelism (CWME)

Orchard, Ronald K., ed. *Witness in Six Continents: Records of the Meeting of the Commission on World Mission and Evangelism of the World Council of Churches Held in Mexico City, December 8th to 19th, 1963.* London: Edinburgh House, 1964.

From Mexico City to Bangkok: Report of the Commission on World Mission and Evangelism, 1963–1972. Geneva: World Council of Churches, 1972.

Bangkok Assembly 1973: Minutes and Report of the Assembly of the Commission on World Mission and Evangelism of the World Council of Churches, December 31, 1972, and January 9-12, 1973. Geneva: World Council of Churches, n.d.

Salvation Today and Contemporary Experience: A Collection of Texts for Critical Study and Reflection. Geneva: World Council of Churches, n.d.

Your Kingdom Come: Mission Perspectives. Report on the World Conference on Mission and Evangelism, Melbourne, Australia, 12-25 May, 1980. Geneva: World Council of Churches, 1980.

Anderson, Gerald H., ed. *Witnessing to the Kingdom: Melbourne and Beyond.* Maryknoll, N.Y.: Orbis, 1982.

B. EVANGELICAL SOURCES

Lausanne Committee on World Evangelization (LCWE)

Douglas, J. D., ed. *Let the Earth Hear His Voice; International Congress on World Evangelization. Lausanne, Switzerland, Official Reference Volume.* Minneapolis: World Wide Publications, 1975.

Padilla, C. Rene, ed. *The New Face of Evangelicalism: An International Symposium on the Lausanne Covenant.* Downers Grove, Ill.: InterVarsity Press; and London: Hodder and Stoughton, 1976.

Lausanne Occasional Papers (LOP). Lausanne Committee for World Evangelization, Box 1100, Wheaton, IL 60187; Monrovia, Calif.: Missions Advanced Research and Communications Center (MARC)—World Vision International, 1978–1982.

No. 1: *The Pasadena Consultation—Homogenous Unit Principle* (1978).

No. 2: *The Willowbank Report: Report of a Consultation on Gospel and Culture Held at Willowbank, Somerset Bridge, Bermuda, from 6-13 January, 1978.*

No. 3: *The Lausanne Covenant: An Exposition and Commentary by John Stott* (1978).

No. 4: *The Glen Eyrie Report: Muslim Evangelization* (1978).

No. 5: *Thailand Report: Christian Witness to Refugees* (1980).

No. 6: _____ *Christian Witness to the Chinese People.*

No. 7: _____ *Christian Witness to the Jewish People.*

No. 8: _____ *Christian Witness to Secularized People.*

No. 9: _____ *Christian Witness to Large Cities.*

No.10: _____ *Christian Witness to Nominal Christians among Roman Catholics.*

No.11: _____ *Christian Witness to New Religious Movements.*

No.12: _____ *Christian Witness to Marxists.*

No.13: _____ *Christian Witness to Muslims.*

No.14: _____ *Christian Witness to Hindus.*

No.15: _____ *Christian Witness to Buddhists.*

No.16: _____ *Christian Witness to Traditional Religionists of Asia and Oceania.*

No.17: _____ *Christian Witness to Traditional Religionists of Latin America and Caribbean.*

No.18: _____ *Christian Witness to People of African Traditional Religions.*

No.19: _____ *Christian Witness to Nominal Christians among the Orthodox* (all 1980).

No. 20: *An Evangelical Commitment to Simple Life-Style: Exposition and Commentary by Alan Nichols* (1980).

No. 21: *Grand Rapids Report: Evangelism and Social Responsibility: An Evangelical Commitment* (1982).

No. 22: *Thailand Report: Christian Witness to the Urban Poor.*

No. 23: *Thailand Report: Christian Witness to Nominal Christians Among Protestants.*

No. 24: *Cooperating in World Evangelization: A Handbook on Church/Para-Church Relationships.*

Dayton, Edward R. *That Everyone May Hear: Reaching the Unreached.* Monrovia, Calif.: MARC, 1979.

Dayton, Edward R., and Fraser, David A. *Planning Strategies for World Evangelization.* Grand Rapids: Eerdmans, 1980.

Dayton, Edward R., and Wilson, Samuel, eds. *The Future of World Evangelization: The Lausanne Movement.* Monrovia, Calif.: MARC, 1984.

C. ROMAN CATHOLIC SOURCES

Second Vatican Council

Flannery, Austin P., ed. *Documents of Vatican II.* Grand Rapids: Eerdmans, 1975.

Apostolic Exhortation

Pope Paul VI. *The Evangelization of the Men of Our Time (Evangelii Nuntiandi).* With an Introduction by Cardinal Agnelo Rossi. Rome: Sacred Congregation for the Evangelization of Peoples, n.d.

Latin America

The Church in the Present Day Transformation of Latin America in the Light of the Council: Second General Conference of Latin American Bishops, Medellin, August 26–September 6, 1968. Vol. 2: Conclusions. Washington: National Conference of Catholic Bishops, 1979.

Eagleson, John, and Scharper, Philip, eds. *Puebla and Beyond: Documentation and Commentary.* Translated by John Drury. Maryknoll, N.Y.: Orbis, 1979.

Asia

Toward a New Age in Mission: The Good News of God's Kingdom to the Peoples of Asia. International Congress on Mission (IMC), Manila, 2-7 December 1979. Three books in two volumes. Manila: Theological Conference Office/International Mission Congress (IMC/TCO), 1981.

Motte, Mary, F.M.M., and Lang, Joseph R., M.M., eds. *Mission in Dialogue: The SEDOS Research Seminar on the Future of Mission, March 8-19, 1981, Rome, Italy.* Maryknoll, N.Y.: Orbis, 1982.

D. LUTHERAN SOURCES

Lutheran World Federation Assemblies

Proceedings of the Lutheran World Federation Assembly, Lund, Sweden, June 30–July 6, 1947. Philadelphia: United Lutheran Publication House, 1948.

Lundquist, Carl E., ed. *The Proceedings of the Second Assembly of the Lutheran World Federation, Hannover, Germany, July 25–August 3, 1952.* Geneva: Lutheran World Federation, 1952.

————, ed. *The Proceedings of the Third Assembly of the Lutheran World Federation, Minneapolis, Minnesota, August 15-25, 1957.* Geneva: Lutheran World Federation, 1958.

Proceedings of the Fourth Assembly of the Lutheran World Federation, Helsinki, July 30–August 11, 1963. Berlin and Hamburg: Lutherisches Verlagshaus, 1965.

Grosc, Lavern K., ed. *Sent Into the World: The Proceedings of the Fifth Assembly of the Lutheran World Federation, Evian, France, July 14-24, 1970.* Minneapolis: Augsburg, 1971.

Sovik, Arne, ed. *In Christ—A New Community: The Proceedings of the Sixth Assembly of the Lutheran World Federation, Dar es Salaam, Tanzania, June 13-25, 1977.* Geneva: Lutheran World Federation, 1977.

Mau, Carl F. Jr., ed. *Budapest 1984: In Christ—Hope for the World. Official Proceedings of the Seventh Assembly of the Lutheran World Federation, Budapest, Hungary, July 22–August 5, 1984.* LWF Report No. 19/20. Geneva: Lutheran World Federation, 1985.

Lutheran World Federation Conference Reports

Mission and Evangelism: A Lutheran World Federation Consultation for North America, the Nordic Countries, and the Federal Republic of Germany, Evangelical Academy, Loccum, FRG, November 26–December 2, 1978. LWF Report No. 4. Geneva: Lutheran World Federation, March 1979.

Scherer, James A. . . . *That the Gospel May Be Sincerely Preached throughout the World: A Lutheran Perspective on Mission and Evangelism in the 20th Century.* LWF Report 11/12. Geneva: Lutheran World Federation, 1982.

Stavanger 1982: LWF Interregional Consultation on Mission and Evangelism, May 18-26, 1982. LWF Report 13/14. Geneva: Lutheran World Federation, 1983.

Stolle, Volker ed. *Kirche aus allen Völkern: Luther-texte zur Mission.* Erlangen: Verlag der Ev.-luth. Mission, 1983.

Lutheran Contributions to the Missio Dei. Geneva: LWF Department of Church Cooperation, 1984.

INDEX

268